Biblical Ethics

The Moral Foundations of Life

The Philosophy of Sin

Discovery House Publishers

Books, music, and videos that feed the soul with the Word of God

Box 3566 Grand Rapids, MI 49501

Biblical Ethics

The Moral Foundations of Life

The Philosophy of Sin

Oswald Chambers

Discovery House Publishers is affiliated with RBC Ministries,
Grand Rapids, Michigan 49512

ISBN 1-57293-035-7

Printed in the United States of America

98 00 02 03 01 99
CHG
1 3 5 7 9 10 8 6 4 2

Contents

The Moral Foundations of Life

The Philosophy of Sin

Foreword to *Biblical Ethics*

This latest book of talks, lectures, and addresses, given by Oswald Chambers at different times and in varied circum-stances—as when the New Theology was making its shallow appeal in 1909, or in the strenuous days of the Bible Training College in London, or when speaking to the soldiers in Egypt in 1917 (just before his own homecall)—covers a wide range of religious thinking.

The earlier chapters on biblical ethics remind us that the *ultimate* aim of Christ's atonement is that God may readjust people to Himself. That calls for a moral response on our part, involving thought and feeling and will. And we need to recognize the ethical demands made in the Scriptures on God's people.

Our Lord gave us the Sermon on the Mount; it appears in the beginning of St. Matthew's gospel. He also taught what appears later in the gospel, that the Son of Man must "suffer many things . . . and be killed, and be raised the third day" (16:21); and that His Life would be "a ransom for many" (20:28). The former without the latter would mock us. Oswald Chambers based all on the Atonement.

I have found in this book some of the most arresting truths I have yet met with. Those who have been most helped by the O.C. literature already published will find fresh pastures here. For he was indeed a scribe bringing forth out of his treasure things new and old, whose ideas never become obsolete or stale, as he is divinely enabled to see old and precious things in new relationships. May God make this book a blessing to many.

David Lambert

Foreword to *The Moral Foundations of Life*

I see sometimes in London the preparations being made for the sure foundations of one of the great modern buildings to be erected there. Far below the surface level, laborers and machines toil patiently on work that soon will be hidden but which alone will make the towering building secure. These talks on moral foundations take us to that depth below the surface of everyday life where the foundations are laid for enduring sainthood. They deal profoundly with such matters as habit, thinking, the will, behavior. The subject of Christian ethical obligation is of paramount importance in the thought life of today. The very basis of our religion, our moral and spiritual standing, is being challenged. Here will be found a valiant answer to the secular, skeptical, and lawless questionings of our time.

The writer was one of God's saints and also one of those sane Christian thinkers who see into the deep places of our strange, perplexing, yet alluring, human lives. These studies will serve for hours of instruction in righteousness as they illumine these dim regions of the soul in the blazing light of Holy Scripture.

David Lambert

Foreword to *The Philosophy of Sin*

The philosophy of sin is a subject of perennial interest, because the dreadful fact of sin is always with us. In every age there are the plain signs of some disruptive force at work among human beings. Hearts are being broken, lives are being spoiled, humanity is overclouded. Our Christian faith sees that the underlying cause is human sin—our fundamental dislocation from God, with all its bitter consequences. A book like this, dealing with sin and its remedy, is to be welcomed, for it helps us come to a clearer understanding of what is wrong with humankind and of how the basic wrong can be put right—through Christ's atonement making possible human repentance and appropriating faith. The salvation that blots out sin is here disclosed. "Sin is the radical twist with a supernatural originator, and salvation is a radical readjustment with a supernatural Originator." That is Good News indeed to every sinner, and everyone finds out at last that one is that, if one is a seeker after the truth. There are many other matters treated here. There are problems of conscience, of outward conduct, of the emotional life, the intellect, the bodily life, of circumstances, nerves, spiritual reality, the natural instincts, and of true inward adjustment to God. No one can ponder these themes as here treated without profit. The one great aim is to show modern Christians the way to the high levels of true holiness and righteousness, so that we may well use Dora Greenwell's prayer:

> And Oh, that He fulfilled may see
> The travail of His soul in me
> And with His work contented be,
> As I with my dear Saviour!

David Lambert

Biblical Ethics

The Moral Imperative—I

(that is, a law universal and binding on every rational will)

How can I do what I ought to do?

Strictly speaking, there is no disobedience possible to an imperative law, the only alternative being destruction. In this sense the moral law is not imperative, because it can be disobeyed and immediate destruction does not follow. Yet the moral law never alters, however much people disobey it; it can be violated, but it never alters. Remember, at the back of all human morality stands God.

God's "Oughts"—Old Testament

The Ten Commandments were not given with any consideration for human ability or inability to keep them; they are the revelation of God's demands made of men and women who had declared that if God would make His law known, they would keep it. "Then all the people answered together and said, 'All that the LORD has spoken we will do' " (Exodus 19:8). "And God spoke all these words saying, . . . You shall . . . . You shall not . . ." (20:1–17). The commandments were given with the inexorable awfulness of almighty God, and the subsequent history of the people is the record of how they could not keep them.

The moral law ordained by God does not make itself weak to the weak, it does not palliate our shortcomings, it takes no account of our heredity and our infirmities; it

13

demands that we be absolutely moral. Not to recognize this is to be less than alive. The apostle Paul said, "I was alive once without the law, but when the commandment came, sin revived and I died" (Romans 7:9). Undress yourself morally and see how much you owe to your upbringing, to the circumstances you are in; when you have gotten rid of all that, there is little to stand before God in, certainly nothing to boast of. As soon as we come into actual human conditions we find inability with regard to the keeping of God's law, then comes in the equivocation: "Of course God won't demand it; of course God will make allowances." God's laws are not watered down to suit anyone; if God did that He would cease to be God. The moral law never alters for the noblest or the weakest; it remains abidingly and eternally the same.

Everyone has an imperative something within that makes her or him say "I ought"; even in the most degraded specimens of humanity the "ought" is there, and the Bible tells us where it comes from—it comes from God. The modern tendency is to leave God out and make the standard what is most useful to people. The utilitarian says that these distinct laws of conduct have been evolved by human beings for the benefit of human beings—the greatest use to the greatest number. That is not the reason a thing is right; the reason a thing is right is that God is behind it. God's "oughts" never alter; we never grow out of them. Our difficulty is that we find in ourselves this attitude—I ought to do this, but I won't; I ought to do that, but I don't want to. That puts out of court the idea that if you teach people what is right they will do it—they won't; what is needed is a power that will enable us to do what we know is right. We may say, "Oh, I won't count this time," but every bit of moral wrong is counted by God. The moral law exerts no coercion, neither does it allow any compromise. "For whoever shall keep the whole law, and yet stumble in one point, he is guilty of all" (James 2:10).

Once we realize this we see why it was necessary for Jesus Christ to come. The Redemption is the reality that alters inability into ability.

Christ's Principles—New Testament

If the "oughts" of the Old Testament were difficult to obey, our Lord's teaching is unfathomably more difficult.

Remember, the commandments were given irrespective of human ability or inability to keep them; then when Jesus Christ came, instead of doing what we all too glibly say He did—put something easier before us—He made it a hundred-fold more difficult, because He goes behind the law to the disposition. There is an idea abroad today that because as Christians we are not under law but under grace, therefore the Ten Commandments have no meaning for us—what did Jesus say? "Do not think that I came to destroy the Law or the Prophets. I did not come to destroy but to fulfill" (Matthew 5:17). The teaching of the Sermon on the Mount is overwhelmingly and disastrously penetrating. Jesus Christ does not simply say, You shall not do certain things; He demands that we have such a condition of heart that we never even think of doing them; every thought and imagination of heart and mind is to be unblameable in the sight of God. Who is sufficient for these things—an unsullied purity that never lusts, a forgiving disposition that loves its enemies, a generous spirit that takes no account of evil? That standard can produce only one thing in an open-eyed individual—absolute despair. What is the use of saying, "All we need is to know what Jesus Christ teaches and then live up to it"? Where are you going to begin? If we are Christians we have to live according to the teaching of the Sermon on the Mount, and the marvel of Jesus Christ's salvation is that He puts us in the place where we can fulfill all the old law and a great deal more.

Be careful not to be caught up in the claptrap of today that says, "I believe in the teachings of Jesus, but I don't see any need for the Atonement." People talk pleasant, patronizing things about Jesus Christ's teaching while they ignore His cross. By all means, let us study Christ's teaching, as we do not think nearly enough along New Testament lines. We are swamped by pagan standards, and as Christians we ought to allow Jesus Christ's principles to work out in our brains as well as in our lives; but the teaching of Jesus apart from His atonement simply adds an ideal that leads to despair. What is the good of telling me that only the pure in heart can see God when I am impure? of telling me to love my enemies when I hate them? I may keep it down but the spirit is there. Does Jesus Christ make it easier? He makes it a hundredfold more difficult! The purity God demands is impossible unless we can be remade from within, and that is what Jesus Christ undertakes to do through the Atonement. Jesus Christ did not come to tell people they ought to be holy—there is an "ought" in every one of us that tells us, and whenever we see a holy character we may bluster and excuse ourselves as we like, but we know that is what we ought to be—He came to put us in the place where we can be holy; that is, He came to make us what He teaches we should be, and that is the difference.

Our Lord's first requirement is a personal relationship to Him and then obedience to His principles. Tolstoy blundered in applying the Sermon on the Mount practically without insisting on the need to be born again of the Spirit first, and he had an enormous following of intellectual faddists, mere spring-cleaners. It is not a question of applying Jesus Christ's principles to your actual life first of all, but of applying them to your relationship to Him; then as you keep your soul open in relation to Him your conscience will decide how you are to act out of that relationship. The principles of Jesus Christ go to the very root of the matter; they have an intensely practical application to our moral lives. "For I say to you, that unless your righteousness exceeds the righteousness of the scribes and Pharisees, you will by no means enter the kingdom of heaven" (Matthew 5:20).

We said that the teaching of Jesus Christ apart from His atonement leads to despair—but if it produces the pauper condition, it is the right kind of despair. "Blessed are the poor in spirit" (v. 3). Conviction of sin will bring a person there, and so will the realization of God's demands. The best expression for us is Psalm 139:23: "Search me, O God"; I cannot make my heart pure, I cannot alter my heredity, I cannot alter the dreams of my mind; "Search me, O God, and know my heart." That is the poverty of spirit Jesus says is blessed; if you are in that condition, He says you can easily enter the kingdom of heaven. Why? Because God gives the almighty gift of salvation from sin to paupers; He gives the Holy Spirit to paupers (see Luke 11:13).

The New Person—Present Day

Jesus Christ, as human representative, accepted the responsibility of exhibiting on the human plane the absolute holiness of God; He lived up to God's standard in every detail of holy living and holy speaking and holy working, and His claim is that through the Atonement He can put us in the place where we can do the same. The very disposition that was in Him is put into me—is it there? If it is not, I will have to answer for it. It is not that God puts the life of Jesus in front of us and says, Do your best to follow Him, but that "the life of Jesus also may be manifested in our body" (1 Corinthians 4: 10); when "Christ is formed" in us by regeneration (Galatians 4:19), we have to see that our human nature puts on the clothing that is worthy of the Son of God. That is where our responsibility comes in—not in being absolutely holy but in seeing that we allow Jesus Christ to be absolutely holy in us. Regeneration does not resolve us into imbecility; it lifts us powerfully into oneness with God in Christ Jesus.

We shall come to find that being not under law but under grace does not mean we are so free from the Law that it does not matter now what we do; it means that in our actual lives we can fulfill all the requirements of the law of God.

The Moral Imperative—II

(that is, a law universal and binding on every rational will)

Why should I do what I ought to do?

Authority, in the final sense, must spring from within. To begin with, we are educated by means of authority on the outside: "you shall" and "you shall not"—but that authority does not treat us as people. The ultimate aim imbedded in all external authority is to produce a standard of authority within ourselves. The authority our Lord obeyed was an internal authority, not an external one; that is, His inner life and the life He exhibited were one and the same, and the purpose of all external authority is to bring us there. We only realize the moral law when it comes with an *if*, which means I have the power not to obey it.

We imagine that if we obey authority we limit ourselves, whereas obedience to authority is not a limitation but a source of power; by obeying we are more. Naturally we are built to command, not to obey; humanity was originally constituted by God to have dominion: "Then God said, 'Let Us make man in Our image, according to Our likeness; let them have dominion' " (Genesis 1:26); consequently there is the natural desire to want to explain things, because everything we can explain we can command. Spiritually we are built not to command, but to obey. Always beware of the tendency to want to have things explained; you may take it as an invariable law that when you demand an explanation in connection with a moral problem it means you are evading obedience.

Authority and Humanity—Conditional

The first standard of authority the Bible reveals is the authority of innocence, a conditional authority (see Genesis 2:16–17). *Innocence* means the absence of legal guilt. As long as Adam obeyed God he was in this state of innocence; God placed him in an external setting so that He might transform his innocence into moral character by a series of choices. It was to be a natural progress of development, not from evil to good, but from the natural to the spiritual. This Adam failed to do; the temptation came—Take dominion over yourself, "and you will be like God" (3:5); he took dominion over himself and by so doing lost dominion over everything else, and the disposition of sin—my claim to my right to myself, I will do what I like—became the inheritance of the whole human race. "Through one man sin entered the world" (Romans 5:12). Children born of natural generation are not innocent in the same way that Adam was innocent, neither does the innocence of a child contain conditional authority; the innocence of regeneration alone corresponds to Adam's innocence.

Some people maintain that innocence should be the only standard of authority; the idea works out magnificently on paper or in thinking, but it does not work out in practical life. If we were all born with the right disposition, development along this line would have been all right, but we quickly find out that there is something drastically wrong—the disposition of sin is at work, this opposing principle that is not true to human nature as God created it. It sounds very delightful to talk about the innocence of children and about living the simple life, but try it in actual experience, and you will find it works out the wrong way every time. Authority based on innocence soon becomes ignorance—not ignorance of ourselves but a determined being without the knowledge of God, and ignorance quickly corrupts into iniquity (see Genesis 3–6).

Another standard of authority is that of conscience, or "the inner light"—what Socrates called "the presiding dæmon," an un-get-at-able, indefinable spirit that gives liberty or check to whatever a person feels impelled to do. Everyone has a conscience, although everyone does not know God. If God had never made known His demands, we might have said that every person was a law to himself or to herself— whatever I think is right, according to my own inner light, must be right. As soon as people become a law to themselves, they begin to do what they like, and if you teach development along the line of obedience to an individual's inner light, what about the person who is born with damnable tendencies—where will it lead that individual? To a moral pigsty. The final standard of authority must be one that can be owned by everyone.

Authority As Happiness—Corrupt

Happiness is the portion of a child; children ought to be thoughtless and happy, and woe be to those who upset their happiness; but if you take happiness as the end and aim for men and women, you have to make its basis a determined ignorance of God, otherwise people will, like Job, remember God and be troubled (see Job 23:15; Psalm 77:3). Read the Seventy-third Psalm. It is the description of people who have made happiness their aim—they are not in trouble as other people, neither are they plagued like other people, they have more than their heart could wish; but once let their moral equilibrium be upset by conviction of sin, and all their happiness is destroyed. The end and aim of human life is not happiness but "to glorify God, and fully to enjoy him forever."

Holiness of character, chastity of life, living communion with God—that is the end of a human life; whether a person is happy or not is a matter of moonshine. Happiness is no standard for men and women because happiness depends on our being determinedly ignorant of God and His demands. Whenever the Spirit of God disturbs people, He brings them back to the Decalogue. The point is that anything that relieves us from the individual responsibility of being personally related to God is corrupt.

Immorality will produce happiness very quickly—the duration of the happiness is another matter; if you go on doing wrong long enough you will be happy doing wrong and miserable doing right—therefore quit doing right! Immorality may be physically clean, but at its heart is this thought: *All I am concerned with is the happiness of the greatest number, and I don't care anything at all about God.* Once personal accountability to God is removed you will get immorality; whether it is bestial or not is a matter of accident. The Bible talks very unvarnishedly; it calls things by the hideous names that belong to them (see, for example, Colossians 3:5; Galatians 5:19–21). Beware of being cute enough to detect immorality only in a moral pigsty; learn to detect it in your own spiritual imagination.

Authority As Holiness—Correct

The commandments of God exhibit not His consideration for humanity but His authoritative demands of humanity. People have to fulfill God's laws in their physical lives, in their mental and moral lives, in their social and spiritual lives, and to stumble in one point is to be guilty of all. Until we realize that God cannot make allowances, the gospel has no meaning for us; if God made allowances He would cease to be God. All through the Bible the authority of God's law is unflinchingly revealed, together with human responsibility to meet its demand; but the problem of problems is—how is it going to be done? When a person reads the teachings of Jesus she or he is obliged to say, "Yes, that is right, but His teaching destroys my peace. I believe that is what I ought to be, but where am I going to begin?"

Holiness is the agreement between a person's disposition and the law of God, as expressed in the life of Jesus. According to the Bible there are only two people, Adam and Jesus Christ; both came into the world directly by the hand of God, innocent. Jesus Christ, the Last Adam, did what the First Adam failed to do: He transformed innocence into holy character. The law of God was incarnated in Jesus Christ; He walked this earth in human guise and lived the perfect life that God desired. Never think of Jesus Christ as an individual, for He is the Federal Head of the race; He not only fulfilled all God's demands, but He made the way for every imperfect human being to live the same kind of life. Jesus Christ does not put us back where Adam was, He puts us where Adam never was—He puts us where He is Himself; He presences us with Divinity, namely, the Holy Spirit. The meaning of the Redemption is that anyone can be regenerated into the life Jesus lived and can have the holiness of God imparted to him or to her—not the power to imitate His holiness, but the very nature of God: "That we may be partakers of His holiness" (Hebrews 12:10). Holiness is the characteristic of the woman or the man after God's own heart.

The holiness that God demands is impossible unless a person can be remade from within, and that is what Jesus Christ has undertaken to do. Jesus Christ does not merely save people from hell: "You shall call His name JESUS, for He will save His people from their sins" (Matthew 1:21)—that is, make totally new, moral people. Jesus Christ came from a holy God to enable people, by the sheer might of His redemption, to become holy. "You shall be holy, for I the LORD your God am holy" (Leviticus 19:2; see 1 Peter 1:16).

N.B.—Notes of this lecture are incomplete.

Moral Institutions—I

In Precept

By "in precept" is meant necessary principles laid down beforehand.

God has ordained that people are to govern people, whether they want to or not. This keeps socialism from being "it"; the socialistic scheme falls to pieces because it ignores the fact that human institutions are not utilitarian; that is, they do not spring from human ingenuity but were deliberately ordained by God for the government of humans by humans. Peter brings this out when he says, "Submit yourselves to every ordinance of man," but he is careful to add "for the Lord's sake" (1 Peter 2:13).

Humanity is responsible to God for the government of the whole world, but if someone succumbs to the temptations of his or her official position, that very position will have the effect of hardening that individual's heart away from God. We read in the Old Testament that "Pharaoh hardened his heart" (Exodus 7:14 and the following); and we read also that "God hardened his heart" (4:21 and the following). The difficulty of this apparent contradiction is purely superficial. It must not be interpreted to mean that God hardened a human heart and then condemned the person for being hardened. The hardening of Pharaoh's heart by himself and by God is the expression of the working of one of God's

24

laws, and God's laws do not alter. Any rulers or ordinary people who refuse to obey the right law will find themselves distinctly hardened away from God. If someone is to govern rightly that person must see that the institutions he or she builds up are based on the stabilities of human nature as God created it; otherwise havoc will be produced.

One of the first general principles to be borne in mind is that we must never think of women and men in the mass. We talk about the struggling mass of humanity—there is no such thing, the mass is made up of separate individuals. The danger of thinking of people in the mass is that you forget they are human beings, each one an absolutely solitary life. Everyone has something or someone to govern; the most ignominious slave has an influence somewhere, and God is going to hold us responsible for the way we govern.

Another thing to be borne in mind is the incalculable element in every life. In the government of people by people, you are not dealing with a mathematical problem but with human beings, and you can never be sure how they will act, any more than you can always be sure how you yourself will act.

These are simply indications of the problems a person has to face in the government of other people, yet God has so constituted things that people have to govern people and to answer to God for the way they govern.

Desire

One of the biggest ingredients in human makeup is what people desire or regard as good. Discouragement or any kind of sulks is accounted for by the fact that the good people aim at is not good enough. People of character will set themselves at nothing less than the highest.

The remarkable thing about the universe of desire is that at any second it may alter. Every now and again a tumult

God may I be a person of character

comes into someone's life and alters what the person desires. For instance, death has an amazing power of altering what a person desires, because death profoundly affects his or her outlook. Or the experience of new birth will do it. When people are born again they stop desiring the things they used to desire, not gradually but suddenly; things begin to matter that did not matter before, and the things that used to matter no longer do so. They experience conflict of desire; at one time they want to do the old things, at another, the new, and for a while they are in an unbalanced state. That is the result ethically and morally of conviction of sin and is exactly what Jesus meant when He said, "Do not think that I came to bring peace on earth. I did not come to bring peace but a sword" (Matthew 10:34).

This sudden alteration in the universe of desire is one of the perplexities in the government of humans by humans. You cannot be sure that the person you are dealing with will always be the same; at any second he or she may alter. You see someone set on a line you know to be wrong, but remember, at any second the universe of that person's desire may change. To remember this will bring a tremendous hopefulness and cure us of our unbelief about any life.

Another thing to bear in mind is the difference between a young life and a mature life. A boy or girl just emerging from the teens is always chaotic; if a young life is normal it is a chunk of chaos; if it is not, there is something wrong, there ought to be the chaotic element. A precocious young life rarely ends well; it becomes ordered too soon. God holds us responsible for the way we judge a young life; if we judge it by the standards by which we would judge a mature life, we will be grossly unjust. As you watch the life, it seems sometimes to lean toward the good, sometimes toward the wrong, and you find yourself getting either excited or depressed over it; but there is one main trend coming out, and that trend can be guarded by prayer. This emphasizes the importance of intercessory prayer. Much misjudgment of young life goes on in the religious domain. There is a stage when a young life manifests a sudden interest in everything to do with religion, but never bank on these awakenings because they are not necessarily awakenings by the Spirit of God, and when the intense stage passes—and it certainly will pass if it is not born of the Spirit—the one who is judging is apt to say that the girl or the boy has backslidden. What has happened is that she or he has passed through a dangerous stage of development. The defects of a growing life are one thing, the vices of a mature life are another. Be as merciless as God can make you toward the vices of a mature life, but be very gentle and patient with the defects of a growing life.

These things make us understand how careful we have to be to recognize God in our government of other lives. If the government of our own lives is upon His shoulder, we will be careful to rely on Him in connection with the lives we are called on to influence and govern.

Moral Institutions—II

In Practice

By "in practice" is meant fitness through regular exercise. If we do not fit ourselves by practice when there is no crisis, we shall find that human nature will fail us when the crisis comes. The grace of God never fails, but we may fail the grace of God. Unless the nervous system is made the ally of the new life from God it becomes a humiliation to us, and we sit down under a tyranny of nerves. Once we have received the Holy Spirit we must sit down to nothing. In these distinctly personal matters it must be borne in mind that the moral institutions ordained by God take no account whatever of nervous disabilities; they take account only of God Himself and the way He has designed the human being. When your nervous system, which has been ruled by the wrong disposition, is inclined to say, "I can't," you must say, "You must," and to your amazement you find you can!

Righteousness

Righteousness is conformity to a right standard, where no one but God sees us. That is where very few of us are Christians.

(a) In Intention

Little children, let no one deceive you. He who practices righteousness is righteous. 1 John 3:7

28

Jesus Christ demands of His disciples that they live in conformity to the right standard in intention. We say, "Though I didn't do well, I meant well"; then it is absolutely certain you did not mean well. Jesus Christ makes no allowance for heroic moods; He judges us by the diligently applied bent of our dispositions. Concentration on the part of a Christian is of more importance than consecration.

"He who *practices* righteousness is righteous." There are different kinds of intention, for example, outer and inner; immediate and remote; direct and indirect. The righteous person is the one whose inner intention is clearly revealed in the outer intention: there is no duplicity, no internal hypocrisy. An individual's outer intention is easily discernible by other people; one's inner intention needs to be continually examined. The marvel of the grace of God is that it can alter the mainspring of human makeup, then when that is altered we must foster in ourselves those intentions that spring from the Spirit of Jesus and make the nervous system carry them out. The Holy Spirit will bring us to the practical test; it is not that I say I am righteous but that I prove I am in my deeds.

(b) In Individuals

> For I say to you, that except your righteousness exceeds the righteousness of the scribes and Pharisees, you will by no means enter the kingdom of heaven. Matthew 5:20

Take Saul of Tarsus as an example of Pharisaism; he says of himself in writing to the Philippians, "as concerning the law, a Pharisee; . . . concerning the righteousness which is in the law, blameless" (3:5–6); Jesus Christ says as disciples we have to exceed that. No wonder we find His statements absolutely shattering. Our righteousness has to be in excess of the righteousness of the person whose external conduct is blameless according to the law—what does that produce? Despair, immediately. When we hear Jesus say "Blessed are the pure in heart" (Matthew 5:8), our answer, if we are awake is, "My God, how am I going to be pure in heart? If ever I am to be blameless down to the deepest recesses of my intentions, You must do something mighty in me." That is exactly what Jesus Christ came to do. He did not come to tell us to be holy but to make us holy, undeserving of censure in the sight of God. If any man or any woman gets there, it is by the sheer, supernatural grace of God. You can't indulge in pious pretense when you come to the atmosphere of the Bible. If there is one thing the Spirit of God does it is to purge us from all sanctimonious humbug—there is no room for it.

(c) In Institutions

> Submit yourselves to every ordinance of man for the Lord's sake: 1 Peter 2:13; see also verses 14–18

Peter's statements in these verses are remarkable, and they are statements the modern Christian does not like. He is outlining what is to be the conduct of saints in relation to the moral institutions based on the government of human beings by human beings. No matter, he says, what may be the condition of the community to which you belong, behave yourself as a saint in it. Many people are righteous as individuals, but they ignore the need to be righteous in connection with human institutions. Paul continually dealt with insubordination in spiritual people. Degeneration in the Christian life comes in because of this refusal to recognize the insistence God places on obedience to human institutions. Take the institution of home life. Home is God's institution, and He says, "Honor your father and your mother" (Exodus 20:12); are we fulfilling our duty to our parents as laid down in God's Book? Guard well the central institutions ordained by God, and there will be fewer problems in civilized life. We have to maintain spiritual reality wherever we are placed by

30   *Biblical Ethics*

the engineering of our circumstances by God; as servants we are to be subject to our masters, to the froward master as well as to the good and gentle. That is where the shoe pinches, and whenever you feel the pinch it is time you go to the death of something.

Rights

By *rights* is meant what one has a just claim to. Every right brings with it an obligation. Legally, people can do what they like with their own; morally, they are under obligation to use it for the general good; spiritually, they are bound to devote it to God.

(a) Of Life

> Whoever sheds man's blood, by man his blood shall be shed. Genesis 9:6

Everyone, in the sight of God, has an equal right to life, and if one person takes away the life of another, that person's own life shall be taken away. The right of life is insisted on all through the Bible. As long as I do not murder anyone outright the law cannot touch me, but is there someone dependent on me to whom in the tiniest way I am not giving the right to live? Someone for whom I am cherishing an unforgiving dislike? "Whoever hates his brother is a murderer," says John (1 John 3:15). One of the terrors of the Day of Judgment will be our indifference to the rights of life.

(b) Of Land

> When you come into the land which I give you, then the land shall keep a sabbath to the LORD. . . . In the seventh year there shall be a sabbath of solemn rest for the land, a sabbath to the LORD. Leviticus 25:2–4

The twenty-fifth chapter of Leviticus is the great classic on the rights of the land. The establishment of human rights on the earth is limited by the rights of the earth itself. If you keep taking from the land, never giving it any rest, in time it will stop giving to you. We talk about the rights of the land and make it mean our right to grab as much from it as we can. In God's sight, the land has rights just as human beings have, and many of the theories that are being advanced today go back to God's original prescription for the land. When God ordained "a sabbath of solemn rest for the land," it was a reiteration of the instructions given to Adam in the Garden of Eden: "Be fruitful, and multiply; fill the earth and subdue it" (Genesis 1:28). Humanity was intended to replenish the earth by looking after it, being its lord not its tyrant; sin has made humanity its tyrant. (Compare Romans 8:19). The rights of the land will probably only be fully realized in the Millennium, because in this dispensation people ignore obedience to God's laws.

In the teaching of Jesus, the earth is never confounded with the world. "Blessed are the meek, for they shall inherit the earth" (Matthew 5:5). The meek, that is, those who have the disposition of the Son of God and are practicing righteousness in accordance with that disposition, are to inherit the earth. The world is the system of things that humanity has erected on God's earth. Today people belong to various *isms* and *ites*, and they say, "We are going to inherit the earth; we are the favored people of God," but that characteristic is not meekness; it is, rather, the spirit of the devil. Jew or Gentile, lost tribe or found, none of it is of any account unless it is based on the principles Jesus Christ lays down. He says that the meek, those who obey the laws of God, shall inherit the earth. The material earth is God's, and the way people treat it is a marvelous picture of the long-suffering of God.

(c) Of Liberty

> All things are lawful for me, but all things are not helpful.
> 1 Corinthians 6:12

Original receipt - an exchange or refund based upon the original tender. Please note: Debit cards using a Personal ID at the pin pad will be refunded cash.

Gift receipt - an exchange or Kohl's Merchandise Return Credit.

No receipt - an exchange, Kohl's Merchandise Return Credit, or credit to Kohl's Charge.

Unworn shoes will be returned/exchanged following the above policies.

Defective Merchandise will be returned/exchanged following the above policies.

For your convenience, bring this receipt along with your purchase at the time of your return.

At Kohl's Complete Satisfaction is Our Goal!

However, if our merchandise does not meet your expectations, we offer the following return options:

iginal receipt - an exchange or refund based
the original tender. Please note: Debit cards
g a Personal ID at the pin pad will be refunded

TELL US WHAT YOU THINK TODAY!
12-01-05   7:30P

GIVE US YOUR FEEDBACK
ON TODAY'S STORE VISIT

GO TO WWW.KOHLS.COM/SURVEY

STORE 0414
ACCESS CODE 01-0010-5925-0

RESPOND WITHIN 48 HRS TO PARTICIPATE.

For your convenience, bring this receipt along with your purchase at the time of your return.

KOHL'S

At Kohl's Complete Satisfaction is Our Goal!

However, if our merchandise does not meet your expectations, we offer the following return options:

Original receipt - an exchange or refund based upon the original tender. Please note: Debit cards using a Personal ID at the pin pad will be refunded cash.

Gift receipt - an exchange or Kohl's Merchandise Return Credit.

No receipt - an exchange, Kohl's Merchandise Return Credit, or credit to Kohl's Charge.

Unworn shoes will be returned/exchanged following the above policies.

Defective Merchandise will be returned/exchanged following the above policies.

For your convenience, bring this receipt along with your purchase at the time of your return.

At Kohl's Complete Satisfaction is Our Goal!

However, if our merchandise does not meet your expectations, we offer the following return options:

KOHL'S

Grand Prairie
Grand Prairie, TX 75052
(972) 263-1099

12-01-05 7:30P 0414/0010/5925/7 1558XXX
ID# 999-8798-9480-6946-9585-8940-7472

CARDS & WRAP   070000191602   2.49 T1

                        SUBTOTAL   2.49
T1=   2.49 @ 8.250% TAX   0.21
                         TOTAL   2.70

CASH   3.00
                       CHANGE   0.30-

Shop KOHLS.COM and
enjoy FREE standard shipping
on purchases of $75 or more
this holiday season

The counterfit of freedom is independence

We call liberty allowing others to please themselves to the same extent as we please ourselves. True liberty is the ability earned by practice to do the right thing. There is no such thing as a gift of freedom; freedom must be earned. The counterfeit of freedom is independence. When the Spirit of God deals with sin, it is independence that He touches; that is why the preaching of the gospel awakens resentment as well as craving. Independence must be blasted right out of a Christian; there must be only liberty, which is a very different thing. Spiritually, liberty means the ability to fulfill the law of God, and it establishes the rights of other people.

The teaching of the Sermon on the Mount is the exact opposite of the modern jargon about equal rights; "Why shouldn't I do this? I'm within my rights." Of course you are, but never call yourself a Christian if you reason like that because a Christian is one who sacrifices his or her liberty for the sake of others, for Jesus Christ's sake. Paul's whole argument is based on this (see 1 Corinthians 8, Romans 14). "Do not use liberty as an opportunity for the flesh," he says (Galatians 5:13). When we receive the Holy Spirit we receive the nature of God, and He expects us to keep our nervous systems obedient to the dictates of the Holy Spirit. All through these studies we have emphasized the principle of obedience to the highest; it is one of the most practical guides for our conduct as individuals. Paul continually dealt with people who under the guise of religion were libertines; they talked about liberty when what they really meant was, "I insist on doing what it is my right to do, and I don't care a jot about anyone else." That is not liberty, that is lawlessness. The only liberty a saint has is the liberty not to use her or his liberty. There is nothing more searching than what the New Testament has to say about the use of liberty. It is never our duty to go the second mile, to give up our possessions or property to someone else, but Jesus says if we are His disciples, that is what we will do.

The Moral Individual—I

Individuality

Individuality is the husk of the personal life, it is all elbows; it separates and isolates. The husk of individuality is God's cre-ated natural covering for the protection of the personal life, but unless individuality gets transfigured it becomes objec-tionable, egotistical and conceited, interested only in its own independence. Individuality is the characteristic of a child, and rightly so, but if we mistake individuality for the personal life we will remain isolated. It is the continual assertion of individuality that hinders our spiritual development more than anything else; individuality must go in order that person-ality may emerge and be brought into fellowship with God.

Independence

A fugitive and a vagabond you shall be on the earth. Genesis 4:12

Individuality is natural, but when individuality is indwelt by sin it destroys personal communion and isolates individu-als, like so many crystals, and all possibility of fellowship is destroyed. The characteristics of individuality are indepen-dence and self-assertiveness. There is nothing dearer to the heart of the natural man than independence, and as long as I live in the outskirts of my prideful independence, Jesus Christ is nothing to me.

Personality, not individuality, is the great Christian doc-trine, but we misunderstand the teaching of our Lord when we confound the natural with the spiritual and individuality with sin. Independence of one another is natural; independence of God is sin. When natural independence of one another is wedded with independence of God it becomes sin, and sin isolates and destroys and ultimately damns the life. Positive individuality in any form is not only anti-Christian, but antihuman, because it instantly says, "I care for neither God nor other people, I live for myself."

Cain stands for positive individuality: "Cain . . . was of the wicked one and murdered his brother. And why did he murder him? Because his works were evil and his brother's righteous" (1 John 3:12). (It is not the act of murder only that is taken into account—our Lord said, "Out of the heart proceed . . . murders" [Matthew 15:19]. The statements of Jesus at times startle us painfully awake.) Cain was the first isolated individual; Adam was not an isolated individual. Before the Fall, Adam was in relationship with God and with the world; when he was driven out from the Garden he was still in relationship with the world. Cain's sin shattered him into absolute solitariness. Being alone is not solitariness; it is the loneliness with an element of moral disesteem in it that is solitariness. There is no comrade for a murderer; he is isolated by the very success of his sin. It is instructive to notice what associates itself with God and what with the sinner: nothing associates itself with the sinner but his or her sin. The sinner is absolutely solitary on God's earth, and as long as the sinner remains proud in that solitariness he or she goes against everything that is anything like God— against humankind, who is most like God, and against the earth, which is also like God, and both humankind and the earth cry out to God against that sinner all the time. "The voice of your brother's blood cries out to Me from the ground" (Genesis 4:10).

For an individual to be isolated is either a sign of sin or of a transition stage, that is, a soul in the making. The most dan-

Are you in isolation?

gerous stage in a soul's development is the no-one-understands-me stage—of course they don't! "I don't understand myself"—of course you don't! If this stage develops unduly the young will find when they get out into the world that they cannot work with others, and they become more and more impossible until the unwholesome idea that they are different from everyone else is knocked out of them. It is well to remember that our examination of ourselves can never be unbiased, so that we are only safe in taking our estimate of ourselves from our Creator instead of from our own introspection, which makes us either depressed or conceited. The oft-repeated modern phrase "self-mastery" is misleading; profoundly speaking, people can never master what they do not understand, therefore the only master of any individual is not himself or herself or another person, but God. Because introspection cannot profoundly satisfy, it does not follow that introspection is wrong; it is right, because it is the only way in which we will discover our need of God. It is the introspective power that is made alert by conviction of sin.

Interdependence

> Neither did anyone say that any of the things he possessed was his own, but they had all things in common. Acts 4:32

> Let us consider one another in order to stir up to love and good works, not forsaking the assembling of ourselves together. Hebrews 10:24–25

These two passages serve to indicate the main characteristic of Christianity, namely, the "together" aspect; false religions inculcate an isolated, holy life. Try and develop a holy life in private, and you find it cannot be done. Individuals can only live the true life when they are dependent on one another. After the Resurrection our Lord would not allow Mary to hold a spiritual experience for herself, she must get into contact with the disciples and convey a message to them: "Do not cling to Me, . . . but go to My brethren and say to them, 'I am ascending to My Father and your Father, and to My God and your God' " (John 20:17). After Peter's denial the isolation of misery would inevitably have seized on him and made him want to retire in the mood of "I can never forgive myself," had not our Lord forestalled this by giving him something positive to do: "When you have returned to Me, strengthen your brethren" (Luke 22:32). As soon as you try to develop holiness alone and fix your eyes on your own whiteness, you lose the whole meaning of Christianity. The Holy Spirit makes people fix their eyes on their Lord and on intense activity for others. In the early Middle Ages people had the idea that Christianity meant living a holy life apart from the world and its sociability, apart from its work and citizenship. That type of holiness is foreign to the New Testament; it cannot be reconciled with the records of the life of Jesus. The people of His day called Him "a friend of tax collectors and sinners" (Matthew 11:19) because He spent so much time with them.

The danger of the Higher Christian Life movements is that the emphasis is put not on the regenerating power of the grace of God, but on individual consecration, individual fasting and prayer, individual devotion to God. The apostle Paul sums up individual human effort under the guise of religion as things that "indeed have an appearance of wisdom in self-imposed religion, false humility, and neglect of the body" (Colossians 2:23). It is simply individualism veneered over with religious phraseology—"What has Jesus done for me? I have done it all for myself; I did it by prayer, by fasting, by consecration." To reason like that is to put our Lord out of it as Savior and Sanctifier. We do not come to Jesus Christ; we come to our own earnestness, to our own consecration; what happens when we do come to Jesus is the miracle of a new creation. The Christian life is stamped all through with

Dont lose sight of your true calling: winning souls?

impossibility. Human nature cannot come anywhere near Jesus Christ's demands, and any rational being facing those demands honestly says, "It can't be done, apart from a miracle." Exactly. In our modern Christianity there is no miracle; it is—"You must pray more"; "you must give up this and that"—anything and everything but the need to be born into a totally new kingdom.

In these talks we have traced all through the insistence that we are brought up in families, and families form communities and communities, institutions and institutions are under governments, and governments are answerable to God—all for one purpose, that we might develop together. In the external aspects of Christianity in civilized life, individuality is not lost, and it is not positive; it is interdependent. Beware of becoming a positive individual in your Christian community and saying, "I must separate myself and start a little place of my own." John wrote, in 1 John 1:7, "If we walk in the light, as He is in the light, we have fellowship with one another"—with everyone else who is in the light. Natural affinity does not count here at all.

Identification

> That they may be one as We are. John 17:11

Christianity is personal, therefore it is unindividual. An individual remains definitely segregated from every other individual; when you come to the teaching of our Lord there is no individuality in that sense at all, but only personality: "that they may be one." Two *individuals* can never merge; two *persons* can become one without losing their identities. Personality is the characteristic of the spiritual man, as individuality is the characteristic of the natural man. When the Holy Spirit comes in, He emancipates the person's spirit into union with God, and individuality ultimately becomes so interde-

You must lose your identity to become one.

pendent that it loses all its self-assertiveness. Jesus Christ prayed for our identification with Him in His oneness with the Father: "that they may be one, *as We are.*" That is infinitely beyond experience. Identification is a revelation—the exposition of the experience. The standard revelation with regard to identification is our Lord Himself, and you can never define Him in terms of individuality but only in terms of personality. When Jesus Christ emancipates the personality, individuality is not destroyed, it is transfigured, and the transfiguring, incalculable element is love, personal, passionate devotion to Him, and to others for His sake.

The Moral Individual—II

The World: In It Worldly: Of It Otherworldly: In It but Not of It

The World—In It

The term *world* is used to mean the material world and the men and women in it—we are all "in it" in this sense. The Bible says that "God so loved the world"—and the unfathomable depth of His love is in that word "so"—yet it also says that "whoever wants to be a friend of the world makes himself an enemy of God" (James 4:4). The apparent contradiction can be explained like this: God's love for the world is the kind of love that makes Him go all lengths in order to remove the sin and evil from it. Love, to be anything at all, must be personal; to love without hating is an impossibility, and the stronger and more emphatic the love, the more intense is its obverse, hatred. God loves the world so much that He hates with a perfect hatred the thing that switched people wrong, and Calvary is the measure of His hatred. The natural human heart would have argued, God so loves the world that of course He will forgive its sin; God so loved the world that He could not forgive its sin. There is no such thing as God overlooking sin, therefore if He does forgive there must be a reason that justifies Him in doing so.

To be a friend of the world means that we take the world as it is and are perfectly delighted with it—the world is all right and we are very happy in it. Never have the idea that

40

Love w/o hate
is impossible.

the worldling is unhappy; he or she is perfectly happy, as thoroughly happy as a Christian. The people who are unhappy are the worldlings or the Christians if they are not at one with the principle that unites them. If worldlings are not worldlings at heart, they are miserable; and if Christians are not Christians at heart, they carry their Christianity like a headache instead of something worth having, and not being able to get rid of their heads, they cannot get rid of their headaches. Worldlings are not immoral; they are those who wisely keep within the bounds of the disposition that the Bible alone reveals as sinful, namely, my claim to my right to myself. The Bible reveals the solidarity of sin, a bond of union that keeps people together; it is the mutual inheritance of the human race: "Through one man sin entered the world, and death through sin, and thus death spread to all men, because all have sinned" (Romans 5:12). Satan is anxious to keep that solidarity intact because whenever it breaks out into immoral acts it disintegrates his kingdom. Two things disintegrate the solidarity of sin—the breaking out into overt acts of sin and the conviction of the Spirit of God. This will be found to be the solution of a number of moral problems.

To love the world as it is is the wrong kind of love; it is that sentiment which is the enemy of God, because it means I am the friend of the system of things that does not take God into account. We are to love the world in the way God loves it and be ready to spend and be spent until the wrong and evil are removed from it. When Jesus said "I do not pray for the world" (John 17:9), it did not mean He was indifferent to the world or despised it; His work for the world is to save it. In thinking about the world we are apt to overlook the greatest factor of all from the Bible standpoint, namely, that we belong to a fallen race. In our intellectual conceptions the Fall has no place at all; the human race is looked upon as a crowd of innocent babes in the wood. The Bible looks upon the human race as it is as the result of a mutiny against God; consequently you find in the Bible something you find in no other book or conception. The modern view of humanity is what a marvelous promise of what it is going to be! The Bible looks at humanity and sees the ruin of what it once was. In the Bible everything is based on the fact that there is something wrong at the basis of things.

Worldly—Of It

To be "of" the world means to belong to the set that organizes its religion, its business, its social life and pleasures without any concern as to how it affects Jesus Christ; as to whether He lived or died matters nothing at all. When our Lord said "Be of good cheer, I have overcome the world" (John 16:33), He obviously did not mean the world in the material, physical sense—the rocks and trees, the seasons, and the beautiful order of nature, the sea and sky; it was not these He overcame, but the world in its ordered system of religion and morality, with all its civilizations and progress, which system reveals in the final analysis that it is organized absolutely apart from any consideration of God. A clean cut from everything that savors of the world in this sense is essential for the Christian. No one can decide the matter for you; you may have to draw the line in one place; I may have to draw it in another, while the Holy Spirit is educating us down to the smallest detail. If I have for my religious ideal a good social life lived among human societies, that is to be of the world, no matter how religious it may be in terms.

It is easy to denounce wrong in the world outside me—anyone without a spark of the grace of God can do that; easy to denounce the sins of others while all the time I may be allowing all sorts of worldly things in my own religious life. We must be continually renewed in the spirit of our minds so that the slightest beginning of compromise with the spirit of the world is instantly detected. "Well, what's the harm; there's nothing wrong in it." When you hear that, you know you have the spirit of the world, because the Spirit that comes from Jesus says, Does this glorify God? The only way we are going to overcome the world as Jesus overcame it is by experimental sanctification. We are to live in heavenly places in Christ Jesus while on this earth and among worldly people. That is the glorious discipline of the sanctified life. The apostle Paul in writing to the Corinthians says, I don't say you are to have no dealings with those that are without, "since then you would need to go out of the world"; but I do say you are to have nothing to do with those who practice wrongdoing within the Christian community (see 1 Corinthians 5:10). Outside the Christian community, we must bear the shame and humiliation of contact with bad people vicariously, like Jesus did, and we may win them to God. "Do you not judge those who are inside? But those who are outside God judges" (vv. 12–13).

"As He is, so are we in this world" (1 John 4:17). Our Lord's own life proved that in the midst of the world where we are placed we can be holy women and holy men, not only talking rightly, but living rightly. The greatest insult you can offer God is pious talk unless it is backed up by holy actions. The attitude of Christians toward the providential order in which they are placed is to recognize that God is behind it for purposes of His own. For example, in our own country the dominance of state machinery stops occasionally and things are reconsidered and readjusted by means of a general election. Then is the time for Christians to work and make their voices heard. As soon as the machinery is at work again, the counsel abides—subjection to the higher powers: "the authorities that exist are appointed by God" (Romans 13:1).

Otherworldly—In It but Not of It

Otherworldly is simply a coined word to express what our Lord prayed for in John 17: "I do not pray that You should take them out of the world, but that You should keep them from the evil one" (v. 15); I don't ask You to take them out of the world, away from human society, but to keep them out of compromise with the Evil One who works in the world. The counsel of the Spirit of God to the saints is that they must allow nothing worldly in themselves while living among the worldly in the world. Those who live otherworldly in this world are the men and women who have been regenerated and who dare to live their lives according to the principles of Jesus. When once the protest is made where your Lord requires you to make it, you will soon find where you stand—exactly where Jesus said you would, outside the synagogue, called purist, narrow, and absurd.

"I have given them Your word; and the world has hated them because they are not of the world, just as I am not of the world" (v. 14). The hatred of the world is its intense objection to the principles exhibited by the saint, and frequently it is the best specimens of the worldly spirit who positively hate and detest the otherworldly spirit of the saint. It is not that they hate you personally—they may be very kind to you—but they hate what you represent of Jesus Christ. Remember what sin is—fundamental independence of God, the thing in me that says, I can do without God, I don't need Him. The hatred of the world has its source there. When you meet the hatred of the whole world-system unspiritual people around you will laugh to scorn the idea that you have a struggle on hand, but you realize that you are wrestling not against flesh and blood, but against the spiritual hosts of wickedness in the heavenly places.

Most of us live our lives in the world without ever dis-covering its hatred, but it is there, and a crisis may suddenly arise and bring it to a head, then we are appalled to find the meaning of our Lord's words, "You will be hated by all for My name's sake" (Matthew 10:22). I have no business to stir up the hatred of the world through a domineering religious opinionatedness—that has nothing whatever to do with the Spirit of Jesus; I am never told to rejoice when people sepa-rate me from their company on that account; but when in all modesty I am standing for the honor of Jesus Christ and a crisis arises when the Spirit of God requires that I declare my otherworldliness, then I learn what Jesus meant when He said, people will hate you. It is the hatred of the world expressed to the otherworldly standpoint once it is made clear.

This age is the last of the ordered ages that condition human life on this earth, and the New Testament writers look on to the time when creation's thralldom ends in deliv-erance and in the manifestation of the sons and daughters of God. "We . . . look for new heavens and a new earth . . ."; nowadays people have gotten tired of the preaching about a future heaven and they have gone to the other extreme and deal only with what is called the practical, consequently they rob themselves of the unfathomable joy of knowing that everything God has said will come to pass. The Redemption covers more than men and women, it covers the whole earth; everything that has been marred by sin and the devil has been completely redeemed by Jesus Christ. ". . . in which righteousness dwells" (2 Peter 3:13)—nothing that defiles can be in it at all; at present that is absolutely inconceivable to us. The world and the earth are not the same; the world represents the human societies on God's earth, and they do as they like; the earth remains God's. "Blessed are the meek, for they shall inherit the earth." The meek bide God's time.

The Moral Individual—III

Conversion

The literal meaning of *conversion* is a change of mind after watching certain facts; for example, we read in Acts 28:6 that the natives "changed their minds" about Paul. We are dealing with conversion here not so much on the religious side as the ethical. Beware of making *conversion* synonymous with *regeneration*. Conversion is simply the effort of a roused human being; the sign of regeneration is that a person has *received* something. When someone fails in Christian experience it is nearly always because he or she has never received anything. There are books that set out to give the psychology of new birth by saying that suddenly something bursts up from one's unconscious personality and alters one: a person is never born again by a subliminal uprush but only by receiving something that was never there before, namely, the Holy Spirit. Certain forms of sin exhaust themselves and we may say of people "Now they are saved," but they may be nothing of the sort. According to the New Testament, the only evidence of new birth is not merely that a person lives a different life, but that the basis of that different life is repentance. The bedrock in the classic experience of the apostle Paul was not only his enthroning of Jesus Christ as Lord, but His enthronement on the basis of a real, ringing repentance wrought in him by the Holy Spirit.

Mental Conversion

A double minded man [is] unstable in all his ways. James 1:8

Instability is an appalling snare in the natural life, and it is disastrous spiritually: "For let not that man suppose that he will receive anything from the Lord," says James (1:7). There may be conversions of heart that are not conversions of mind; the last thing a person comes to is the conversion of the mind. Our Lord refers to this instability in His parable of the sower and the seed: "The ones on the rock are those who, when they hear, receive the word with joy; and these have no root, who believe for a while and in time of temptation fall away" (Luke 8:13)—quicksilver Christians. They may have as many conversions as there are days in the year, and at the end of the year they remain the same unreliable, emotional people, utterly incapable of resting in a stable point of truth, and they become eager adherents of every new interest. The main characteristic of young modern life today is an intense craving to be interested—literature, amusements, all indicate this tendency, and in religion the church is apt to pander to the demand to be interested; consequently people won't face the rugged facts of the gospel, because when the Holy Spirit comes in He challenges a person's will, demands a reconstruction of the whole life, and produces a change of mind that will work havoc in the person's former complacency.

Moral Conversion

Unless you . . . become as little children. Matthew 18:3

Our Lord teaches that moral progress must start from a point of moral innocence and is consequently only possible to a person when he or she has been born again. A child's life is implicit, not explicit. To "become as little children" means to receive a new heredity, a totally new nature, the essence of which is simplicity and confidence toward God. In order to develop the moral life, innocence must be transformed into virtue by a series of deliberate choices in which the present pleasure is sacrificed for the ultimate joy of being good. This aspect of truth is familiar in all Paul's epistles, namely, that the natural has to be transformed into the spiritual by willing obedience to the Word and will of God. Such passages as Romans 12:2: "Be transformed by the renewing of your mind," and Ephesians 4:23: "Be renewed in the spirit of your mind," apply directly to the moral lives of those who have been supernaturally saved by the grace of God, those in whom the Holy Spirit dwells and is at work. To "renew" means to transform to new life. These passages make it clear that we can be renewed in our minds when we choose. We have no choice about being born into this world, but to be born again, if we will but come to Jesus and receive His Spirit, is within our own power. This is true all along in the Christian life, you can be renewed in the spirit of your mind when you choose, you can revive your mind on any line you like by sheer force of will. Always remember that Jesus Christ's statements force an issue of will and conscience first, and only as we obey is there the understanding with the mind (see John 7:17). The challenge to the will comes in the matter of study, as long as you remain in the "stodge" state there is no mental progress— "I am overwhelmed by the tremendous amount there is to know and it's no use my going on." If you will forge through that stage you will suddenly turn a corner where everything that was difficult and perplexing becomes as clear as a lightning flash, but it all depends on whether you will forge ahead. When people say, "Preach us the simple gospel," what they mean is, "Preach us the thing we have always heard, the thing that keeps us sound asleep, we don't want to see things differently"; then the sooner the Spirit of God sends a thrust through their stagnant minds the better. Continual renewal of mind is the only healthy state for a Christian. Beware of the ban of finality about your present views.

Mystical Conversion

> To them God willed to make known what are the riches of the glory of this mystery among the Gentiles: which is Christ in you, the hope of glory. Colossians 1:27

Mystical is a word that is easily abused; it means the type of mind the Holy Spirit develops in us whereby we see things by intuition. Intuition in the natural world is the power to see things at a glance without reasoning, and the Spirit of God develops that power in the saint. The accuracy of intuitive judgment is in proportion to the moral culture of the one who judges. A child and a good woman are the best examples of intuitive judgment. It is a bad look-out when anything blurs intuition, because it is an indication that something is wrong with the moral character. All this is common to human beings apart from the Holy Spirit; spiritual intuition lives in the same sphere as natural intuition *plus* the Holy Spirit. "My sheep hear My voice," said Jesus (John 10:27). Keep the intuitive, secret life clear and right with God at all costs; never blunt intuition. Whenever people come into personal contact with Jesus Christ they know at once whether they are good or bad; they do not reason it out, they know it intuitively. These are the moments when the spirit's true endowments stand out plainly from its false ones."

"If anyone loves Me, he will keep My word, . . . and We will come to him and make Our home with him" (John 14:23)—the Triune God, Father, Son, and Holy Spirit, abiding with the saint. These words of our Lord refer to mystical communion with God in all matters of mental and moral judgment and imply sympathy with all that the heart of God holds dear.

Spiritual Evolution

Evolution means a gradual working out or development. There is a difference between natural evolution and spiritual evolution: in natural evolution we do not know the final goal; in spiritual evolution the goal is given before the start: "till we all come to the unity of the faith . . . to a perfect man, to the measure of the stature of the fullness of Christ" (Ephesians 4:13).

Spiritual Biogenesis

> In Him was life, and the life was the light of men. John 1:4

> Most assuredly, I say to you, Unless you eat the flesh of the Son of Man and drink His blood, you have no life in you. John 6:53

No one by nature has the life of the Son of God within; everyone has the life that God creates in all human beings, but before anyone can have in actual life the life that was in the Son of God, he or she must be born from above. "You have no life in you," said Jesus, that is, the life He had. The life of Jesus is imparted to us on the ground of the Redemption, but we have to come to Him for it. A person may say, "I have the life of God in me by nature, all I have to do is to develop it, Jesus will assist me; He is the great type-Christian." If you take that view, namely, that people become spiritual as they pay attention to the best elements in themselves, you make the Atonement unnecessary. "Unless one is born again, he cannot see the kingdom of God" (John 3:3). Unless my personal life so assimilates the life of Jesus that I can manifest it, I have not gotten the life that characterized Him. Life can only come from preexisting life: I must get the life of God from the One who has it. "He who has the Son has life; he who does not have the Son of God does not have life" (1 John 5:12). "You are not willing to come to Me that you may have life" (John 5:40).

Spiritual Birth

Do not marvel that I said to you, "You must be born again." John 3:7

Drummond's thesis in his *Natural Law in the Spiritual World* makes it too easy; it does not recognize the factor of sin and consequently does not cover all the facts. According to the New Testament, a person can only be lifted into the kingdom of God by being born into it. Here Drummond's illustration holds good, but remember, it was the tragedy caused by sin that made new birth necessary. It sounds much more sensible to say that if someone goes on evolving and developing she or he will become a spiritual being, but once you get a dose of the plague of your own heart and you will find that things are as the Bible says they are, tragically wrong. As long as people have no experience of tragedy in their own lives they remain ignorant of the need for the Redemption. "I was alive once without the law," says the apostle Paul in verse 9 of that little-understood chapter, Romans 7, which deals with his alternating experiences. When once a person recognizes the gap sin has made between God and humankind, the meaning of the Atonement is clear—that in the Cross Jesus Christ bridged the gap and made it possible for anyone to be lifted to where the whole human race was designed to be, namely, in perfect communion with God.

God formed Adam of the dust of the ground, *a* son of God. *The* Son of God was born of the Holy Spirit. If I am ever going to have the heredity of the Son of God I must have a similar experience, I must be born of the Spirit; my personal life must be impregnated by the Holy Spirit: "My little children, for whom I labor in birth again until Christ is formed in you" (Galatians 4:19). You cannot illustrate new birth by natural birth. Natural birth is by means of a process of procreation; new birth is not in the least like it. The only symbol for being born from above is the advent of Jesus Christ into this world. Jesus Christ entered into the human race from outside it; He entered it through the door of the Virgin's womb by the conception of the Holy Spirit: "Therefore also that Holy One who is to be born will be called the Son of God" (Luke 1:35).

Adam was created a son of God, that is, he was innocent in relation to God, and God intended him to take part in his own development by a series of moral choices whereby he was to sacrifice the natural life to the spiritual. If Adam had done this there would have been no death, but transfiguration, as in Jesus Christ, the Last Adam. But Adam refused to let God be his Ruler; he took his right to himself and became his own god, thereby cutting himself off from the domain of God. The New Testament phrase is that we are "dead in trespasses and sins" (Ephesians 2:1), dead toward all that Jesus Christ stands for.

The two realms, the natural and the spiritual, ought to be one and the same: to be born human should be to be a child of God, as Adam was in the beginning. But God's original order for humankind was broken into: "sin entered the world, and death through sin" (Romans 5:12); consequently the necessity of the new birth is insisted on all through. "Do not marvel that I said to you, 'You must be born again.' " It is a statement of foundation fact. The words were spoken not to a sinner, as people count sin, but to an upright, godly individual. Before anyone can be in the realm of God he or she must be born into it.

New birth is not the working of a natural law. The introduction of anything into this world is cataclysmic: before a tree can grow it must be planted; before a human being can evolve it must be born—a distinct and emphatic crisis. Every child born into the world involves a cataclysm to someone; the mother has practically to go through death. The same thing is true spiritually. Being born from above is not a simple, easy process; we cannot glide into the kingdom of God. Commonsense reasoning says we ought to be able to merge into the life of God, but according to the Bible, and in actual experience, that is not the order. The basis of things is not rational, it is tragic, and what Jesus Christ came to do was to put human life on the basis of Redemption, whereby anyone can receive the heredity of the Son of God and be lifted into the domain where He lives.

The historic Jesus represents the personal union of God and humanity. He lived on the human plane for thirty-three years and during that time He presented what God's normal human being was like. When we are regenerated, we enter into the kingdom of God, we begin to grow, and the goal is certain: "We know that when He is revealed, we shall be like Him, for we shall see Him as He is" (1 John 3:2). But before I can begin to see what Jesus Christ stands for I have to enter another domain: "Unless one is born again, he cannot . . . enter the kingdom of God" (John 3:3, 5). I enter the life of God by its entering me; that is, I deliberately undertake to become the home of the life of the Son of God—"Bethlehem." I do not draw my life from myself, I draw it from the One who is the Source of life.

Spiritual Breath

> And the spirit of the LORD shall rest upon Him. . . . His delight is in the fear of the LORD. Isaiah 11:2–3

Literally, "he shall draw his breath in the fear of the LORD." Most of us draw our breath from the ordinary human life we all live. The time Christians give to prayer and communion with God is not meant for their natural lives but meant to nourish the life of the Son of God in them. God engineers the circumstances of His saints in order that the Spirit may use them as the praying-house of the Son of God. If you are spiritual the Holy Spirit is offering up prayers in your bodily temple that you know nothing about, it is the Spirit making intercession in you (see Romans 8:26–27). We hear it said that "Prayer alters things"; prayer not so much alters things as alters the one who prays, and that one alters things. When I am born from above, the life of the Son of God is born in me, and I have to take time to nourish that life. The essential meaning of prayer is that it nourishes the life of the Son of God in me and enables Him to manifest Himself in my mortal flesh.

The secret of our Lord's life is given us in His own words: "Most assuredly, I say to you, unless a grain of wheat falls into the ground and dies, it remains alone; but if it dies, it produces much grain" (John 12:24). Spiritual life is always of that order: just when you think it is going to be successful, it disappears; it is not time for it yet, it will appear in another order. Ultimately, "the meek shall inherit the earth," and then we shall have a system of national life without any of the materialistic crudities seen everywhere today. There are views abroad of a federation of nations, but it can only be brought about by the Lord Jesus Christ, by our adherence entirely to Him. Whenever a religious community begins to get organized it ceases to "draw its breath in the fear of the LORD"; the old way of talking is kept up, but the life is not there, and people who used to be keen on proclaiming the gospel are keen now only on the success of the organization.

The verse God gave me that morning before my dad died.

Talks on Spiritual Construction given at Zeitoun, Egypt, April 1917

Spiritual Construction—I

So we built the wall. Nehemiah 4:6 (see verses 1–6)

The first essential in spiritual construction is to clear away the rubbish. Nehemiah could not begin to build until the rubbish had been dealt with (v. 2). Rubbish is waste matter, and there is the moral equivalent of rubbish that must be dealt with before you or I can begin to build a spiritual character. We do not start with a clean sheet, we start with a sheet that is like a palimpsest, a manuscript that has been written on twice, and if the right chemical is used, the first writing is seen. We all have hereditary writing in us that is so much rubbish to be removed.

rubbish to be removed from past generations

Destruction by Neglect

> Therefore put to death your members which are on the earth: fornication, uncleanness, passion, evil desire, and covetousness, which is idolatry. Colossians 3:5

In this passage Paul mentions things that are of the nature of rubbish, and he mentions them in their complete ugliness. They are the abortion of the stuff human nature is made of, and he says, put them to death by neglect. Certain things can only be dealt with by ignoring them; if you face them you increase their power. It is absurd to say, Pray about them; when once a thing is seen to be wrong, don't pray about it, it fixes the mind on it; never for a second brood on it; destroy it by neglect. We have no business to harbor an emotion that we can see will end in any of the things Paul mentions. No man or woman on earth is immune; each one of us knows the things we should not think about or pray about but resolutely neglect. It is a great thing for the moral character to have something to ignore. It is because these things are not understood that there is so much inefficiency in spiritual life. What Christianity supplies is "the expulsive power of a new affection." We cannot destroy sin by neglect; God deals with sin, and we can get the effective measure of His dealing with it in our actual lives.

Direction by Sacrifice

> If your right eye causes you to sin, pluck it out and cast it from you; for it is more profitable for you that one of your members perish, than for your whole body to be cast into hell. Matthew 5:29–30

Sacrifice is spoken of in the Bible in its disciplinary, chastening aspect as well as in its worshiping aspect. The worshiping aspect means that I give back to God the best He has given me, and in this way He makes it His and mine for ever. What is the best God has given me? My right to myself. Jesus Christ is always unyielding on one point, namely, that I must give up my right to myself to Him. He does not teach the annihilation of self; He shows how self can be rightly centered in personal, passionate devotion to God. Self-sacrifice may be a disease; we are not to sacrifice for our own sakes or for the sake of anyone else, but for God's sake. Why should God make it that the natural had to be sacrificed to the spiritual? God did not; God intended the natural to be transformed into the spiritual by obedience; sin made it necessary to sacrifice the natural. It was God's permissive will, not His order. Sanctification means not only that we are delivered from sin, but that we start on a life of stern discipline. It is not a question of praying but of performing, of deliberately disciplining ourselves. There is no royal road there; we each have it entirely in our own hands. It is not wrong things that have to be sacrificed, but right things. "The good is the enemy of the best"—not the bad, but the good that is not good enough. The danger is to argue on the line of giving up only what is wrong; Jesus Christ selected things essential to a full-orbed life—the right hand and the eye, these are not bad things, they are creations of God. Jesus Christ talked rugged, unmitigated truth, He was never ambiguous, and He says it is better to be maimed than damned. There was never a saint yet who did not have to start with a maimed life. Anyone will give up wrong things if she or he knows how to, but will I give up the best I have for Jesus Christ? If I am only willing to give up wrong things, never let me talk about being in love with Him! We say, "Why shouldn't I do it, there is no harm in it?" For pity's sake, go and do it, but remember that the construction of a spiritual character is doomed once you take that line.

Designed by Desires

Delight yourself also in the LORD, and He shall give you the desires of your heart. Psalm 37:4

If you abide in Me, and My words abide in you, you will ask what you desire, and it shall be done for you. John 15:7

We have any number of instincts but very few desires. *Desire* is what you determine in your mind and settle in your heart and set yourself toward as good, and that is the thing God will fulfill if you delight in Him—that is the condition. God deals with us on the line of character building: "You will ask what you *desire*," said Jesus—not what you like but what your will is in, and we ask very few things. If our desires are distorted we are apt to say that God gave us a stone when we asked for bread, whereas God always hears our prayers, but He answers them according to His own nature.

The basis of spiritual construction is implicit faith in Jesus Christ. If I stake all on His astute mind, I will find I have struck bedrock. The majority of us only believe in Jesus Christ as far as we can see by our own wits. If we really believed Him, what a mighty difference there would be in us! We would trust His mind instead of ours, we would stop being amateur providences over other lives, and we would be fit to do our twenty-four hours' work like no one else. "Unless you become as little children"—simple-hearted, trusting, and not afraid.

You can never become a Christian by thinking—you can only become a Christian by receiving something from God; but you must think after you are a Christian. Some folks have a cowardly fear of intellect in spiritual matters. After the war the most energetic thinking will have to be done by Christians; we must think as we have never thought before, otherwise we will be outstripped by those who think on lines that ignore Jesus Christ and endeavor to prove that the Redemption is not necessary.

Spiritual Construction—II

The Alloy

The Divine and the Human

> We have this treasure in earthen vessels, that the excellence of
> the power may be of God and not of us. 2 Corinthians 4:7

In spiritual reconstruction, after the war, the purely spiritual
line, if it ignores the human, will be useless, and the purely
human will not be any good; there must be the amalgam, that
is, the pure divine and the pure human mixed—not divine and
sinful, but divine and human. Paul is not despising the
earthen vessel—it is in the earthen vessel that the excellence
of God's power is to be manifested.

In the Incarnation we see the amalgam of the Divine and
the human. Pure gold cannot be used as coin—it is too soft; in
order to make gold serviceable for use it must be mixed with
an alloy. The pure gold of the Divine is of no use in human
affairs; there must be an alloy, and the alloy does not stand
for sin but for that which makes the Divine serviceable for
use. God almighty is nothing but a mental abstraction to me
unless He can become actual, and the revelation of the New
Testament is that God did become actual: "the Word became
flesh" (John 1:14). Jesus Christ was not pure Divine, He was
unique: Divine and human.

The Christian doctrine of the Incarnation is not only that
"God was manifested in the flesh" (1 Timothy 3:16), but that
the same thing will take place in anyone who receives the
Holy Spirit: that individual receives from God a totally new

heredity, the life of the Son of God, "until Christ is formed in you" (Galatians 4:19). Human nature is the home where the Divine manifests itself. Holiness movements are apt to ignore the human and bank all on the Divine; they tell us that human nature is sinful, forgetting that Jesus Christ took on Him our human nature, and "in Him there is no sin" (1 John 3:5). It was God who made human nature, not the devil; sin came into human nature and cut it off from the Divine, and Jesus Christ brings the pure Divine and the pure human together. Sin is a wrong thing altogether and is not to be allowed for a moment. Human nature is earthly, it is sordid, but it is not bad—the thing that makes it bad is sin. Sin is the outcome of a relationship set up between humanity and the devil whereby human beings become bosses over themselves, their own gods (see Genesis 3:8). No one was ever created to be her or his own master or to master other people; there is only one Master of humanity, and that is Jesus Christ. We can be fanatical and ignore the human, or sinful and ignore the divine, or we can become the mixture of the divine and the human. No one is constituted to live a pure, divine life on earth; we are constituted to live human lives on earth, presenced with Divinity. When the pure Divine comes in, we have the difficulty of making the human nature the obedient servant of the new disposition; it is difficult, and thank God it is! God gives us the fighting chance. A saint is not an ethereal creature too refined for life on this earth; a saint is a mixture of the divine and the human that can stand anything.

The Preacher and the Philosopher

> It pleased God through the foolishness of the message preached to save those who believe. 1 Corinthians 1:21

Preachers are there not by right of personality or oratorical powers but by right of the message they proclaim. Who is the preacher who attracts us today? The one with a striking personality, and we don't care about the message. Paul said, "Yes, woe is me, if I do not preach the gospel!" (9:16). An orator rouses human nature to do what it is asleep over; the New Testament preacher has to move people to do what they are dead set against doing, namely, giving up the right to themselves to Jesus Christ; consequently the preaching of the gospel awakens a terrific longing—but an equally intense resentment. The aspect of the gospel that awakens desire in a person is the message of peace and goodwill—but I must give up my right to myself to get there. The basis of human life has been put on Redemption, and on the ground of that Redemption anyone can be lifted into right relationship with God. The gospel is "the power of God to salvation to everyone who believes" (Romans 1:16). There is no room for despair on the part of anyone who will only believe what the New Testament preacher proclaims—but it takes some believing. No thinking will ever make me a Christian; I can only become a Christian through listening to what is preached and accepting salvation as a gift, but I must think after I am a Christian.

The shaking, through this war, has revealed the shallowness of our Christianity; there is no moral power in it—not sufficient moral power to make someone live as a disciple of Jesus Christ in home life, let alone business life or camp life. The consequence is the moral emphasis has been coming from the world, not from the church. There needs to be a radical change in many of us who name the name of Christ if we are going to measure up to the nobility and self-sacrifice exhibited by women and men of the world. Now is the time when the preaching of the Cross will have a chance it never had before. The war has hit rationalism a severe blow, but rationalism will gather itself together and take its revenge. Rationalism fundamentally is rotten. The boldness of rationalism is not in what it does but in the way it criticizes. The basis of things is not rational, it is tragic; there is something wrong at the heart of life that reason cannot account for. According to rationalism there is no need to be born again—"develop the best in yourself." That was God's original design for the human race, namely, that people should take part in their own development by a series of moral choices whereby they would transfigure the natural into the spiritual, but sin entered and there came a hiatus, a break, and human development is not now based on the rational progression God designed but on the Redemption, which deals with the tragedy caused by sin. No one can get at God as Jesus Christ presents Him by philosophy. The philosopher has vision, so has the poet, but neither of them has any memory; the preacher of the gospel has vision and memory; preachers realize there is a gap between God and humanity and know that the only way that gap can be bridged is by Jesus Christ making the divine and the human one. The goal of human life is to be one with God, and in Jesus Christ we see what that oneness means.

In spiritual construction, after the war, the emphasis must be laid on what the preacher proclaims, not on what the philosopher reasons about. The great message of the Incarnation is that there the Divine and the human became one, and Jesus Christ's claim is that He can manifest His own life in anyone who will cooperate with Him. If I am going to nourish the pure divine in my human life I must first of all let God deal drastically with sin; by my own willing agreement I must let Him put His ax to the root of sin, and then when His life has come into me, I must obey it. Do I as a preacher of the gospel really believe the gospel I preach? The test is in the souls of the preachers themselves, in the ones who say they believe the gospel. For instance, do I believe that that man or that woman who did me a cruel wrong, that individual who thwarted me, can be presented perfect in Christ Jesus?

We are rarely taught to think along these lines. Thinking is not of first importance, but it is of mighty importance secondarily. The one who prefers to be lazy in the spiritual life may do well enough, but it is the one who has thought on the basis of things who is able to give intelligent help to those who are up against it. People have been hit during the war and few of us have been able to help them, we are inarticulate, we don't know how to put things because we have not thought about them. "My people do not consider," says God (Isaiah 1:3), they do not think. We are not called on to preach a philosophy of thought, which is the tendency nowadays—but to preach "Jesus Christ and Him crucified" (1 Corinthians 2:2), because that preaching enables God to create His miracles in human lives. If I prefer to preach my philosophy, I prevent God creating His miracles, but when I am simple enough to preach the Cross, God performs His miracles every time.

Spiritual Construction—III

Do It!

John 13:13–18

We have to recognize that we are one-half mechanical and one-half mysterious; to live in either domain and ignore the other is to be fools or fanatics. The great, supernatural work of God's grace is in the incalculable part of human nature; we have to work out in the mechanical realm what God works in in the mysterious realm. People accept creeds, but they will not accept the holy standards of Jesus Christ's teaching. To build on the fundamental work of God's grace and ignore the fact that we have to work it out in the mechanical life produces humbugs, those who make a divorce between the mysterious life and the practical life. In John 13 the mysterious and the mechanical are closely welded together.

The Lordship of Jesus

> You call Me Teacher and Lord, and you say well, for so I am. If I then, your Lord and Teacher, have washed your feet, you also ought to wash one another's feet. John 13:13–14

Verse 13 refers to the spiritual mastery of Jesus over His disciples; verse 14 states how that mastery is to be expressed in the mechanical life. You can't wash people's feet mysteriously; it is a purely mechanical, matter-of-fact job; you can't do it by giving them devotional books or by praying for them; you can only wash people's feet by doing something mechanical. Our Lord did not tell the disciples how they were to do it, He simply says, Do it. He is not questioning whether or not they can do it; He is saying that they must do what the mastery of His ruling shows them they should do. Our bodily habits are purely mechanical, and the revolution caused in individual lives by our Lord's salvation is that He enables us to do what He commands us to do, if we will but practice the doing. Habits are built up not by theory but by practice. The one great problem in spiritual life is whether we are going to put God's grace into practice. God won't do the mechanical—He created us to do that—but we can only do it while we draw on the mysterious realm of His divine grace. "If you love Me, keep My commandments" (John 14:15). We have to remember that there is a domain of our lives that is handed over to mechanism; God will not work it for us, but if we obey His Spirit we shall find we can make this mechanism work out God's will exactly. Beware of any spiritual emotion that you do not work out mechanically; whenever, in devotion before God, His Spirit gives a clear indication of what He wants you to do, do it.

The way to examine whether we are doing what Jesus Christ wants us to do is to look at the habits of our lives in three domains—physical, emotional, and intellectual. The best scrutiny we can give ourselves is along this line: Are my bodily habits chaste? Is my emotional nature inordinate? Is my intellectual life insubordinate? When we begin to work out what God has worked in, we are faced with the problem that this physical body, this mechanism, has been used by habit to obeying another rule, called sin; when Jesus Christ delivers us from that rule, He does not give us new bodies; He gives us power to break and then remold every habit formed while we were under the dominion of sin. Much of the misery in our Christian lives comes not because the devil tackles us but because we have never understood the simple laws of our makeup. We have to treat the body as the servant of Jesus Christ: when the body says "Sit" and He says "Go," go! When the body says "Eat" and He says "Fast," fast! When the body says "Yawn" and He says "Pray," pray!

Education is for the purpose of behavior, and habits are the stuff out of which behavior is formed. The difference between educated and uneducated people lies just here— when educated people are put into new circumstances, they always know how to behave because their minds are stored with examples of right behavior. When uneducated people come into new situations, they do not know what to do and behave in an ignorant manner. Spiritual education and habit go together in this connection: I learn to make my body act quickly along the line of education the Holy Spirit has given me, then when I find myself in new circumstances I shall not be helpless because I have educated myself according to the laws of God's grace.

The Example of Jesus

> For I have given you an example, that you should do as I have done to you. 13:15

Jesus did not tell the disciples to imitate Him in washing one another's feet; the one thing He condemned was imitation before the life was there. For instance, when He set before them a little child and said "Unless . . . you become as little children" (Matthew 18:3), He did not mean they were to act like babies; He was telling them to be as simple and artless in their relationships to God as a child is in relation to its father. If we try to imitate Jesus Christ we produce a mechanical exhibition of what we are ourselves; the life is not there, we are spiritual frauds, and everybody knows it. But our Lord's teaching is clear: If I am your Lord and Teacher, it means you have received My Spirit, then you will do what I do—and our habits are copies of the true, indwelling Spirit of Jesus.

The disciples had not always been in the relation of disciples to Jesus, but now they are His disciples and as such He says to them, "Do as I have done to you." When you see a thing should be done, the command of Jesus is always: Do it. Beware of saying, "I must go and tell Mrs. So-and-so to do that, she is just suited for it"; it is for you to do. There must be a mechanical outlet for spiritual inspiration. You must do what you see, or become blind in that particular. In order to obey our Lord we must accumulate all possible circumstances to reinforce the right motive. It is easy to sit in a drawing room and think about the terrible condition of things in the world and pray and sentimentalize over it endlessly, but Jesus says, "I have given you an example," that you should go and do to others what I have done to you. If all Jesus Christ had done was to sit before His Father's throne and pray for us, we would have been exonerated for leaving things undone, but He has given us an example to follow. Never allow your circumstances to exonerate you from obeying any of the commands of Jesus. The lessons that have to be repeated are those we have not bothered our heads to learn.

The Warning of Jesus

> I do not speak concerning all of you. I know whom I have chosen; but that the Scripture may be fulfilled, "He who eats bread with Me has lifted up his heel against Me." verse 18

Any one of us can lift the "heel," the mechanical life, against Jesus Christ's dominion and, while eating His bread, play the traitor to Him in private. No one preaches more earnestly, talks more earnestly than we do; we are absolutely sincere, but we are not real because we have never acted when the opportunity occurred along the line Jesus Christ wants us to. The thing the world is sick of today is sincerity that is not real.

So much depends on a simple understanding of the mechanical laws of human nature. The only One who knows the mysterious, unfathomable depths of human personality is God; we have to deal with the practical part and see that we have faith in God with regard to the mysterious part, while we obey Him in the practical domain. Jesus Christ lived the only sane life that ever was lived. In His life the mysterious and the mechanical were wrought into one wonderful unique personality, and it is His life that is to be "manifested in our mortal flesh".

"Now is the day of salvation," and to do it now is the "thank You" of our acceptance of that salvation.

The Fundamental Offense

Apart from shedding of blood there is no remission. Hebrews 9:22

1. **Christ Is the Blood of God.**
   The Cross is the Blood of Christ. 1 John 2:2

   When we speak of the blood of Christ we mean that what He did drew upon what was the very citadel of His personality and involved His total self.

2. **Sin Is the Blood of Satan.**
   Self-realization is the Blood of Sin. 1 John 3:8

   What in us harrows the heart, in Him harrowed Hell. He revolutionizes the eternal foundations of our moral world.

3. **Sanctification is the Blood of the Saint**
   Repentance is the Blood of Sanctification. 1 John 1:7

   The sinner could only be saved by something that damned his sin.

Dr. P. T. Forsyth

Christ Is the Blood of God

And He is the propitiation for our sins; and not for ours only, but also for the whole world. 1 John 2:2

The expression, "the blood of Christ," means not only that Christ shed His blood, but that He poured out His very life before God. In the Old Testament the idea of sacrifice is that the blood, which is the life (see Genesis 4:4), is poured out to God, its Giver. When Jesus Christ shed His blood on the cross it was not the blood of a martyr or the blood of one human for another; it was the life of God poured out to redeem the world. It is easy to be thrilled by the sacrifices people make; it takes the Spirit of almighty God to get us even interested in the cost to God of our redemption. There is a good deal of talk today to the effect that the people who sacrifice their lives are thereby redeemed. It is said in an earnest mood, but it reveals a total lack of understanding of the Cross, which is not the cross of a human being but the Cross of God, that is, the offering of God for the purpose of bringing back the human race into fellowship with Himself. Either the Cross is the only way there is of explaining God, the only way of explaining Jesus Christ, and of explaining the human race, or there is nothing in it at all. If the human race apart from the Cross is all right, then the Redemption was a useless waste.

Our Lord did not sacrifice Himself for a cause; He poured out His life for a purpose in the mind of God. We will sacrifice ourselves endlessly for another part of ourselves, but the meaning of Jesus Christ's passion is that He poured out His total self. The Cross is the expression of the very heart of God, and when my eyes are opened I see that Jesus Christ has made the basis of life redemptive, and it cost Him everything to do it. The death of Christ was not the death of a martyr, it was God manifesting Himself in the heart of the human race when the human race was saying, "Crucify Him."

The Christian revelation is not that Jesus Christ stands to us as the representative of God, but that He is God. If He is not, then we have no God. "God was in Christ reconciling the world to Himself" (2 Corinthians 5:19). We do not worship an austere, remote God—He is here in the thick of it. The Cross is a reality, not a symbol—at the wall of the world stands God with His arms outstretched. There is nothing more certain in time or eternity than what Jesus Christ did on the Cross: He switched the whole human race back into right relationship to God and made the basis of human life redemptive, consequently any member of the human race can get into touch with God now. It means not simply that people are saved from hell and put right for heaven, but that they are freed from the wrong disposition and can have imparted to them the very disposition of the Son of God, namely, the Holy Spirit. The dangerous tendency of today is not so much the antireligious tendency as the pietistic tendency, that by prayer and consecration, by giving up things and devoting ourselves to God, He will recognize us. We can never get to God in that way; we can get to God at once, irrespective of what we are, on the basis of the Redemption. On that basis I can be forgiven, and through the forgiveness I can be turned into another person.

2 Sin Is the Blood of Satan

> For this purpose the Son of God was manifested, that He might destroy the works of the devil. 1 John 3:8

The Bible makes a distinction between the devil and Satan; only occasionally are the terms used synonymously, for example, Revelation 20:2. The devil is the antagonist of God; Satan is the result of a relationship set up between humanity and the devil. God took on Himself the responsibility of having created the being who became the devil and the being who became the sinner, and the proof that He did so is the Cross. God never lays the sin of the human race on anyone except Himself; the revelation is not that God punished Jesus Christ for our sins, but that "He made Him who knew no sin to be sin for us" (2 Corinthians 5:21). The relationship set up between Adam and the devil was self-realization—not immorality and vice—but my claim to my right to myself, whether it is manifested in clean living or unclean living is a matter of indifference; sin is the fundamental relationship underneath. Sin is not wrongdoing, it is wrong being, inde-

continue

pendence of God; God has undertaken the responsibility for its removal on the ground of the Redemption. The condemnation is not that people are born with a heredity of sin; people begin to get the seal of condemnation when they see the Light and prefer the darkness (see John 3:19).

 The great miracle of the Redemption is that I can receive an absolutely new heredity, namely, the Holy Spirit, and when that heredity begins to work out in me, I manifest in my mortal flesh the disposition of the Son of God. The result of the Redemption in my life must be that I justify God in forgiving me. I can mouth my salvation, I can thank God for it, but if I do not produce "goods up to sample," my religious life is a travesty. Always beware of the presentation of Redemption that produces a dangerous state of priggishness in moral life—that I can receive forgiveness and yet go on being bad; if I do, God is not justified in forgiving me. If you are justified by faith, show it by your works, says the apostle James (see 2:14–24); in what way are you different in your life? Does the reality of the Redemption at work in you justify God in having forgiven you? People have to clear the conscience of God in forgiving them. Present-day evangelism is inclined to go much more strongly on the line of the passion for souls than the passion for sanctification; everyone has gone aslumming to save the lost; it suits our religious passion to help the men and women who are down and out. Saving souls is God's work, human work is discipling those souls (see Matthew 28:18–20). When Jesus Christ faced people with all the forces of evil born in them and people who were clean living and moral and upright, He did not look at the immorality of the one group or the morality of the other. He looked at something we do not see—self-realization. If my religion is based on my right to myself, that spells "Satan" in my soul; I may be right-living, but I am anti-God. If you are going to be My disciple, Jesus says, you must give up your right to yourself. Jesus

Christ came to do what I could not do, namely, alter my heredity, and the point for me is, am I going to let Him do it? "Without shedding of blood there is no remission" (Hebrews 9:22). God redeemed the world by shedding His blood, by putting the whole passion of the Godhead into it. He did not become interested and put one arm in to help the human race up; He went into the Redemption absolutely, there was nothing of Him left out. Am I willing to put my whole self into becoming His? Or am I one of those who accept His salvation but thoroughly object to giving up my right to myself to Him? Unless I am willing to shed my blood for Him, my Christianity is not worth anything. The trouble is that we have never come to the realization of what *sin* is; we confound it with *sins*. Sin has to be cleansed, sins must be forgiven; the Redemption of Jesus Christ deals with sin. Do I agree with God's judgment on sin and self-realization on the Cross? If so, I see where that judgment hits me and I agree that God is right. Self-realization and God cannot live together. In the history of the human race, when God appeared in the person of Jesus Christ, we crucified Him. When I am born from above I realize that if I am going to obey the Holy Spirit I must enter into identification with Jesus Christ, otherwise I will kill the life of God in me. If I agree with God's judgment on self-realization, then the salvation of Jesus Christ will be manifested in me. It is a moral decision. There is no shirking the point and saying, "Oh, I'm not as bad as other people"; it is a question of agreeing with God's verdict on sin. Will I go through the condemnation now? If I will, there is no more condemnation for me, the salvation of Jesus Christ is made actual.

3 Sanctification Is the Blood of the Saint

If we walk in the light as He is in the light, . . . the blood [the essential life] of Jesus Christ His Son cleanses us from all sin. 1 John 1:7

The one condition is that we walk in the light as God is in the light. God does not give people a clean thing to look after, He puts a life within that keeps them clean as long as they walk in the light—a superabounding life, "a fountain of water springing up into everlasting life" (John 4:14).

Repentance is the blood of sanctification, the exhibition of a real gift of God; not only am I sorry for my sin—that is human—but in the sorrow for sin God slips in something else: the power never to do the thing again. Many a woman or man is kept away from Jesus Christ by a sense of honor, "I don't deny what you say, that God is able to save, but it can't mean me—if you only knew me! the mistakes I have made, the wrong things I have done, the blundering things; I would be a perfect disgrace to Him." There are more people in that attitude than is commonly supposed, but when people realize what Jesus Christ undertakes to do—not tell them to do their best but to surrender to Him and He will put into them the power to do right, they are emancipated right away.

Is Christianity Worthy of God?

2 Corinthians 5:18–21

The Redemption is God's battle unto death with sin.

—Forsyth

There is a presentation of Christianity that is sentimental and weak and unworthy of God; the Christianity of the New Testament is something "angels desire to look into" (1 Peter 1:12). God has paid the price of redeeming a race that had become degenerate; He is not going to redeem it, He has redeemed it. The gospel is just that—Good News about God, that He has redeemed the human race. "God was in Christ reconciling the world to Himself" (2 Corinthians 5:19). Is the gospel, as it is popularly presented, good news about God, or is it a misrepresentation of God? It is not good news about God unless it presents the revelation that God has put the basis of human life on redemption. The Redemption means a great deal more than my personal salvation and yours—that is a mere outcome; pseudoevangelism is apt to make it the great thing. The great thing according to the New Testament is not that the Redemption touches me but that it avails for the whole human race. The Cross is not the cross of a martyr; it is the mirror of the nature of God focused in one point of history. If I want to know what God is like, I see it in the Cross. Jesus Christ is not Someone who leads me to God—either He is God, or I have none.

Christ's Cross the Conscience of the Race

> How much more shall the blood of Christ, who through the eternal Spirit offered Himself without spot to God, cleanse your conscience from dead works to serve the living God? Hebrews 9:14

> If we do not take as much pains that our conscience is true, the pains we take to be true to our conscience is wasted.
>
> —Forsyth

Christianity is not consistency to conscience or to convictions; Christianity is being true to Jesus Christ. Over and over again my personal relationship to Jesus Christ gets into my convictions and splits them, like new wine put into old wineskins, and if I stick to my convictions, before long I will become anti-Christ. The standard for my conscience and for the conscience of the whole human race is the Cross, and if I do not take care to rectify my individual conscience by the Cross I become "pernicketty" and end in criticizing God. The standard for the Christian is never: Is this thing right or wrong? but: Is it related to the blood and passion and agony of the cross of Christ? Does it identify itself with the death of self-realization?

Wherever Christianity has ceased to be vigorous it is because it has become Christian ethics instead of the Christian evangel. People will listen more readily to an exposition of the Sermon on the Mount than they will to the meaning of the Cross, but they forget that to preach the Sermon on the Mount apart from the Cross is to preach an impossibility. What is the good of telling me to love my enemies, and "Blessed are the pure in heart"? You may talk like that endlessly, but it does not amount to anything. Jesus Christ did not come to teach people to be or do any of these things; He did not come primarily to teach, He came to make people the possessors of His own disposition, the disposition portrayed in the Sermon on the Mount.

The conscience of the race, that is, the standard whereby people are judged, is the Cross. I do not make my own conscience the standard or the Sermon on the Mount the standard; the cross of Christ, not His teaching, is the central thing, and what God condemns in the Cross is His standard for me. My conscience may be a competitor against Jesus Christ; I may be conscientious to the backbone, as Saul of Tarsus was, and be anti-Christ: "Indeed, I myself thought I must do many things contrary to the name of Jesus of Nazareth" (Acts 26:9). Conscientious objectors take as the standard not the Cross—which is a cruel thing, a thing that sheds blood and blasts life—but the teachings of Jesus, which have no meaning apart from His cross; consequently they are in danger of becoming a bloodless kind of individual. As soon as you come face-to-face with realities there has to be war to the death. It is absurd to call Christianity a system of nonresistance; the great doctrine of Christianity is resistance "to bloodshed" (Hebrews 12:4) against sin. If a person does not resist physically it is only in order that he or she may resist all the more morally; where moral resistance does not tell, then physical resistance must. Take our Lord Himself; we read that He went into the temple and cast out those who sold and bought, overthrew the tables of the moneychangers, and in a voice of thunder ordered the whole crowd out. Is He the meek and mild and gentle Jesus there? Up to the time of the war, we had a Christianity that had lost the element of fight, the element of grit and judgment; the war has brought back these elements. There is something appalling about human life, and if we make our own private consciences the standard and remain in the offing on the conscientious line, we shall come under the curse of Meroz who "did not come to the help of the LORD . . . against the mighty" (Judges 5:23).

My aim is not to be the saving of my own soul, getting myself put right for heaven, but battling to the death for what the cross of Christ stands for. The great thing is not the teaching of Jesus but what He came to do for the human race, namely, to make the way back to God. It cost Him His life to do it, and the writer to the Hebrews says, "Consider Him . . . , lest you become weary and discouraged in your souls. You have not yet resisted to bloodshed, striving against sin" (12:3–4). Have I got the iron of the cross of Christ into my conscience, or am I a weak sentimentalist, kind and generous, but with nothing of the nature of the Cross in me? Is there anything in me that would go to the death for Jesus Christ's sake, or do I easily knuckle under because I base all on the teachings of Jesus instead of on His cross? Conscientiousness is an ingre-dient in human nature, but the first and foremost relationship in Christianity is the sovereign preference for Jesus Christ.

Christ's Cross the Consecration of the Human Race

For what the law could not do in that it was weak through the flesh, God did by sending His own Son in the likeness of sinful flesh, on account of sin: He condemned sin in the flesh. Romans 8:3

The process and progress of the Kingdom of God in history only unfolds this final achievement of His universal person.

—Forsyth

The cross of Christ consecrated the human race to God, and the human race cannot be run with success on any other line—we are certain it can. It cannot be run on imperial lines or democratic lines, it can only be run on the lines on which Jesus Christ consecrated it.

Where it touches my individual life is that in the Cross, God "condemned sin in the flesh," not sins. Sins I look after;

sin God looks after. The Redemption deals with sin. When the disposition of sin rules in my body it takes my organs and uses them for lust. Lust means, I will satisfy myself; whether I satisfy myself on a high or a low level makes no difference, the principle is the same. It is the exercise of my claim to my right to myself, and that has to go; in the final windup of the human race there won't be a strand of it left. Where we blunder is in confounding regeneration with the Redemption; the experience of regeneration is rare, the majority of people don't come anywhere near it, but that does not alter the fact of the Redemption. The meaning of regeneration is that in my actual life I become of some account to Jesus Christ, I become His disciple and recognize that my body is the temple of the Holy Spirit. We say we can do what we like with our bodies—we cannot. If I try to satisfy any appetite on the basis of my right to myself, it means there is a spirit of antagonism to Jesus Christ at work in me; if I recognize that my body is the temple of the Holy Spirit, it is a sign that my life is based on the Cross.

Christ's Cross the Concentration of the Human Race

Knowing this, that our old man was crucified with Him, that the body of sin might be done away with. Romans 6:6

Mankind's acquirement of its soul is Christ's moral and bloody victory worked into detail; His justice made to triumph and sin made to yield its opposite.

—Forsyth

There are two mystical bodies, the body of Christ and the body of sin; both are outside me. The disposition of sin inside me, called the "old man," connects me with the body of sin; when I am born from above I have the disposition of holiness imparted to me, and this connects me with the body of Christ and I go to the death of the old man, and in this way the body of sin is going to be destroyed. Sanctification is not a question of being delivered from hell but of identifying myself with the death of Christ. Am I based in the moral center of my life on the cross of Christ? Have I ever been moved for one second by the Cross? Those of us who are Christians ought to give a great deal more time to thinking on the fundamentals of our religion. Take it in your actual life, if you are not delivered from any particular element of sin, the reason is either you don't believe God can deliver you or you don't want Him to. As soon as you want Him to deliver you, the power of God is yours and it is done, not presently, but now, and the manifestation is wonderful. Let someone give up the right to himself or to herself to Jesus Christ, and the efficacy of His redemption works out at once.

Great Questions!

The Ethics of Enthusiasm

Ephesians 5

Enthusiasm means, to use the phrase of a German mystic, "intoxicated with God"; the word has come down in the world and popularly means anything that enthuses. Christianity takes all the emotions, all the dangerous elements of human nature, the things that lead us astray, all feelings and excitabilities, and makes them into one great power for God. Other religions either cut out dangerous emotions altogether or base too much on them. The tendency is in us all to say, "You must not trust in feelings"; perfectly true, but if your religion is without feeling, there is nothing in it. If you are living a life right with God, you will have feeling, most emphatically so, but you will never run the risk of basing your faith on feelings. The Christian is one who bases his or her whole confidence in God and His work of grace, then the emotions become the beautiful ornament of the life, not the source of it.

The Excitable Course of Personal Energy (Ephesians 5:1–13)

Anything that awakens the strong emotions of a person will alter the mental outlook—for example, the incoming of the Holy Spirit breaks every habit and every arranged set of ideas people have, and if they will obey the Spirit, they can remake themselves according to God's plan.

(a) The Drift of Ideas

If people are unexcited, their ideas are dull, they drift impersonally; but let the excitement of anger or of love or hate or jealousy come in or let the Holy Spirit come in, and the drift stops and the whole mind is concentrated at once along one line. Human nature, if it is healthy, demands excitement, and if it does not obtain its thrilling excitement in the right way, it will take it in the wrong. That is a law of human nature that the Spirit of God does not contradict but exalts. Every false religion and false order of culture tries to make out that we ought to be absolutely unmoved—the passionlessness of exhaustion—but a healthy, full-orbed life is continually seeking excitement. God never makes us bloodless Stoics, He makes us passionate saints. The word used of Jesus Christ has in it the very essence of Christianity—our Lord's *passion*; you could never speak of His passionlessness; the one characteristic of our Lord's life was its condensed intensity.

(b) The Direction of Ideas

Obedience to the Holy Spirit will mean that we have power to direct our ideas. It is astonishing how we sit down under the dominance of an idea, whether a right or wrong idea, and saints have sat down under this idea more than any other, that they cannot help thoughts of evil. Thank God that's a lie—we can. If you have never realized this before, put it to the test and ask yourself why the Spirit of God through the apostle Paul should say, "bringing every thought into captivity to the obedience of Christ" (2 Corinthians 10:5), if we cannot do it? Never sit down under ideas that have no part or lot in God's Book; trace the idea to its foundation and see where it comes from. The Bible makes it plain that we can help thoughts of evil; it is Satan's interest to make us think we cannot. God grant the devil may be kept off the brains of the saints!

(c) The Divine Inhibition of Ideas

The Holy Spirit not only instructs us, but as we obey Him He inhibits our ideas. Those of you who have been a while in grace, examine yourselves and you will be astonished to find how much has been shed off your life, like autumn leaves. Ideas you never imagined you could get rid of have gone completely because God's Spirit has been definitely selecting out of your mind the ideas He can use, and, as you obey Him and keep on that line, the other ideas die out. It is only done by obedience, not by impulses, but by keeping at it.

The Emotional Center of Personal Energy (Ephesians 5:14–20)

(a) The Scarcity of Emotions

Awake, you who sleep, arise from the dead. verse 14

The Bible reveals that apart from the Spirit of God people have no moving emotion toward God, they are described as "dead"; the preaching of the gospel, the reading of the Word of God, has no answering emotion. Religious enterprise that has not learned to rely on the Holy Spirit makes everything depend on the human intellect. "God has said so-and-so, now believe it and it will be all right"—but it won't. The basis of Jesus Christ's religion is the acceptance of a new Spirit, not a new creed, and the first thing the Holy Spirit does is to awaken us out of sleep. We have to learn to rely on the Holy Spirit because He alone gives the Word of God life. All our efforts to pump up faith in the Word of God is without quickening, without illumination. You reason to yourself and say, "Now God says this and I am going to believe it," and you believe it and re-believe it and re-re-believe it, and nothing happens, simply because the vital power that makes the words living is not there. The Spirit of

God always comes in surprising ways: "The wind blows where it wishes. . . . So is everyone who is born of the Spirit" (John 3:8). No creed or school of thought or experience can monopolize the Spirit of God. The great snare of some aspects of presenting the gospel is that everything is put in the head, everything must be rational and logical, no room is left for the great power of life that shows itself in surprising ways. In natural life people without any emotions are undesirable to have as friends, and a Christian life that is without the continual recurrence of divine emotion is suffering from spiritual sleeping sickness.

(b) The Successive Emotions

See then that you walk circumspectly. Ephesians 5:15

Emotions in nature and in grace succeed one another very rapidly and need a strong controlling power. In natural life people who have successive emotions are in danger of becoming sentimentalists; in spiritual life successive emotions lead to being driven about by every wind of doctrine that savors of piety. Sentimentalists are those who like to live in a great swim of emotions but are unfit to meet the facts of life and, when real trouble comes their way, try to hide themselves away from it and become intensely selfish. The anxiety lest you should suffer—"It is such a distress to me to see you in pain," is really anxiety lest they should suffer. In spiritual life successive emotions are more dangerous. If you are without the control of the Spirit of God, devotional emotion and religious excitement always end in sensuality. Emotions that stir feelings must act themselves out, whether rightly or wrongly will depend on the person. If you feel remarkably generous, then be generous at once, act it out; if you don't, it will react and make you mean. If you have a time of real devotion before God and see what God wants you to do and you do not work it out in your practical life, it will react in secret immorality. That is not an exceptional law, it is an eternal law, and I wish it could be blazed in letters of fire into the mind of every Christian. Very often you will find that God paralyzes your emotional nature and allows you to feel nothing; it is a sure sign that He is guiding, because your life has been too full of emotions you have not been working out.

(c) The Sovereign Emotions

Be filled with the Spirit. verse 18

The sovereign emotions are guided and controlled by love, but bear in mind that love in its highest moral meaning is the preference of one person for another person. A Christian's love is personal, passionate devotion to Jesus Christ, and Christians learn to grip on the threshold of their minds, as in a vice, every sentiment awakened by wrong emotions. God holds the saints responsible for emotions they do not have and ought to have, as well as for the emotions they have allowed that they ought not to have allowed. If we indulge in inordinate affection, anger, anxiety, God holds us responsible, but He also insists that we have to be passionately filled with the right emotions. The emotional life of a Christian is to be measured by the exalted energy exhibited in the life of our Lord. The language applied to the presence of the Holy Spirit in the saint is descriptive of the energy of emotion that keeps the inner and outer life like our Lord's own life. We must find out for ourselves the particular "psalms and hymns and spiritual songs" that will keep our emotional lives right with God, and we shall find that the Holy Spirit insists on intellectual fasting as well as on intellectual control. The apostle Paul continually urges the saints to stir up their minds; we have no right to be stagnant and dull. If you have no emotional life, then you have disobeyed God. "Be filled with the Spirit"; it is as impossible to be filled with the Spirit and be free from emotion as it is for a person to be filled with wine and not show it. The reason some of us are so amazingly dull and get sleeping sickness is that we have never once thought of paying attention to the stirring up the Spirit of God gives the mind and the emotional nature. How many of us are terrified out of our wits lest we should be emotional! Jesus Christ demands the whole nature, and He demands the part of human nature the devil uses most, namely, the emotional part. We have to get the right bedrock for the nature, the life of Jesus Christ, and then glean the things that awaken our emotions and see that those emotions are expressed in ways that are like the character of our Lord.

The Expansive Character of Personal Energy (Ephesians 5:21–33)

(a) Transformation of Selfhood

Submitting to one another in the fear of God. verse 21

When the Holy Spirit first comes into us He seems to put us into a prison house, then He opens our eyes and causes us to expand in the realization that "all things are yours" (1 Corinthians 3:21), from the tiniest flower that blooms to God on His throne. When you have learned the secret that God Himself is the source of your life, then He can trust you with the expansion of your nature. Every expansion of your nature transforms selfhood into unselfishness. It is not peculiar to Christians, it is true of human nature apart altogether from the grace of God. Inspiration, either true or false, unites the personality, makes you feel at one with yourself and with everyone else, and you are unselfish as long as the inspiration lasts. Paul says, "Do not be drunk with wine," which is the counterfeit of the true transformation, "but be filled with the Spirit" (Ephesians 5:18), and all self-interested considerations are transformed at once, you will think only, without trying to, of the good of others and of the glory of God. Be careful what you allow to unite you and make you feel unselfish; the only power we must allow as Christians is the Holy Spirit, who will so transform us that it will be easy to submit to one another in the fear of God.

(b) Transfiguration of Selfhood

> Wives, submit to your own husbands, as to the Lord. Ephesians 5:22

With a sudden abruptness Paul mentions the closest practical relationships in life, and immediately it becomes clear why he does so. If the expansive character of the Holy Spirit is at work in us as saints, it will transfigure our lives in all these relationships. The Holy Spirit keeps us on the line of the transfiguration of selfhood and the thought of good to ourselves never enters in, unless it is introduced by someone else.

(c) Tenderness of Sainthood

The characteristic of the expansive power of the Holy Spirit in a saint appears in a tenderness just like Jesus Christ's: "just as Christ also loved the church and gave Himself for her" (v. 25). These characteristics never come by impulse. Impulse is the impertinence of human nature keeping on tiptoe to try and look as big as God. The Holy Spirit always checks impulse, and the saint learns through humiliation to bring it to heel. Watch how Jesus Christ not only checked, but rebuked impulse in the disciples. The vagaries of modern spiritual life come in because our impulses are insubordinate: "No, I won't submit, I have illumination." The Holy Spirit never works like that. "Be filled with the Spirit," and as we walk in the light the life of God is worked out moment by moment—a life of glorious discipline and steady obedience.

Personality—I

Personality is the perplexing fact of my self that is continually changing and yet remains the same. Personality is an enigma; its only answer is God. Never confound personality with consciousness; all that can be dealt with psychologically is consciousness, but a person's salvation is not limited to his or her consciousness.

The Disposition of Darkness

> The natural man does not receive the things of the Spirit of God; for they are foolishness to him. 1 Corinthians 2:14

The word disposition is used here in the sense of the mainspring that moves me. Apart from a knowledge of Jesus Christ and apart from being crumpled up by conviction of sin, people have dispositions that keep them perfectly happy and peaceful. The natural man is not in distress, not conscious of any disharmony in the self, not "in trouble as other men" (Psalm 73:5), and is quite content with being once-born; the things Jesus Christ stands for have no meaning for the natural man. The Bible refers to this disposition as one of darkness: "having their understanding darkened" (Ephesians 4:18). We preach to people as if they were conscious of being dying sinners—they are not, they are having a good time, and all our talk about the need to be born again is from a domain they know nothing about; because some people try to drown unhappiness in worldly pleasures, it does not follow that all people respond like that. There is nothing attractive about the gospel to the natural man; the only one who finds the gospel attractive is the one who is convicted of sin. Conviction of sin and being guilty of sins are not the same thing. Conviction of sin is produced by the incoming of the Holy Spirit because conscience is promptly made to look at God's demands and the whole nature cries out, in some form or other, "What must I do to be saved?"

For one to be undisturbed and in unity with oneself is a good condition, not a bad one, because a united personality means freedom from self-consciousness; but if one's peace is without any consideration of Jesus Christ it is simply the outcome of this disposition of darkness that keeps people alienated from the life of God. When Jesus Christ comes in He upsets this false unity; He comes not as a Comforter but as a thorough Disturber. "If I had not come, . . . they would have no sin" (John 15:22)—then why did He come? If I was peaceful and happy, living a clean, upright life, why should Jesus Christ come with a standard of holiness I never dreamt of? Simply because that peace was the peace of death, a peace altogether apart from God. The coming of Jesus Christ to the natural man means the destruction of all peace that is not based on a personal relationship to Him.

The Disposition Divided

> For we know that the law is spiritual, but I am carnal, sold under sin. For what I am doing, I do not understand. For what I will to do, that I do not practice; but what I hate, that I do. Romans 7:14–15

Romans 7 is the classic for all time of the conflict a person experiences whose mind is awakened by the incoming of the light of God. Never say, "We must get out of the seventh of Romans"—some of us will never get into it; if we did, we would be in hell in two minutes. The seventh of Romans represents the profound conflict that goes on in the consciousness of a person without the Spirit of God, facing the demands of God. Only to one in a thousand can God lift the veil to show what the seventh of Romans means. It is the presentation by someone who stands now as a saint, looking back on the terrific conflict produced by his conscience having been awakened to the law of God but with no power to do what his mind assigned he should. A lot of tawdry stuff has been written on this chapter simply because Christians so misunderstand what conviction of sin really is. Conviction of sin such as the apostle Paul is describing does not come when one is born again, nor even when one is sanctified, but long after, and then only to a few. It came to Paul as an apostle and saint, and he could diagnose sin as no other. Knowledge of what sin is is in inverse ratio to its presence; only as sin goes do you realize what it is; when it is present you do not realize what it is because the nature of sin is that it destroys the capacity to know you sin.

The problem in practical experience is not to know what is right but to do it. My natural spirit may know there are a great many things I ought to do, but I never can do what I know I should until I receive the Life that is life indeed, namely, the Holy Spirit. "For the good that I will to do, I do not; but the evil I will not to do, that I practice" (v. 19). That is the picture of one conscious of a dislocation within oneself. "O wretched man that I am! Who will deliver me from this body of death?" (v. 24). The consciousness of a personality at this stage is that of a house divided against itself; it is the stage technically known as conviction of sin. "I was alive once without the law"—at peace till I saw what Jesus Christ was driving at, "but when the commandment came, sin revived, and I died" (v. 9). "If all God can do for me is to destroy the unity I once had, make me a divided personality, give me light that makes me morally insane with longing to do what I cannot do, I would rather be without His salvation, rather remain happy and peaceful without Him." But if this experience is only a stage toward a life of union with God, it is a different matter.

The Disposition Divorced

> For the flesh lusts against the Spirit, and the Spirit against the flesh; and these are contrary to one another, so that you do not do the things that you wish. Galatians 5:17

After being born again you experience peace, but it is a militant peace, a peace maintained at the point of war. The wrong disposition is no longer in the ascendant, but it is there, and you know it is. You are conscious of an alternating experience, sometimes you are in ecstasy, sometimes in the dumps; there is no stability, no real spiritual triumph. To take this as the experience of full salvation is to prove God not justified in the Atonement.

"For the flesh lusts against the Spirit, and the Spirit against the flesh." The Spirit of God entering into a person wars against "the flesh," not flesh and blood, but the disposition of sin. Paul calls the product of this friction between the Spirit and the flesh carnality. A worldly person has no carnality; she or he is not conscious of any conflict between the Spirit and the flesh; when the individual is born again the conflict begins, and there is a disclosure of the carnal mind, which "is enmity against God" (Romans 8:7). People don't know they have that enemy on the inside until they receive the Holy Spirit.

The carnal mind is not something that has to be removed; it either is or is not. As soon as you agree to the dethronement of the disposition that lusts against the Spirit, the carnal mind is not. The flesh and the Spirit are daggers drawn, so to speak, and I have to decide which shall rule. If I am going to decide for the Spirit, I will crucify the flesh; God cannot do it, I must do it myself. To "crucify" means to put to death—not counteract, not sit on, not whitewash—but kill. If I do

Personality—I   91

not put to death the things in me that are not of God, they will put to death the things that are of God. To belong to Christ means I have deliberately chosen to depose the disposition of the flesh and be identified with Christ; "Yes, I agree with the Spirit and go to the death of the old disposition; I agree with God's condemnation in the Cross of self-interest and self-realization, though these things have been dearer to me than life." Jesus Christ is merciless to self-realization, to self-indulgence, pride, unchastity, to everything that has to do with the disposition you did not know you had till you met Him. The Redemption does not tinker with the externals of a person's life; it deals with the disposition. "And those who are Christ's have crucified the flesh with its passions and desires" (Galatians 5:24). No one is really Christ's till that is done.

The Disposition Divine

> Through these [exceedingly great and precious promises] you may be partakers of the divine nature. 2 Peter 1:4

At this stage a person's personality is again united into peace. Jesus Christ's one aim is to bring us back into oneness with God. The whole purpose of the Redemption is to give back to humankind the original source of life, and in a regenerated person this means "Christ is formed in you" (Galatians 4:19). Am I willing that the old disposition should be crucified with Christ? If I am, Jesus Christ will take possession of me and will baptize me into His life until I bear a strong family likeness to Him. It is a lonely path, a path of death, but it means ultimately being presenced with Divinity. The Christian life does not take its pattern from good people but from God Himself, that is why it is an absolutely supernormal life all through. "Therefore you shall be perfect, just as your Father in heaven is perfect" (Matthew 5:48).

Personality—II

Self-Realization versus Christ-Realization

Self-realization is a modern phrase; "Be moral, be religious, be upright, in order that you may realize yourself." Nothing blinds the mind to the claims of Jesus more effectually than a good moral life based on the disposition of self-realization. Paul says, "If our gospel is veiled, it is veiled to those who are perishing, whose minds the god of this age has blinded, who do not believe" (2 Corinthians 4:3–4). The issue is not with external sins and wrongdoing but with the ideal of self-realization, because it is this disposition that divides clean asunder from all Jesus Christ stands for. In using Bible terms, remember they are used from God's standpoint, not humanity's. From the human standpoint, self-realization is full of light and wisdom; from God's standpoint, it is the dark night of the soul. Romans 7 describes the giving way of the foundations of self-realization.

Separate Self-Consciousness

The notion that we conceive of ourselves as separate from everyone else is erroneous, it is the rarest thing—unless we have done wrong, then immediately we realize not our oneness with others but our separateness. The guilty person is the one who wants to be alone, the person who is right with God does not; neither does a child. Separate self-consciousness is the realization that I am other than what I see and am troubled by all that is not "me." The "I" of separate self-consciousness is the manifestation of sin; the final curse of a disobedient soul is that it becomes a separate, self-conscious individual.

God did not create Adam holy. He created him innocent, that is, without self-consciousness (as we understand the word) before God; Adam was conscious of himself only in relation to the Being whom he was to glorify and enjoy. Consciousness of self was an impossibility in the Garden until something happened, namely, the introduction of sin. To begin with, Adam was not afraid of God; he was not afraid of the beasts of the field, or of anything, because there was no consciousness of himself apart from God. As soon as he disobeyed, he became conscious of himself and he felt afraid: "I heard Your voice in the garden, and I was afraid" (Genesis 3:10); he had ceased to be a child and had become a sinner. That is why our Lord says we have to become children all over again. Through the miracle of regeneration we are placed back into a state of innocence. "Sin kills the child out of us and creates the bitter sinner in us." In other words, God's right to me is killed by the incoming of my self-conscious right to myself—"I can do without God." Sin is not a creation, it is a relationship set up between the devil (who is independent entirely of God) and the being God made to have communion with Himself. Disobey God, separate yourself from Him, and you will be "like God, knowing good and evil" (Genesis 3:5; see v. 22). The entrance of sin meant that the connection with God was gone and the disposition of self-realization had come in its place.

Our Lord never denounced wrongdoing and immorality so strongly as He denounced self-realization. Have you ever been puzzled by His attitude to the people of His day—why He told the chief priests that "tax collectors and harlots enter the kingdom of God before you" (Matthew 21:31)? He could not have meant that social sins were not abominable; He was

To be placed back in the state of innocence.

looking at something we do not see, namely, the disposition at the basis of right- and wrongdoing. If either my goodness or my badness is based on the disposition of self-realization, I am anti-Christ. Modern culture and much of the Higher Christian Life type of teaching goes on the line of perfecting my natural individual self until I am in such a condition that God will say, Now you have done so well I will call you My child. Could anything be more alien to the New Testament? Our Lord's teaching is always anti-self-realization. "He who finds his life will lose it"—Why do we ignore what Jesus said? When we come across something we don't like we say we don't understand it; it is too plain not to be understood. Jesus Christ says that the relationship to Him is to be supreme: "and he who loses his life for My sake will find it" (10:39).

We know experimentally what it is to be born again, but we do not think along that line, consequently barriers come in the way, for example, self-conscious piety, sanctimonious sincerity. Anything that makes me conscious of myself or of my experience is of the nature of sin and brings the bondage of self-consciousness. In a religious person self-consciousness dresses itself up in the guise of piety; you can't be "pi" without feeling self-conscious. The truly godly person is one who is entirely sanctified, and he or she is never sanctimonious but absolutely natural. The characteristic of a saint is freedom from anything in the nature of self-consciousness. Our Lord was conscious of only one thing: "I and My Father are one" (John 10:30).

Solidarity in Christ

If I am prepared to have the disposition of self-realization destroyed and the disposition of Christ-realization put in its place, I get to the bedrock of identification with the death of Jesus, and there begins the possibility of my being something

that will show my gratitude for His redemption. Identification with the death of Jesus is a most powerfully practical
experience. The dominating principle at work now is toward
Christ-realization; experimentally it means that I am ruled by
the very disposition of Jesus. Once we are reinstated in the
life of God through the Redemption, self-consciousness gets
feebler and feebler until it disappears altogether, and we are
conscious only of personality as a means of knowing God.

The beginning of the Christian life is characterized by an
abomination of self-interest; it is what the Lord said to me,
and what I said to Him; it is a stage through which many a
life goes, but it is not in agreement with the life Jesus pic-
tures, not the life of a child. There is never any trace of self-
conscious sainthood in abandonment to Jesus; there is only
one consciousness:

> Jesus only, Jesus ever,
> Jesus all in all I see.

Some people are everlastingly badgered by self-consciousness, full of nervous troubles, but let something like
war or a bereavement strike the life and all the morbid self-
interest is gone, and the abandonment in concern for others
marks the beginning of real life. That is an ordinary natural
law and has nothing to do with the Spirit of God. Apply it to
what our Lord teaches about discipleship—He makes abandonment to Him the condition (see Luke 14:26).

Whenever our Lord talked about the relation of a disciple to Him it was in terms of mystical union: "I am the vine
[not the root of the vine, but the vine itself], you are the
branches" (John 15:5). We have not paid enough attention to
the illustrations Jesus uses. This is the picture of sanctification in the individual, a completeness of relationship between
Jesus Christ and me. Pharisaic holiness means that my eyes

are set on my own whiteness and I become a separate individual. I have the notion that I have to be something; I have not, I have to be absolutely abandoned to Jesus Christ, so one with Him that I never think of myself apart from Him. Love is never self-conscious.

We are one with God only in the manner and measure we have allowed the Holy Spirit to have His way with us. The fruit of the Spirit is the fruit of a totally new disposition, the disposition of Christ-realization. Instead now of self-realization, self-consciousness, and sin, there is sanctity and spiritual reality, bringing forth "fruit to holiness" (Romans 6:22).

Do you allow the Holy Spirit to have His way in your life?

Personality—III

Psalm 139

Intercessory Introspection

The Supernatural Intimacy of God
(Psalm 139:1–6)

> O LORD, You have searched me and known me. verse 1

Psalm 139 ought to be the personal experience of every Christian. My own introspection or exploration of myself will lead me astray, but when I realize not only that God knows me, but that He is the only One who does, I see the vital importance of intercessory introspection. All of us are too big for ourselves; thank God for all who realize it and, like the psalmist, hand themselves over to be searched out by God. We only know ourselves as God searches us. "God knows me" is different from "God is omniscient"; the latter is a mere theological statement; the former is a child of God's most precious possession: "O Lord, You have searched me and known me."

No matter what our Christian experience may be the majority of us are nowhere near where the psalmist was; we will rest in our experience instead of seeing that the experience is meant to bring us to the place of knowing God's supernatural intimacy.

"You comprehend my path and my lying down, and are acquainted with all my ways. For there is not a word on my tongue, but behold, O LORD, You know it altogether" (vv. 3–4). To say, "Of course God is omniscient and knows everything," makes no effect on me, I don't care whether God is omni-anything; but when by the reception of the Holy Spirit I begin to realize that God knows all the deepest possibilities there are in me, knows all the eccentricities of my being, I find that the mystery of myself is solved by this besetting God. Do I really believe I am too big a mystery to solve by myself? Or am I so desperately ignorant that I imagine I understand myself thoroughly? If so, I am likely to have a rude awakening. The psalmist implies, "You are the God of the early mornings, the God of the late at nights, the God of the mountain peaks, the God of the sea, but, my God, my soul has further horizons than the early mornings, deeper darkness than the nights of earth, higher peaks than any mountain, greater depths than any sea—You who are the God of all these, be my God. I cannot search to the heights or to the depths; there are motives I cannot trace, dreams I cannot get at; my God, search me out and explore me, and let me know that You have." Look back over your past history with God and you will see that this is the place He has been bringing you to: "God knows me, and I know He does." You can't shift the person who knows that; there is the sanity of almighty God about such a person. It is an interpretation of what Jesus Christ said: "The very hairs of your head are all numbered. Do not fear therefore" (Matthew 10:30–31).

> Never shall I think
> Of anything that thou might'st overlook:—
> In faith-born triumph at thy feet I sink.
>   —George MacDonald

The Surprising Presence of God (Psalm 139:7–12)

Where can I go from Your Spirit? Or where can I flee from Your presence? verse 7

The psalmist states further that the presence of God is the secure accompaniment of His knowledge; not only does God know everything about him, but He is with him in the knowledge. Where is the place that God is not?—hell? No, hell is God; if there were no God, there would be no hell. "If I make my bed in hell, behold, You are there" (v. 8). The first thing the fool does is to get rid of God: "The fool has said in his heart, 'There is no God' " (14:1); then he gets rid of heaven and hell; then he gets rid of all moral consequences—no such thing as right and wrong. The psalmist is stating that wherever he may go in accordance with the indecipherable providence of God, there the surprising presence of God will meet him. As soon as you begin to forecast and plan for yourself, God will break up your program—He delights to do it—until we learn to live like children based on the knowledge that God is ruling and reigning and rejoicing, and His joy is our strength. When we say: "Even there Your hand shall lead me, and Your right hand shall hold me" (139:10), there is no foreboding anxiety, because His love in times past enables us to rest confidently in Him. The only rest there is is in abandon to the love of God. There is security from yesterday, security for tomorrow and security for today: "You have hedged me behind and before, and laid Your hand upon me" (v. 5). It was this knowledge that gave our Lord the imperturbable peace He always had. We must be like a plague of mosquitoes to the Almighty, with our fussy little worries and anxieties and the perplexities we imagine, all because we won't get into the elemental life with God that Jesus came to give.

This psalm is the expression of the Atonement at work in human experience, at-one-ment with God. The marvel of the Atonement is that Jesus Christ can create endlessly in lives the oneness that He had with the Father. When the Holy Spirit emancipates my personality, no attention is paid to my individuality, to my temperament or to my prejudices; He brings me into oneness with God entirely when I am willing to waive my right to myself and let Him have His way. No individual gets there without a crisis, a crisis of a terrific nature in which he or she goes to the death of something.

God is never far enough away from His saints to think about them—He thinks about them, we are taken up into His consciousness. This is expressed in the life of our Lord. How we get there we cannot say, but it is by the processes of God's training of us. God won't leave us alone until the prayer of His Son is answered, that we may be one with the Father even as He is one.

Personality—IV

I have been crucified with Christ; it is no longer I who live, but Christ lives in me; and the life which I now live in the flesh I live by faith in the Son of God, who loved me and gave Himself for me. Galatians 2:20

The Sacrifice of Soul

When you make His soul an offering for sin. Isaiah 53:10

Galatians 2:20 is a complete statement of the life "hidden with Christ in God" (Colossians 3:3) in personal experience, and the prophecy in Isaiah that the soul of our Lord was made "an offering for sin" has exactly the same idea. The sacrifice of body may be an un-Christian sacrifice: "Though I give my body to be burned, but have not love, it profits me nothing" (1 Corinthians 13:3); but the sacrifice of soul is a willing love-offering.

"I have been crucified with Christ." The teaching of self-realization is the great opponent of the doctrine of sanctification—"I have to realize myself as a separate individual, educate and develop myself so that I fulfill the purpose of my being." Self-realization and self-consciousness are ways in which the principle of sin works out, and in Galatians 2:20 Paul is referring to the time and the place where he got rid of his "soul" in this respect. There is nothing in the nature of self-realization or of self-consciousness in our Lord.

People will say glibly, "Oh, yes, I have been crucified with Christ," while the whole life is stamped with self-realization; once identification with the death of Jesus has really taken place, self-realization does not appear again. To be crucified with Christ means that in obedience to the Spirit granted to me at regeneration, I eagerly and willingly go to the Cross and crucify self-realization for ever. The crucifixion of the flesh is the willing action of an obedient, regenerate man or woman. "And those who are Christ's have crucified the flesh with its passions and desires" (Galatians 5:24). Obey the Spirit of God and the Word of God, and it will be as clear as a sunbeam what you have to do; it is an attitude of will toward God, an absolute abandon, a glad sacrifice of the soul in unconditional surrender. Then comes the marvelous revelation: "I have been crucified with Christ"; not, "I am being crucified," or, "I hope to be crucified by and by"; not, "I am getting nearer to the place where I shall be crucified with Christ," but, "I have been crucified with Christ," I realize it and know it.

The Surprise of Sacrifice

For to me, to live is Christ. Philippians 1:21

"It is no longer I who live, but Christ lives in me." Paul still says "I," but the "I" is so taken up with Christ that all he sees is Christ-realization, not self-realization. "Knowing this, that our old man was crucified with Him" (Romans 6:6)—the "old man" is the Scriptural name for self-realization, and it is my old man that connects me with the body of sin. Sin is infinitely more than my old man; there is a supernatural body of sin that backs me up in wrong, it is an impulsion to wrong on the outside that is far more powerful than the disposition to sin on the inside. By the identification with the death of Christ Paul refers to, the old man, self-realization in me, is crucified, and in this way the body of sin is "done away"—not crucified but destroyed. There are two mystical bodies—the body of sin ruled over by Satan, and the body of Christ built up of the men and women who have been made one in Him.

That is why Paul refers to our Lord as the Last Adam; He is the Federal Head of a totally new conception of humanity. When I am lifted by the Atonement into oneness with God I do not lose my personal identity, my identity becomes that of conscious union with God. The human relationship with God in the beginning was such that the consciousness of union with Him was a delight; as soon as sin entered, that went and people became self-conscious: they realized they were no longer in union with God and tried to hide themselves from His presence.

Paul says, "I have been crucified with Christ; it is no longer I who live, but Christ lives in me"; my personal identity, as created by God and restored in Christ Jesus, is still there, but the "I" is no longer ruled by the disposition of sin—that has been identified with the Cross, and it is Christ who lives in me. Paul's whole life was so identified with Christ that it was not only not untrue for him to say "Christ lives in me," it was the only truth. When he says, in writing to the Corinthians, "I fear, lest . . . your minds may be corrupted from the simplicity that is in Christ" (2 Corinthians 11:3), he is referring to the fundamental simplicity of this relationship. Our Lord Himself continually reminded His disciples of this simplicity: "Assuredly, I say to you, unless you are converted and become as little children" (Matthew 18:3); "I thank You, Father, . . . that You . . . have revealed [these things] to babes" (11:25)—out of the complication, out of the torture of self-consciousness, out of the strenuousness and effort, into the simplicity of the life hidden with Christ in God, where God is at liberty to do with us what He likes, even as He did with His own Son.

The Summit of Substitution

Whoever eats My flesh and drinks My blood abides in Me, and I in him. John 6:56

> The life which I now live in the flesh I live by faith in the Son of God, . . .

The doctrine of substitution in the Bible is "Christ for me" that it may be "Christ in me," until the personal oneness can only be expressed in the language of our Lord in John 6. "The life which I now live," says Paul, not hereafter, but the life you can see, the life I live in the flesh, the life exhibited through my tongue, through all the organs of my body, the way I eat and drink, and the way I do my work. That is the life Paul has the audacity to say he lives "by faith in the Son of God." It is the life of the Spirit made manifest in the flesh, and that is always the test of identification with Christ, not prayer meetings and times of devotion. If I have been identified with the cross of Christ it must show through my fingertips.

> . . . who loved me and gave Himself for me.

Paul is identified forever with the interests of the Son of God in other lives; he attracted to Jesus Christ all the time, never to himself; he became a sacramental personality; wherever he went Jesus Christ helped Himself to his life. "To me, who am less than the least of all the saints, this grace was given, that I should preach [that is, sacramentally express] among the Gentiles the unsearchable riches of Christ" (Ephesians 3:8).

Where Jesus Christ Tells

In the Domain of Struggle and Sin

If Jesus Christ does not mean anything to you it is because you have not entered into the domain where He tells; you may have to enter that domain through a ruthless doorway. As soon as you go through the bottom board of self-complacency and come to the elemental, you enter the domain of struggle and sin, and Jesus Christ begins to tell at once. People are alive physically and intellectually apart from Jesus Christ, and as long as they are satisfied with that attitude to life Jesus Christ is not a necessity; the wholesome-minded type is totally oblivious to Jesus Christ. "Those who are well have no need of a physician, but those who are sick," said Jesus. "I have not come to call the righteous, but sinners, to repentance" (Luke 5:31–32).

There are numbers of women and men who are materially satisfied, their reach does not exceed their grasp; they are not moral renegades, but they remain outside the domain in which Jesus Christ figures. They have no disrespect for Jesus Christ, but they have no use for Him—He seems to be untouched by the reality of things. It is quite possible to live in that domain and never come across the need for Jesus Christ; in fact you can work out a better philosophy of life without Him because He comes in as an interruption. But once one realizes that one's actual life spits at one's creed, then begins the struggle. Boys and girls in their teens think higher and nobler than at any other time, then they begin to find that actual life comes nowhere near their ideals—"I can't begin to be actually what I see I ought to be." The struggle represented by that type of mind is an agony, and that is the first domain where Jesus Christ begins to tell. If someone has begun this struggle there is only one way out: "Come to Me, all you who labor and are heavy laden, and I will give you rest" (Matthew 11:28). If you are not struggling, you don't need to bother your head, but if it is a struggle worthy of the name, remember the only way out is by going to Jesus. So long as I have no struggle, no sense of sin, I can do well enough without Him.

In the Domain of Suffering and Sorrow

Another domain in which Jesus Christ tells is the domain of suffering and sorrow. You cannot think of a home today that is without suffering. The war has knocked on the head the stupid, temperamental idea that every cloud has a silver lining; there are clouds in countless lives with an inkier lining inside than outside. It is an insult to tell such people to cheer up and look on the bright side; their lives are blasted for all time from every standpoint except Jesus Christ's. The remarkable thing is that it is rarely the one who suffers who turns against God; it is the lookers-on who turn against God because they do not see the one fact more in the life that gives God room to work. Those who look on are apt to come to the conclusion either that the one who suffers is a sinner or that God is cruel; they take the line of Job's comforters. Why there should be suffering we do not know, but we have to remain loyal to the character of God as revealed by Jesus Christ in the face of it.

There is a type of suffering caused because we do not see the way out. A person may say that the basis of things is rational—"Get to the bottom of things and you will find it all simple and easy of explanation"—well, that simply is not true. The basis of things is not rational but tragic, and when you enter the domain of suffering and sorrow you find that reason and logic are your guide amongst things as they are, but nothing more. Is it rational that I should be born with a heredity over which I have no control? Is it rational that nations that are nominally Christian should be at war? The basis of things is tragic, and the only way out is through the Redemption. Many a one in mental stress of weather is driven to utter what sounds like blasphemy, and yet that one may be nearer God than in the complacent acceptance of beliefs that have never been tried. Never be afraid of someone who seems to you to talk blasphemously—he or she is up against problems you may never have met with; instead of being wrathful, be patient with such a person. The one to be afraid of is the one who is indifferent, what morality that one has got is well within his or her own grasp, and Jesus Christ is of no account at all.

In the Domain of Spirit and Sublimity

It is in the implicit domains that Jesus Christ tells. By *implicit* is meant the thing you can't put into words but that makes you, you. It is in the moments when the implicit is awakened that Jesus Christ becomes the only One who does tell. You cannot get there when you like—there are moral conditions. Jesus Christ makes Himself the great Decider of human destiny: "But who do you say that I am?" (Matthew 16:15). Beware of the subtlety that likes to listen to the teaching of Jesus but says, "There is no need for all this talk about the Atonement and the Cross, all that is necessary is to live out the Sermon on the Mount, to follow in the steps of Jesus." If Jesus Christ came to teach people to be what they never can be, would He had never come! He is the greatest tantalizer of humankind if all He came to do was to tell us to be pure in heart, to be so holy that when God scrutinizes us He can see nothing to censure. But what He came to do was to make it possible for anyone to receive the disposition that ruled Him, namely, the Holy Spirit. When someone is born again what happens is that he or she receives the heredity of Jesus Christ. That is the meaning of regeneration. There is only one disposition that can live out the teaching of Jesus, and that is His own disposition. When I have received the disposition of Jesus Christ, God does not shield me from any requirements of a son; I have the opportunity of proving actually worthy of His great redemption. "If the Son makes you free, you shall be free indeed," said Jesus (John 8:36)— free from the inside, free in essence; there will be no pretense, no putting yourself on a pedestal and saying "This is what God has done for me"; you will be free, the thing will be there ostensibly.

With Christ in the School of Philosophy

The New Thinking of Pentecost

The things of the Spirit of God. 1 Corinthians 2:14

Everywhere the charge is made against Christian people, not only the generality of Christians, but really spiritual people, that they think in a very slovenly manner. Very few of us in this present dispensation live up to the privilege of thinking spiritually as we ought. This present dispensation is the dispensation of the Holy Spirit. The majority of us do not think according to the tremendous meaning of that; we think ante-Pentecostal thoughts, the Holy Spirit is not a living factor in our thinking; we have only a vague impression that He is here. Many Christian workers would question the statement that we should ask for the Holy Spirit (see Luke 11:13). The note struck in the New Testament is not "Believe in the Holy Spirit," but "Receive the Holy Spirit." That does not mean the Holy Spirit is not here; it means He is here in all His power, for one purpose, that people who believe in Him might receive Him. So the first thing we have to face is the reception of the Holy Spirit in a practical, conscious manner.

Always distinguish between yielding to the Spirit and receiving the Spirit. When the Spirit is at work in a time of mighty revival it is very difficult not to yield to the Spirit, but it is quite another thing to receive Him. If we yield to the power of the Spirit in a time of revival we may feel amazingly blessed, but if we do not receive the Spirit we are left decidedly worse and not better. That is first a psychological fact and then a New Testament fact. So as Christians we have to ask ourselves, does our faith stand "in demonstration of the Spirit and of power" (1 Corinthians 2:4)? Have we linked ourselves up with the power of the Holy Spirit, and are we letting Him have His way in our thinking?

(a) The Material of This Thinking

> You will know them by their fruits. Matthew 7:16; see verses 15–20

The touchstone of truth is not a big intellect but a pure heart—a holy person; but an unholy person can test the reality of a person's holiness. Jesus told His disciples to test preachers and teachers not by the fact that they prophesied in His name but by their fruits. How many of us do? How many of us know experimentally what Jesus meant when He said: "My sheep hear My voice" (John 10:27), but "they do not know the voice of strangers" (v. 5)? We must never test our teachers by our spiritual prejudices. Jesus laid down as the one principle for testing teachers not that God was at work through them, but by their fruits. God will honor His Word whether a saint or a bad individual preaches it; this is one of the startling things that our Lord says (see Matthew 7:21–23). Jesus demands that we submit our teachers to the test He Himself submitted to (see John 18:20). A teacher sent from God never teaches in secret or teaches the special esoteric line of things that only the initiated few can get into.

Take it individually, are we thinking on the sane, vigorous lines we have indicated generally? Do the things we teach demonstrate themselves in practical living? "Therefore by their fruits you will know them" (Matthew 7:20). If someone's character does not back up what he or she teaches, we must brand that person as a false prophet. We all know the boomerang effect of messages; after we have preached, the

Spirit of God comes and says, "What about you?" It is this kind of thinking that puts the death blow to the sentimental evangelism and Higher Lifeism that is not robust enough to pay its debts or to be clean and upright, to be absolutely beyond suspicion in every detail of the life.

(b) The Method of This Thinking

Test all things. 1 Thessalonians 5:21

The only way we can prove spiritual things is by experience. Are we thinking along ante-Pentecostal lines? Are we thinking, that is, without making room for the supernatural? Much of the thinking of today belongs to a day before Pentecost; the majority of us are out of date. To think along Pentecostal lines means that we have received the Holy Spirit, and this should be sufficient for us to see that we have the ability to do the things that are demanded by God. It is a crime for a saint to be weak in God's strength. "For this is the will of God, your sanctification" (4:3). Have we thought about that? Have we proved it by experience? We can prove it only by having the mind of the person who said it put into us. It is no use inquiring of John Wesley or of saved and sanctified saints; we must come to one place only, namely, five minutes' concentration before God, "Lord, I want to test this thing, I am willing to go the whole length." That is the only way we can test spiritual things, the only way we become vigorous New Testament thinkers—not working signs and wonders— that is child's play, froth; it may indicate the tremendous ocean underneath, or it may not. The great thing that the Holy Spirit reveals is that the supernatural power of God is ours through Jesus Christ, and if we will receive the Holy Spirit He will teach us how to think as well as how to live. Always refer back to the receiving of the Holy Spirit, we receive Him to do His work in us. Just as Jesus glorified God, so the Holy Spirit glorifies Jesus; He makes us written epistles not only in living, but in thinking.

(c) The Mind of the Thinker

> Let this mind be in you which was also in Christ Jesus.
> Philippians 2:5

To have the Spirit of Christ is one thing, to form His mind is another. To have the mind of Christ means that we are willing to obey the dictates of the Holy Spirit through the physical machines of our brains and bodies till our living bears a likeness to Jesus. Every Christian ought to be living in this intense, vigorous atmosphere—no sentimental weaknesses. The majority of us scorn self-pity along physical and moral lines, but I am not so sure that we scorn self-pity along spiritual lines. We must form the mind of Christ till it works out in a strong family likeness to Jesus. *This is how people should feel after being around me.*

Every time we come in contact with a Christian of this sort we feel as if we are brought face-to-face with the Lord Himself. That alone is the evidence of the Holy Spirit. The great, glorious power of the Holy Spirit, if He has been received by us, manifests itself in the way we think. It is not sufficient to know God said a thing, but, relying on the Holy Spirit, we must test it. God brings us into circumstances where we have to "test all things," where we form the mind of Christ and make our thinking like His—robust, vigorous and strong, right toward God, not because we are in earnest but because we have received the earnest Holy Spirit.

The New Thinking about Christ

> But Christ as a Son over His own house. Hebrews 3:6

(a) The Reminiscent Christ

> Though we have known Christ according to the flesh.
> 2 Corinthians 5:16

Pentecost made Christ spiritual to us. We mean by *reminiscent* what Paul implies here, trying to picture by desperate efforts of imagination what Christ was like, searching the Bible records and trying by sheer effort of mind to bring back to our minds what Christ would tell us if He were here now. All that belongs to a dispensation we have no business to be living in. The Holy Spirit makes Jesus Christ both present and real. He is the most real Being on earth, "closer is He than breathing, and nearer than hands and feet." Simply receive the Holy Spirit, rely on Him and obey Him and He will bring the realization of Christ.

(b) The Realization of Christ

Lo, I am with you always. Matthew 28:20

When the Lord Jesus is revealed from heaven. 2 Thessalonians 1:7

The Scriptures make a distinction between the Parousia and the *Apokalupsis*. The Parousia is spiritual and invisible; the *Apokalupsis* is a hope. We rejoice in the presence of the Lord, we wait in hope for the revelation of the Lord Jesus Christ from heaven. Are any of us struggling to remember what Christ was like, saying, "I wish that His hands had been placed on my head"? By receiving the Holy Spirit we may know Him ten thousandfold better! The very life of Jesus will be in us by the sheer supernatural grace of God. That is the marvel of this present dispensation. The Holy Spirit is seeking to awaken people out of lethargy; He is pleading, yearning, blessing, pouring benedictions on people, convicting and drawing them nearer, for one purpose only, that they may receive Him so that He may make them holy men and women, exhibiting the life of Jesus Christ. How the devil does rob Christians who are not thinking on Pentecostal lines of the tremendous power of the presence of Jesus made real by the Holy Spirit!

(c) The Revelation of Christ

> He will give you another Helper. John 14:16

The Holy Spirit is not a substitute for Jesus; the Holy Spirit is all that Jesus was and all that Jesus did, made real in personal experience now. The Holy Spirit alone makes Jesus real, the Holy Spirit alone expounds His cross, the Holy Spirit alone convicts of sin; the Holy Spirit alone does in us what Jesus did for us. It is thinking along these lines that makes it a burden insuperable when one sees men and women who ought to be princes and princesses with God bound up in a show of things, taken up with duties that are not the supreme duty. Instead of applying the supreme law, which we ought to do in every case of conflict, namely, "You shall love the LORD Your God with all your heart," the second commandment is put first: "You shall love your neighbor as yourself" (Matthew 22:37, 39). Whenever Jesus dealt with the closest relationships and with our own self-interest, He always put Himself first. His meaning is perfectly clear, that if His claims clash with those relationships, it must be instant obedience to Him (see Luke 14:26). Men and women who ought to be living in the glorious privileges of this Pentecostal dispensation are very often bound up by duties that are right from every standpoint but one, the standpoint of the Holy Spirit; right according to the logic of morality and common sense and justice but not according to the logic of Pentecost, the Spirit does not witness, His illumination does not come. Some people spend their lives sacrificing themselves for other people, with the only result that the people for whom the sacrifice is made become more and more selfish. Whenever the Holy Spirit inspires the sacrifice, it is the sacrifice of ourselves for Jesus' sake, and that never blights but always blesses. Half the heartbreaks and difficulties that some of us have hurried ourselves into would have been prevented if we had only dared to obey God in the power of the Spirit.

The New Thinking about God

> No one has seen God at any time. John 1:18

(a) The Eternal God

> He who has seen Me has seen the Father. John 14:9

Pentecost has made God spiritual to us. Jesus Christ was God Incarnate; Pentecost is God come in the Spirit. The essential nature of God the Father, of God the Son, and of God the Spirit is the same. The characteristics that marked God the Father in the old dispensation and that marked God the Son when He lived on this earth mark God the Holy Spirit in this present dispensation. "God is Spirit" (John 4:24). Apart from the Spirit of God we cannot think about anything that has not its basis in space and time, consequently when people without the Spirit think of God, they think of a Being sitting somewhere or ruling somewhere. We cannot think about God until we have received the Spirit, our natural hearts are atheistic. We have a dumb blind instinct that feels after God (see Acts 17:27), but it leads nowhere. When we receive the Holy Spirit, He opens the eyes of our understanding, convicts of sin, and shows us what Jesus came to do. "No one knows the things of God except the Spirit of God" (1 Corinthians 2:11). Is it not astounding the amount of persuasion that is necessary before some of us will receive the Holy Spirit—we will argue and debate and do everything under heaven before we will waive our preconceived notions, our doctrinal points of view, and come as simple children and ask for the Holy Spirit. "If you knew the gift of God, . . . you would have asked Him, and He would have given you living water" (John 4:10). Jesus did not speak these words to a learned person, but to a sinful one. He told that woman of Samaria to ask for the Holy Spirit, and there would be done in her what was done at Pentecost for the disciples, and that is where we ought to be living today.

(b) The Eternal Spirit (Universal)

I will pour out of My Spirit on all flesh. Acts 2:17

The dispensation of Pentecost is not confined to the Jews, not confined to Christendom; it is confined nowhere, it is absolutely universal, the sweep and sway and majesty of the power of the Holy Spirit is at work in every crook and cranny of the universe. For what purpose? That people may receive Him. We imagine that God has special favorites, and by trying to prescribe the movements of the Holy Spirit we exploit Him. We do not say so, but we are apt to think that unless people come the way we came, the Holy Spirit will not teach them. The great truth is that God's Spirit in this dispensation is absolutely universal for one purpose, that the life of Jesus may be made manifest in our mortal flesh.

(c) The Eternal Spirit (Ubiquitous)

Where can I flee from Your presence? Psalm 139:7

If we try to drown God's presence in the depths of iniquity, it is there; if we go to the heights and speculate, it is there—insisting, wooing, drawing; the hand of Christ knocking at the door, for one purpose—to get in. The Spirit of God is everywhere—would that people would yield to Him! The reason we do not yield is that in the deep recesses of our hearts we prefer the captaincy of our own lives, we prefer to go our own ways and refuse to let God govern. A human being cannot alter us; God almighty Himself cannot alter us. Jesus Christ Himself stood absolutely powerless before people with the spiritual "nod." Do you know what the spiritual nod is? Disbelief in anything but my own point of view. "He did not do many mighty works there because of their unbelief" (Matthew 13:58).

Have you received the Holy Spirit? If not, why not receive Him now?

I. How to Think about God

Philip said to Him, "Lord, show us the Father, and it is sufficient for us."

Jesus said to him, "... He who has seen Me has seen the Father; so how can you say, 'Show us the Father'?" John 14:8–9

How do we think about God habitually? Jesus said, "He who has seen Me has seen the Father." In the face, in the character, in the walk and the work of Jesus, we have God the Father revealed. The Christian faith affirms the existence of a personal God who reveals Himself. Pseudo-Christianity departs from this, we are told we cannot know anything at all about God, we do not know whether He is a personal Being, we cannot know whether He is good. The Christian revelation is that God is a personal Being and He is good. By good, I mean morally good. Test all beliefs about God by that; do they reveal clearly that God is a good God and that all that is moral and pure and true and upright comes from God?

Instinct and Revelation

As I was passing through and considering the objects of your worship, I even found an altar with this inscription: To The Unknown God. Therefore, the One whom you worship without knowing, Him I proclaim to you. Acts 17:23

The evangelical teaching about this intuition and instinct in human nature is that it is to be recognized as being there but requiring a revelation from outside to discover what it wants. The Christian affirmation is that this instinct and intuition is not God, but a dumb, inarticulate feeling after

God. "That they should seek the Lord, in the hope that they might grope for Him and find Him, though He is not far from each one of us" (v. 27). That is the first point of divergence of the modern tendency from the Christian affirmation. We see at once how it works out in practical religious life; it means that we have the Spirit of God in us by nature, we do not need to be born again of the Spirit. This line of thinking could not be more diametrically opposed to the New Testament conception. The New Testament reveals that the deepest instinct in us is to feel after God, but that instinct is never to be taken for the Spirit of God.

Honeycombing all our Christian teaching today is the idea that the instinct in us is God and that as we allow the deepest instinct in us expression, we reveal ourselves as more or less God, and that the Being in whom this instinct had its greatest expression was the Lord Jesus Christ; therefore He stands in the modern movements, and to everyone who follows that line of thinking, as the best expression of God. The New Testament reasoning is that if we are going to enter into contact with the God whom the Bible reveals we must be born from above, be lifted into a totally new realm by means of the Atonement. "Do not marvel that I said to you, 'You must be born again' " (John 3:7). Jesus Christ is a distinct break in our order and not the product of our order. Just as our Lord came into human history from the outside, so He must come into us from the outside. The meaning of new birth is that we know God in a vital relationship (see John 1:12-13).

Paul puts as the Christian attitude to God that "we are the offspring of God" (Acts 17:29). The term the "Fatherhood" of God is rarely used nowadays in the New Testament sense; it is only used in the sense of God as Creator, not in the sense that Jesus Christ used it; the consequence is great havoc is produced in our Lord's teaching. If God is our

Father by creation in the sense Jesus says He is by the experience of regeneration, then the Atonement is nonsense. What was the good of Jesus Christ living and dying and rising again? Where is the need for all this teaching that we have to be born again? If our instinct is God, we need only be sufficiently well-educated to allow the instinct that is in us to come out. But does this satisfy you and me regarding ourselves? Are we consciously, solemnly, and satisfyingly confident that if we let the deepest instincts in us have expression, we are letting God express Himself? According to the Bible, the very essence of Satan is self-rule, and there are two mighty forces at work, one against and one for God.

Paul argues, "For what man knows the things of a man except the spirit of the man which is in him? Even so no one knows the things of God except the Spirit of God" (1 Corinthians 2:11). It is the same insistence on the need to be born from above, and if we will take Jesus Christ's way and face facts as He asks us to face them, we will find all the mystery of doing right amid entrancing wrong, all the mystery of attaining the highest when the lowest is the most attractive, all the mystery of complete deliverance from the disposition of sin opened up and made possible. Doctrine is expounded not by our intelligence, not by our searching, but by the indwelling of a completely new Spirit imparted to us by the Lord Jesus Christ.

It is necessary to give a note of warning against the tyranny of abstractions. An ideal has no power over us until it becomes incarnate. The idea of beauty lies unawakened until we see a thing we call beautiful. God may be a mere mental abstraction; He may be spoken of in terms of culture or poetry or philosophy, but He has not the slightest meaning for us until He becomes incarnate. When once we know that God has "trod this earth with naked feet, and woven with human hands the creed of creeds," then we are arrested.

When once we know that the almighty Being who reigns and rules over His creation does not do so in calm disdain but puts His back to the wall of the world, so to speak, and receives all the downcast, the outcast, the sin-defiled, the wrong, the wicked, and the sinful into His arms, then we are arrested. An intellectual conception of God may be found in a bad, vicious character. The knowledge and vision of God is dependent entirely on a pure heart. Character determines the revelation of God to the individual. The pure in heart see God. Jesus Christ changes the worst into the best and gives the moral readjustment that enables us to love and delight in the true God. Of a great, almighty, incomprehensible Being we know nothing, but of our Lord Jesus Christ we do know, and the New Testament reveals that the almighty God is nothing that Jesus was not.

Ideas and Revelation

> For in Him we live and move and have our being. . . . We are the offspring of God. Acts 17:28–29

Our ideas of God are no greater than ourselves, and we ought to receive from God other ideas by revelation, so that the working human mind may receive the power to live a larger, grander life than lies in any of its own ideas. Our ideas of God are indistinct, and when we make those ideas in their indistinctness the ground of our understanding of God, we are hopelessly at sea. We are never told to walk in the light of our convictions or instinctive ideas; according to the Bible, we have to walk in the light of our Lord. Nothing is known about God except in and through our Lord Jesus Christ. "Nor does anyone know the Father except the Son, and the one to whom the Son wills to reveal Him" (Matthew 11:27). I can only have a personal, passionate love for a Being who is not myself, and the whole meaning of the Atonement is to destroy the idolatry of self-love, to extract the pernicious poison of self-interest, and presence us with the Divinity that enables us to love God with all the heart, soul, mind, and strength. The New Testament reveals that we are not ultimately to be absorbed into God; we are distinctly and eternally to be the passionate lovers of God. No one was ever created to be his or her own god, and no one was ever created to be the god of another person, and no system of ideas was ever made to dominate humanity as god. There is one God, and that God was incarnate in the Lord Jesus Christ. And as that marvelous Being has His dominant sway over us, the whole of time, the whole of eternity, and the threshold between the two will be shot through with the dawn of an endless day that shall never end in night, when "God will wipe away every tear from their eyes" (Revelation 7:17; 21:4) and heaven prove the complement of earth.

II. How to Think about the Lord Jesus Christ

> All things have been delivered to Me by My Father, and no one
> knows the Son except the Father. Matthew 11:27

In Matthew 11:27 the unique position of Jesus Christ to His
own consciousness is clearly exhibited. The mystery of the
person of Jesus resides in its nature from the beginning;
before we begin to understand His person we must be quick-
ened from above by the Holy Spirit. That is where the battle
rages today—around the person of Jesus Christ (compare 1
John 4:2–3). The call for every Christian worker is to thoroughly equip herself or himself with right thinking about
Jesus Christ.

The Bible has no respect for mental abstractions. Jesus
Christ did not talk about the Infinite or the Incomprehensible; whenever He talked about God He brought it down to
concrete reality: "He who has seen Me has seen the Father"
(John 14:9). Unless God has become a concrete reality in
Jesus Christ, He has no meaning for us at all. Jesus nowhere
said, he who has seen humanity has seen the Father; He
emphatically states that He is the only medium God has for
revealing Himself. The trend of thought at the heart of all
the modern ethical movements is based on the idea that God
and humanity are one and the same. Jesus nowhere taught
that God was in humanity, but He did teach that God was
manifest in human flesh in His person, that He might become
the generating center for the same thing in every human

being, and the place of His travail pangs is Bethlehem, Calvary, and the Resurrection.

"I and My Father are one" (10:30). Do we accept Jesus Christ's thinking about Himself? According to His own thinking He was equal with God, and He became incarnate for the great purpose of lifting the human race back into communion with God, not because of their aspirations but because of the sheer omnipotence of God through the Atonement. The life of Jesus Christ is made ours not by imitation but by means of His death on Calvary and by our reception of His Spirit. Our Lord's marvelous message for all time is the familiar one: "Come to Me, . . . and I will give you rest" (Matthew 11:28).

"The wayfaring people, yea fools, shall not err therein." When people do err in the way of God, it is because we are wise in our own conceits. When the facts of life have humbled us, when introspection has stripped us of our own miserable self-interest and we receive a startling diagnosis of ourselves by the Holy Spirit, we are by that painful experience brought to the place where we can hear the marvelous message—profounder than the profoundest philosophies earth ever wove, "Come to Me, all you who labor and are heavy laden, and I will give you rest." Until this experience comes, people may patronize Jesus Christ, but they do not come to Him for salvation. The only solution is the one given by Jesus Christ Himself to a good, upright individual of His day: "Do not marvel that I said to you, 'You must be born again' " (John 3:7).

"However, when He, the Spirit of truth, has come . . . He will glorify Me" (16:13–14). There is abroad today a vague, fanatical movement that bases everything on spiritual impulse—"God gave me an impulse to do this and that," and there are the strangest outcomes to such impulses. Any impulse that does not lead to the glorification of Jesus Christ, has the snare of Satan behind it. People say, "How am I to know whether my impulse is from the Holy Spirit or from my own imagination?" Very easily. Jesus Christ gave us the simplest, most easy-to-be-understood tests for guidance: "The Holy Spirit . . . will teach you all things, and bring all things to your remembrance all things that I said to you" (14:26); the Holy Spirit "will guide you into all truth; for He will not speak on His own authority" (16:13). Beware of any religious experience that glorifies you and not Jesus Christ. It may use the right phrasing, it may praise Jesus Christ and praise the Atonement—that is one of the subtlest powers of the insinuations of Satan—but the life does not glorify Jesus, it does not magnify and uplift the crucified Son of God. Living much in the presence of Jesus, coming in contact with His mind, simplifies life to believers and makes them unflurried skeptics of everything that is not true to the nature of God.

The central citadel of Christianity is the person of our Lord Jesus Christ. The final standard for the Christian is given at the outset: "to be conformed to the image of His Son" (Romans 8:29).

III. How to Think about Man

What is man, that You are mindful of him, and the son of man, that You visit him? Psalm 8:4

The Christian faith declares the spiritual nature and dignity of humanity, that its creation is in the Divine image and its destination is to bear the likeness of God in a perfected Parent-child relationship: "to be conformed to the image of His Son" (Romans 8:29). When we read the history of the race, our thoughts must fit into one of two fundamental categories: either we are wonderful beings in the making or we are wonderful ruins of what we once were. The latter is the view of the Bible. In John 3, we find our Lord recognized the unmaking of humanity so keenly that He told Nicodemus not to marvel when he was told he must be born again. A person never grows out of a natural into a spiritual person without being re-created. The apostle Paul bases his reasoning entirely on this fundamental revelation; he argues, "Therefore, if anyone is in Christ, he is a new creation" (2 Corinthians 5:17). According to the Bible, we do not evolve into better manifestations of God or even into nearness to God, but only by a violent readjustment to God through regeneration are we remade to bear the family likeness to God that we were at first designed to have. It is much easier to live a holy life than to think on Jesus Christ's lines. Are we traitors intellectually to Jesus Christ while professing to be His disciples?

Man's Creation

So God created man in His own image. Genesis 1:28; see Colossians 1:16–17

127

The modern view is that the human race is continually evolving and developing, each phase being better than the last and the last gives us the best revelation of God; from this standpoint Jesus Christ is looked upon as the manifestation of all the best in the evolutionary processes of humanity. The evolutionary conception starts from something un-get-at-able, incalculable, with a power within itself to evolve end-lessly. The great word we bow down and worship today is *progress*; we are progressing and developing, and the conse-quence is we are blind to the facts of history and blind to moral facts. The Bible revelation about humanity is that humanity, as it is, is not as God made it.

As soon as we get the idea that we are part of God, and the universe is His thought about Himself, we are unable to accept the idea that God created us. It is far more natural for us to suppose ourselves emanations from the Being of God, time-manifestations of God, as Jesus was, all of the same kin-dred. Such conceptions have a wonderful element of truth in them when applied to regenerated humanity, but the Bible reveals the presence in unregenerated humanity of a positive anarchy against God (see Romans 8:7). It is possible to be so full of love and sympathy for unregenerate human beings as to be red-handed anarchists against God. This is exactly what the New Testament states, especially in the reasonings of Saint Paul regarding the "old man," the disposition of self-interest that entered into human nature and unmade God's creation so that the human likeness to God in disposition was blotted out. The New Testament reveals that this dispo-sition cannot be educated, it cannot be disciplined or altered, it must be removed and a new mainspring to human nature put in its place. The marvel of the Atonement is that all who will make the moral decision that the old man ought to be crucified and will accept the gift of the Holy Spirit, which was manifested in Jesus Christ, will receive the new disposition that introduces them into the kingdom of God and raises them to sit in heavenly places in Christ Jesus, which surely means a present experience, not a future one.

It is always fascinating to follow an intellectual process, that more or less blinds one to facts, because whatever hinders that intellectual process must either be absorbed or removed. In practical experience, when the deep within us calls to the deep without, there is tumult and upset, and we find a tremendous force that works away from God and will never work in harmony with Him. When in the experience of individuals or of nations the upburst of this disintegrating power occurs, we turn with wistful glance to the Book that has been discarded and to the one Being who has the key to all the problems of life and death, first things and last things, the beginning and ending of things, namely, the Lord Jesus Christ.

Man's Calling

The Bible reveals that humanity's calling is to stand before God and develop by obedience from the lowest point of conscious innocence to the highest reach of conscious holiness, with no intermediaries. This is our calling as God created us, and that is why God will never leave us alone until the blaze and pain of His fire has burned us as pure as He is Himself (compare Matthew 3:11).

It is the moment of unique crisis when one realizes for the first time the hiatus between oneself and God, when the cry goes out from the depths of one's nature, "Oh, that I knew where I might find Him!" or, "My God, what must I do to be saved?" This is not the cry of a person crumpled up by moral irregularities, it is the cry wrung from the depths of human nature. In this crisis, which is the immortal moment of one's conscious life, the meaning of the gospel first comes into play (see Matthew 1:21; 1 John 3:8). Jesus Christ claims that He can do in human nature what human nature cannot do for itself, namely, "destroy the works of the devil" (1 John 3:8), remove the wrong heredity and put in the right one. He can satisfy the last aching abyss of the human heart, He can put the key into our hands that will give the solution to every problem that ever stretched before our minds. He can soothe by His pierced hands the wildest sorrow with which Satan or sin or death ever racked humanity. There is nothing for which Jesus Christ is not amply sufficient and over which He cannot make us more than conquerors. The New Testament does not represent Jesus Christ as coming to us in the character of a celestial lecturer; He is here to recreate us, to presence us with Divinity in such a way that He can remake us according to God's original plan, eternal lovers of God Himself, not absorbed into God but part of the great Spirit-baptized humanity: "till we all come to the unity of the faith and of the knowledge of the Son of God, to a perfect man, to the measure of the stature of the fullness of Christ" (Ephesians 4:13).

Man's Communion

And Enoch walked with God. Genesis 5:24; see John 14:23

The Bible reveals humanity's communion to be consciously with God not in spasms or ecstasies, but under the figure of a walk in the Old Testament and the abiding inmates of a home in the New Testament; it is not absorption but communion. In the Bible people are revealed as created beings, intended to be God's lovers, not a part of God but to be brought back into the relationship of conscious, passionate devotion to God, even as our Lord Himself expressed it. Jesus Christ showed us during a life of thirty-three years what a normal person should be; in what He did and said, and in what He was, He showed us how to think about people, namely, that people are to be the companions and lovers of God.

Many today are seeking reconciliation between the modern views and the New Testament views. It is being attempted ably, but it is a perfectly useless attempt, as useless as trying to make black white; as trying to make wrong right, as trying to make the old man the new man by whitewash. It can never be done. There is only one solution, and that solution comes along the line of the personality of truth, not the abstraction of truth. "I am the way, the truth, and the life" (John 14:6)—the Way in the waylessness of this wild universe; the Truth amidst all the contending confusions of human thought and existence; the Life amidst all the living deaths that sap people's characters and their relationships and connections with the highest. Only by being recreated and readjusted to God through the atonement of our Lord Jesus Christ can we understand the marvelous unity between God and human beings for which God destined us: "that they all may be one, as You, Father, are in Me, and I in You; that they also may be one in Us, that the world may believe that You sent Me" (John 17:21).

IV. How to Think about Sin

Then, when desire has conceived, it gives birth to sin; and sin, when it is full-grown, brings forth death. James 1:15

How do we think about sin habitually, as Christians? If we have light views about sin, we are not students in the school of Christ. The fact of sin is the secret of Jesus Christ's cross; its removal is the secret of His risen and ascended life. Do we think along these lines? It is quite possible to be living in union with God through the Atonement and yet be traitors mentally. It is easy to be traitors unless we are disciplined along the lines that Jesus taught, namely, the need to submit our intellects to Him as He submitted His intellect to His Father. Do we think along the line that salvation is only possible through the Cross? We do not think, and we do not like to think, along Jesus Christ's line; we are told it is old-fashioned and ugly, and so it is; it is awful, it is so awful that it broke God's heart on Calvary.

Every subject we have touched on during this series of talks has been important, but the subject of sin is the vital pivot on which all the rest turn. The slightest deflection from the real truth about sin and all the rest of the reasoning goes wrong. Once placed fundamentally right regarding the doctrine of sin, and the reasoning follows in good order. If you read carefully the modern statements regarding sin you will be amazed to find how often we are much more in sympathy with them than with the Bible statements. We have to face the problem that our hearts may be right with God while our heads have a startling affinity with a great deal that is antago-

132

nistic to the Bible teaching. What we need, and what we get if we go on with God, is an intellectual rebirth as well as a heart rebirth.

The trouble with the modern statements regarding sin is that they make sin far too slight. Sin, according to the modern view, simply means selfishness, and preachers and teachers are as dead against selfishness as the New Testament is. As soon as we come to the Bible we find that sin is much deeper than that. According to the Bible, sin in its final analysis is not a defect but a defiance, a defiance that means death to the life of God in us. Sin is seen not only in selfishness, but in what people call unselfishness. It is possible to have such sympathy with other people as to be guilty of red-handed rebellion against God. Enthusiasm for humanity as it is is quite a different thing from the enthusiasm for the saints that the Bible reveals, namely, enthusiasm for readjusted humanity.

Sin, intellectually viewed, is never anything else than defective development, because the intellect will not allow for gaps that destroy its main principle of outlook. The Bible supplies the facts for the gaps that intellect will not accept. According to the Bible, sin is doing without God. Sin is not wrongdoing, it is wrong being, deliberate and emphatic independence of God. That may sound remote and far away from us, but in individual experience it is best put in the terms of my claim to my right to myself. Every one of us, whether we have received the Holy Spirit or not, will denounce selfishness, but who amongst us will denounce my right to myself? As long as my right to myself remains, I respect it in you, you respect it in me, and the devil respects it in the whole crowd and amalgamates humanity under one tremendous rule that aims at blotting the one true God off His throne. The Bible shows that human nature as it is is one vast strike against God. Paul states that "through one man, sin entered the

Sin is not a defect but a defiance!

world" (Romans 5:12), but we must remember that that individual was not someone like you or me; he was the federal head of the human race. Sin entered into the world through that man's disobedience to God's rule (see Genesis 3). From that moment the strike against God began and has gone on all down the dispensations, and never was there such a big, massive, organized strike as there is today against God and God's rule.

All the great movements of the modern mind are on the line of a combine that swamps individual value. People detest the doctrine of individual responsibility and react against a doctrine of salvation through Jesus Christ because it fixes on the value of the individual. The Bible reveals that the losing of the sense of personal responsibility is the result of sin (see Genesis 4:8–9). The characteristic of sin is to destroy the capacity to know we sin, and the Bible talks about unregenerate people as dead—not dead physically but dead toward God (see Ephesians 2:1).

The recovery of the Bible affirmation about sin is what is needed. The Bible distinctly states that sin is not the natural result of being a finite being but a definite stepping aside from what that finite being knew to be right. How one wishes that people who read books about the Bible would read the Bible itself! Read Ezekiel 18: "The soul who sins shall die" (v. 4); and again: "The wages of sin is death" (Romans 6:23). The Bible does not deal with sin as a disease; it does not deal with the outcome of sin, it deals with the disposition of sin itself. The disposition of sin is what our Lord continually faced, and it is this disposition that the Atonement removes. As soon as our evangelism loses sight of this fundamental doctrine of the disposition of sin and deals only with external sins, it leaves itself open to ridicule. We have cheapened the doctrine of sin and made the Atonement a sort of moral lavatory in which people can come and wash themselves from sin and then go and sin again and come back for another washing. This is the doctrine of the Atonement: "He made Him who knew no sin" (not sins)—He who had not the disposition of sin, who refused, steadfastly and to the death on Calvary, to listen to the temptations of the prince of this world, who would not link Himself with the ruling disposition of humanity but came to hew a way single-handedly through the hard face of sin back to God—"to be sin for us, that we might become the righteousness of God in Him" (2 Corinthians 5:21).

The disposition of sin that rules human nature is not suppressed by the Atonement, not sat on, not cabined and confined—it is removed. Human nature remains unaltered, but the hands and eyes and all our members that were used as the servants of the disposition of sin can be used now as servants of the new disposition (see Romans 6:13). Then comes the glorious necessity of militant holiness. Beware of the teaching that allows you to sink back on your oars and drift; the Bible is full of pulsating, strenuous energy. From the moment a person is readjusted to God, then begins the running, being careful that "the sin which so easily ensnares us" (Hebrews 12:1) does not clog our feet.

I believe that God so radically, so gloriously, and so comprehensively copes with sin in the Atonement that He is more than master of it and that a practical experience of this can take place in the life of anyone who will enter into identification with what Jesus Christ did on the Cross. What is the good of saying, "I believe in Jesus Christ as the Savior of the world," if you cannot answer the blunt question, What has He saved you from? The test is not in theories and theologies but in practical flesh and blood experience. Jesus Christ is our Savior because He saves us from sin, radically altering the ruling disposition. Anyone who has been in contact with the Lord when He alters the ruling disposition knows it, and so do others. But there is a painful, tremendous repentance first. The whole teaching of the Bible on the human side is based on repentance. The only repentant person is the holy person, and the only holy person is the one who has been made so by the marvel of the Atonement. And here comes the wonder—let the blunders of lives be what they may, let hereditary tendencies be what they like, let wrongs and evils crowd as they will, through the Atonement there is perfect readjustment to God, perfect forgiveness, and the gift of a totally new disposition that will manifest itself in the physical life just as the old disposition did (see Romans 6:19). Jesus Christ comes as the Last Adam to take away the abnormal thing (which we call natural), the disposition of my right to myself, and He gives me a new disposition, namely, His own heredity of unsullied holiness, the Holy Spirit.

V. How to Think about the Atonement

God was in Christ, reconciling the world to Himself. 2 Corinthians 5:19; see verses 18–21

The modern view of the Atonement is that it simply reveals the oneness of God and humanity; as soon as we turn to the New Testament we find that the doctrine of the Atonement is that God can readjust humanity to Himself, indicating that there is something wrong, something out of joint, something that has to be put right. The Bible reveals that there is anarchy somewhere, real thorough-going anarchy in the hearts of human beings against God; therefore the need is strong that something should come into us from the outside to readjust us, to reconcile us, to turn us round, to put us right with God. The doctrine of the Atonement is the explanation of how God does that. The doctrine of the Atonement is that "while we were still sinners, Christ died for us" (Romans 5:8). All heaven is interested in the cross of Christ, all hell terribly afraid of it, while people are the only beings who more or less ignore its meaning.

No one can believe in the teaching of Jesus unless he or she believes in the Cross. Those who say, "I believe in the Sermon on the Mount," mean that they give their mental assent to it: "It is a good ideal for whoever can come up to it." But if all Jesus came to do was to tell me I must have an unsullied career, when my past has been blasted by sin and wickedness on my own part, then He but tantalizes me. If He is simply a teacher, He only increases our capacity for misery, for He sets up standards that stagger us. But the teaching of Jesus Christ is not an ideal; it is the statement of the life we will live when we are readjusted to God by the Atonement. The type of life Jesus lived, the type of character He expressed is possible for us by His death, and only by His death, because by means of His death we receive the life to which His teaching applies.

"He made Him who knew no sin to be sin for us, that we might become the righteousness of God in Him" (2 Corinthians 5:21). The idea of substitution popularly understood is that Jesus Christ was punished for me, therefore I go scot-free. The doctrine of substitution in the Bible is always twofold: Christ for me, that He might be substituted in me. There is no Christ for me if there is no Christ in me. The doctrine of substitution is the most practical, radically working thing in the world; it is the very essence of our Lord's teaching. "Unless you eat the flesh of the Son of Man and drink His blood, you have no life in you" (John 6:53). When the apostle John says "He who practices righteousness is righteous" (1 John 3:7), he is not talking of the righteousness of good moral conduct but the righteousness that is impossible to people unless they have been readjusted to God. "When it pleased God . . . to reveal His Son in me," says Paul (Galatians 1:15–16). That is the doctrine of substitution; not, "I believe in God the Father, God the Son, and God the Holy Spirit," and remain the same miserable, selfish, crooked sinner all the time.

How are we to get to the place where the mighty efficacy of the Lord's life is ours? As soon as we are willing to recognize that God condemned sin forever in the death of His Son. If we will accept His verdict and go to God just as we are, the Holy Spirit will apply the Atonement to us personally, and we will know with a knowledge that passes knowledge that we have been born again from above into the realm where Jesus lives, and all the marvelous efficacy of His life comes into our mortal frames. The consequence is we can do all that God commands. The only sign of a readjusted life to God is not a head-belief at all, but a manifestation in our mortal flesh that we can keep the commandments of God.

Now examine the Sermon on the Mount. Can a person by praying, by letting the generous impulse of his or her nature have its way, produce a heart so pure that it sees God? Can a person by doing those things that are easily within the reach of morality produce a life unblameable in holiness before God? Paul says He "became for us. . . righteousness" (1 Corinthians 1:30). That is the doctrine of the Atonement—that we are made undeserving of censure in God's sight, so that God looking down into the motives of our hearts can see nothing to blame. Will I let God identify me with the cross of Christ until I can say not merely with my lips but by my life: "I have been crucified with Christ; it is no longer I who live, but Christ lives in me; and the life which I now live in the flesh I live by faith in the Son of God, who loved me and gave Himself for me" (Galatians 2:20)? From that position it becomes possible for God to take us into His counsels regarding His redemptive purpose. Our understanding of the Atonement depends on our spiritual growth not on our Bible study or on our praying. As we "grow up in all things into Him" (Ephesians 4:15), the one thing about which we get more and more understanding is the mystery of Redemption, and we understand why Jesus said, "Blessed are the pure in heart, for they shall see God" (Matthew 5:8).

VI. How to Think about the Scriptures

For the word of God is living and powerful, and sharper than any two-edged sword, piercing even to the division of soul and spirit, and of joints and marrow, and is a discerner of the thoughts and intents of the heart. Hebrews 4:12

"Why should I believe a thing because it is in the Bible?" That is a perfectly legitimate question. There is no reason why you should believe it, it is only when the Spirit of God applies the Scriptures to the inward consciousness that a person begins to understand their living efficacy. If we try from the outside to fit the Bible to an external standard or to a theory of verbal inspiration or any other theory, we are wrong. "You search the Scriptures, for in them you think you have eternal life; and these are they which testify of Me. But you are not willing to come to Me that you may have life" (John 5:39–40).

There is another dangerous tendency, that of closing all questions by saying, "Let us get back to the external authority of the Bible." That attitude lacks courage and the power of the Spirit of God; it is a literalism that does not produce written epistles but persons who are more or less incarnate dictionaries; it produces not saints but fossils, people without life, with none of the living reality of the Lord Jesus. There must be the Incarnate Word and the interpreting word, that is, people whose lives back up what they preach: "You are our epistle written in our hearts, known and read by all men" (2 Corinthians 3:2). Only when we receive the

Holy Spirit and are lifted into a total readjustment to God do the words of God become "living and powerful" to us. The only way the words of God can be understood is by contact with the Word of God. The connection between our Lord Himself, who is the Word, and His spoken words is so close that to divorce them is fatal. "The words that I speak to you are spirit, and they are life" (John 6:63).

The Bible does not reveal all truth, we have to find out scientific truth and commonsense truth for ourselves, but knowledge of the Truth, our Lord Himself, is only possible through the reception of the Holy Spirit. "However, when He, the Spirit of truth, has come, He will guide you into all truth" (John 16:13). The Holy Spirit alone makes the Word of God understandable. The regenerating and sanctifying work of the Holy Spirit is to incorporate us into Christ until we are living witnesses to Him. S. D. Gordon put it well when he said, "We have the Bible bound in morocco, bound in all kinds of beautiful leather; what we need is the Bible bound in shoe leather." That is exactly the teaching of our Lord. After the disciples had received the Holy Spirit they became witnesses to Jesus, their lives spoke more eloquently than their lips: "They realized that they had been with Jesus" (Acts 4:13). The Holy Spirit being imparted to us and expressed through us is the manifested exhibition that God can do all that His Word states He can. It is those who have received the Holy Spirit who understand the will of God and "grow up in all things into Him." When the Scriptures are made living and powerful by the Holy Spirit, they fit every need of life. The only Interpreter of the Scriptures is the Holy Spirit, and when we have received the Holy Spirit we learn the first golden lesson of spiritual life, which is that God reveals His will according to the state of our characters (compare Psalm 18:25–26).

VII. How to Think about Our Fellowman

A new commandment I give to you, that you love one another; as I have loved you, that you also love one another. John 13:34.

There is no subject more intimately interesting to modern humanity than our relationship to other people, but people get impatient when they are told that the first requirement is that they should love God first and foremost. "The first of all the commandments is: '. . . you shall love the Lord your God with all your heart, with all your soul, with all your mind, and with all your strength.' this is the first commandment" (Mark 12:29–30). In every crisis in our lives, is God first in our love? In every perplexity of conflicting duties, is He first in our leading? "And the second, like it, is this: 'You shall love your neighbor as yourself' " (v. 31). Remember the standard: "as I have loved you." I wonder where the best of us are according to that standard? How many of us have turned away over and over again in disgust at people, and when we get alone with the Lord Jesus He speaks no word, but the memory of Him is quite sufficient to bring the rebuke: "as I have loved you." It takes severe training to think habitually along the lines Jesus Christ has laid down, although we act on them impulsively at times.

How many of us are letting Jesus Christ take us into His school of thinking? The saint who is thoughtful is like a person fasting in the midst of universal intoxication. People of the world hate a thoughtful saint. They can ridicule a living saint who does not think, but a thinking saint—I mean of

142

course, one who lives rightly as well—is the annoyance, because the thinking saint has formed the mind of Christ and re-echoes it. Let us from this time forth determine to bring into captivity every thought to the obedience of Christ.

The Moral Foundations of Life

The Will in Discipleship

Luke 9:61–62

Beware of thinking of will as a faculty. Will simply means the whole nature active. We talk about someone having a weak will or a strong will, it is a misleading idea. When we speak of people having weak wills, we mean they are without any impelling passion, they are the creatures of every dominating influence; with good people they are good, with bad people they are bad, not because they are hypocrites but because they have no ruling passion, and any strong personality knits them into shape. Will is the essential element in God's creation of human beings. I cannot give up my will: I must exercise it.

The Want To

Lord, I will follow You. Luke 9:61

Want is a conscious tendency toward a particular end. My wants take shape when something awakens my personal life. Invalids, if left alone, have no wants; they want neither to live nor to die; but when they see people full of bounding physical health, a want to be like them is instantly awakened. Whatever awakens my person awakens a want. In this incident the presence of Jesus awakened a conscious want to follow Him, a want to be like Him.

(a) The Want in Conscience

The first appeal was to conscience and could be expressed in this way: "Follow Him, He is your supreme Lord." The presentation of Jesus Christ always awakens that desire, the presentation of abstract ideals never does. You can present morality, good principles, the duty of loving your neighbor, and never arouse anyone's conscience to want anything; but when you present Jesus Christ, instantly there is a dumb awakening, a want to be what He would like me to be. It is not conviction of sin but an awakening out of the sleep of indifference into a want.

There are some things that are without meaning for us. For instance, to be told that God will give us the Holy Spirit if we ask Him may be a dead proposition, but when we come in contact with a person filled with the Spirit of God we instantly awaken to a want. Or again, if you tell half a dozen clean-living, upright, sterling individuals that God so loved them that He gave His Son to die for them, only their good breeding will keep them from being amused— "Why should Jesus Christ die for me?" It is not a living proposition to them, not in the sphere of their lives at all. Their morality is well within their own grasp, they are clean-living and upright, all that can be desired; they will never be awakened in that way, but present them with Jesus Christ or with a life that is like His life, and instantly there will awaken in them a want they were not conscious of before. That is why Jesus said, "If I had not come . . . , they would have no sin, but now they have no excuse for their sin" (John 15:22). You can never argue anyone into the kingdom of heaven, you cannot argue anyone anywhere. The only result of arguing is to prove to your own mind that you are right and the other person wrong. You cannot argue for truth, but as soon as Incarnate Truth is presented, a want awakens in the soul that only God can meet. Conscience is that faculty of the spirit which fits itself onto the highest someone knows, and when the light of Jesus Christ is thrown on what is regarded as the highest, conscience records exactly, and the reason is startled and amazed (compare Acts 26:9).

(b) The Want in Heart

The presence of Jesus awakened a want in this man's heart. Heart is the center of all the vital activities of body, soul, and spirit. Never think of the heart in the way the old psychology thought of the will, namely, as a compartment, a kind of hatbox into which you put all your convictions and dole them out occasionally when you lift the lid. The heart is the center of human personality. "For out of the heart proceed . . . ," said our Lord (Matthew 15:19). You can never tell from someone's life to date what he or she is going to want next, because the real element of want is not logical. A person's reasoning is based on something more than reason; there is always an incalculable element.

(c) The Want in Desire

out of the heart the mouth speaks.

The want in conscience and in heart urges someone to immediate action: "Lord, I will follow You." It was the finest, profoundest element in the man that made him say it. In his conscience, in the deep depths of his personality, there was awakened the desire to follow Jesus and to be like Him. The measure of a person's want is seen in the nature of the power that awakened it. No one can stand in front of Jesus Christ and say, "I want to make money." People can stand before a successful commercial leader and find the desire awakened to be like that man or that woman and make money. This man was in contact with the Prince of persons, the Lord Jesus Christ, consequently the deep desire of his heart was for the very highest—"Lord, I want to follow You, and I not only want to but I will."

The Wish To

A wish is often of an abstract character, directed towards some single element into a concrete event, without reference to accompanying circumstances.

—Mackenzie

The Will in Discipleship 149

When I see Jesus Christ I simply want to be what He wants me to be. A wish is more definite than a want, which is inarticulate, something I am conscious of and that is all. Contact with a personality will always harden our wishing into a clear initiative along certain lines. For example, when children see a soldier they wish to be soldiers; when they see an engineer they wish to be engineers, and so on. We have to select the domain of our wishes. At a time of religious awakening, when Jesus Christ is in the ascendant and I come into close contact with Him, I wish to be a Christian. I have never known conviction of sin, never seen the need for the removal of the wrong disposition and identification with Jesus, but I wish to be like Him. The "wish to" simply sees the end of the desire and takes no account of the means to that end.

(a) Resensitized Sympathy

Our wishes move in various domains. We cannot hold ourselves in a handful for we are never sure what is going to happen in the domain of our wishes. We may have all our wishes in a certain domain and be perfectly master of them, with everything clear and simple; then a bereavement comes, and instantly the domain of our wishing is completely altered, we are suddenly put into sensitive sympathy with things we never thought about before. When Jesus Christ is in the ascendant the wish moves in the domain in which He lives, the sensitivity of our wishing answers to Him in a general softening of the whole nature. We are not conscious of wishing to possess any particular virtue, of wishing to be this or that; we simply wish to be in perfect sympathy with Him and His purposes. The only point of rest is for us to have our sympathies sensitized by Jesus Christ, because the basis of human nature is always open to let us into some unsuspected "hell" until we have been dominated by our Lord. When our Lord speaks of discipleship He catalogues the other loves (see Luke 14:26) and says that our love to Him must be the dominant love of all, because any of those other loves may be a trapdoor to something entirely removed from God's purposes.

(b) Reflection of Sublimity

Abstract principles have no more power to lift one than one has to lift oneself; but anyone, no matter how sunk in sin, will answer to Jesus Christ when He is presented. To tell people who are down and out to get up and do the right thing can never help them, but when once Jesus Christ is presented to them there is a reflected wish to be what Jesus wants them to be. It is appalling how many books and sermons there are today that simply present abstract truths. Jesus Christ appeals to the highest and the lowest, to the rich young ruler type of individual, and to the individual whom no ethics or moral principles can touch. Always keep Jesus Christ in the front; He says Himself He is to be there. "I, if I am lifted up from the earth, will draw all peoples to Myself" (John 12:32).

(c) Recession of Second Thought

Lord, I will follow You, but . . .

The wish ought to be followed by immediate obedience. I must take the wish and translate it into resolution and then into action; if I don't, the wish will translate itself into a corrupting power in my life instead of a redeeming power. This principle holds good in the matter of emotions. A sentimentalist is one who delights to have high and devout emotions stirred whilst reading in an armchair, or in a prayer meeting, but a sentimentalist never translates those emotions into action. Consequently sentimentalists are usually callous, self-centered, and selfish, because the emotions they like to have stirred do not cost them anything, and when they come across the same things in the domain where things are real and not sentimental, the revenge comes along the line of selfishness and meanness, which is always the aftermath of an unfulfilled emotion. The higher the emotion, the purer the desire, the viler is the revenge in the moral character unless the emotion is worked out on its right level. It is better never to have seen the light, better never to wish to be what you are not than to have the desire awakened and never to have resolved it into action. Always do something along the line of the emotion that has been stirred; if you do not, it will corrupt that which was good before. The curbing of the outward action revenges itself in a meaner disposition on the inside, and the higher the religious emotion, the more appalling is the reaction unless it is worked out on its own level. There are those whose language and habits are coarse, yet they are not vile in their inner dispositions, and suddenly they manifest graces and beauties of character that amaze you. They answer to the call given by Jesus Christ, while others of the Pharisee type do not answer (compare Matthew 21:28–32). Jesus Christ said it was impossible for those who are self-centered in their particular impression of themselves to believe in Him (see John 5:44).

The Will To

> But Jesus said to him, "No one, having put his hand to the plow, and looking back, is fit for the kingdom of God.

The will to means I must act; it is not sufficient to want to, to wish to, I must act on the wish instantly, no matter what it costs. Whenever the conviction of God's Spirit comes there is the softening of the whole nature to obey, but if the obedience is not instant there will come a metallic hardening and a corrupting of the guidance of God.

(a) The Inspired Instinct

Whenever you stand in the presence of Jesus Christ, as He is portrayed in the Scriptures and made real to you by the Holy Spirit, the instincts of your heart will always be inspired; let them lead. We read that when Jesus preached His first public sermon, all the people "marveled at the gracious words which proceeded out of His mouth" (Luke 4:22); their hearts were inspired as they listened to Him, their instincts turned in the right direction; then their prejudices came in the way and they closed down the witness of their hearts, broke up the service and tried to fling Him over the brow of the hill (see vv. 16–30). Always let the instinct that rules you in the presence of Jesus lead. That is why it is so necessary in an evangelistic meeting to push people to an issue of will. It is a terrible thing to awaken people up to a certain point and never give them the chance to act in the same atmosphere. If I preach a particularly searching discourse and never give the people a chance to act according to their inspired instincts at the time, their blood is on my head before God. If I make the issue clear and give them the opportunity to act, I clear my soul from their blood, whether they answer or not. The devil's counterfeit for this is wanting to see how many people we can get out to the penitent form. As preachers and teachers we have to bring people to the point of doing something.

(b) The Inverting Impulse

> No one, having put his hand to the plow, and looking back . . .

Never postpone a moral decision. Second thoughts in moral matters are always deflections. Give as many second thoughts as you like to matters of prudence, but in the presence of God never think twice—act. Our Lord puts it very clearly in Matthew 5:23–24: when you are at the altar, that is, in the presence of God, and your heart answers to the conviction of the Spirit of God, you know exactly what you must do: First, go. There is no midway. If you say, "I don't mind going halfway, but I was not altogether in the wrong," God's touch is gone instantly. The slightest revision of what I know God is telling me to do is the first element in the damnation of my character in that particular (see John 3:19). As soon as I see what God wants me to do, when I am in His presence, I must do it and care nothing for the consequences. "Lord, let me first go and bury my father" (Luke 9:60). The reply of Jesus sounds harsh, but remember the man's meaning was that he must stay with his father till he died. It was a point of view that put Jesus Christ right out of court. So with the rich young ruler—the wish to be all that Jesus wanted him to be awoke as soon as he came in contact with Him, but when it came to the first step of the will in acting it out, to become a mere conscious man, separated from all his wealth, dead fundamentally to the whole thing, then his countenance fell and he went away sorrowful. It is better never to have had the light than to refuse to obey it.

(c) The Intrinsic Incapacity

. . . is fit for the kingdom of God.

Not "fit" does not mean not good enough, it means out of the machine. We can never earn our places in the kingdom of God by doing anything. As soon as we obey the instinct born in us of God's Spirit we are fitted into the kingdom of God. Always act according to the wish that is born in you by the Spirit of God. Take the initiative to obey, never wobble spiritually. Wobble means that we bring in other considerations that ought never to demean the presence of God, because those considerations mean that Jesus has not thought things out properly; He has forgotten I have a duty to my father and mother, that I have this thing the matter with my body; He has forgotten my circumstances. All these things are unconscious blasphemy against the wisdom of God. We must always get to the point of acting on the want and the wish born in us when we are in the presence of Jesus Christ.

Direction of the Will

John 7:17

> If anyone wills to do His will, he shall know concerning the doctrine, whether it is from God or whether I speak on My own authority.

The Will to Do

If any one wills to do His will . . . John 7:17

In John 7: 17, our Lord is not so much laying down the principle that obedience is the gateway to knowledge as specifically stating that the only way to know whether or not His teaching is of God is conditioned by obedience. The only way to know is to will to do His will.

(a) Think

The only way to progress in spiritual matters is to think voluntarily. A great amount of stuff we call thinking is not thinking but merely reverie or meditation. Thinking is a voluntary effort, and in the initial stages it is never easy; voluntary effort must be made to keep the mind on some particular line. The teaching of some of the Higher Christian Life movements is apt to put thinking out of it altogether. According to that teaching we have to be semiswooning invalids in the power of God, letting the Spirit of God take us as so much driftwood, and all our impulses and dreams are taken to be the will of God. When we become spiritual we have to exercise the power of thinking to a greater degree than ever before. We starve our minds as Christians by not thinking. If we are going to succeed in the natural world we must think voluntarily about things, and it is the same in the spiritual world. In order to think we must stop woolgathering, check our impulses, and set the mind on one line.

(b) Think Habitually

Habit is a mechanical process of which we have ceased to become conscious. The basis of habit is always physical. A habit forms a pathway in the material stuff of the brain, and as we persist in thinking along a certain line we hand over a tremendous amount to the machine and do things without thinking. Habit becomes second nature. "Habit a second nature! Habit is ten times nature!" (Duke of Wellington). For instance, when you begin to use a muscle in a particular way, it hurts badly, but if you keep on using that muscle judiciously it will get beyond hurting, until you are able to use it with mechanical precision. The same thing is true in regard to thinking. It is a difficult matter to begin with. If thinking gives you a headache, it is a sign that you have brains. The brain is not ethereal or mystical, it is purely a machine. The thing that is not mechanical is the power of personality that we call thought. At first we find our brains do not work well, they go in jerks, we are bothered with associated ideas; but as we persist in thinking along a particular line our brains become the allies of our personalities. Not only are our bodies capable of becoming our best friends, but the places where the body has become used to thinking become a strong assistance also. We infect the places we live in by our ruling habit. If we have made our bodies the allies of our personalities, everything works together to aid the body wherever it is placed. People complain about their circumstances because they have not begun to make their bodies their allies.

(c) Think Habitually to Do

Our Lord says, in effect, that if anyone will habitually think, that person will come to know where His teaching comes from. The only way to prove spiritual truth is by experiment. Are we willing to set our minds determinedly to work out habitually what we think is God's will? We talk about justice and right and wrong, are we prepared to act according to what we think? Are we prepared to act according to the justice and the right that we believe to be the character of God? If we are, we shall have no difficulty in deciding whether or not the teaching of Jesus Christ comes from God.

The first moment of thinking alters our lives. If for one moment we have discerned the truth, we can never be the same again; we may ignore it or forget it, but it will not forget us. Truth once discerned goes down into the subconscious mind, but it will jump up in a most awkward way when we least expect it. In the matter of intercession, when we pray for someone, the Spirit of God works in the unconscious domain of that person's being—about which we know nothing and about which the one we pray for knows nothing, and after a while the conscious life of the one prayed for begins to show signs of softening and unrest, of inquiry and a desire to know something. It seems stupid to think that if we pray all that will happen, but remember to whom we pray; we pray to a Being who understands the unconscious depths of human personality, and He has told us to pray. The great Master of the human spirit said "Greater works than these he will do; . . . and whatever you ask in My name, that I will do" (John 14:12–13). This is true also in preaching the Word. We may see no result in our congregations, but if we have presented the truth and anyone has seen it for one second, that person can never be the same again, a new element has come into her or his life. It is essential to remember this and not to estimate the success of preaching by immediate results.

Our Lord was always stern with disbelief, that is, skepticism, because there is always a moral twist about skepticism. Never place an agnostic in the same category as a skeptic. An agnostic is one who says, "There is more than I know, but I have not found anyone who can tell me about it." Jesus is never stern with that attitude, but He is stern with people who object to a certain way of getting at the truth because they do not like that way. If people refuse to try the way Jesus Christ puts before them, they cease from that second to be honest doubters; they must try it and put Jesus Christ's teaching to the proof. People cannot say they are honest intellectual doubters if they refuse one way of getting at the truth; that is mental immorality.

The Way to Know

... he shall know concerning the doctrine ...

If I find it hard to be a Christian it is a sign that I need the awakening of new birth. Only a spiritually ignorant person tries to be a Christian. Study the life of Jesus Christ and see what Christianity means, and you will find you cannot be a Christian by trying; you must be born into the life before you can live it. There are a great many people trying to be Christians; they pray and long and fast and consecrate, but it is nothing but imitation, it has no life in it. As soon as we have life imparted to us by the Holy Spirit, we realize that it is the very life that was in Jesus that is born into us; we are loosened from the old bondage and find that we can fulfill all the expectations of the life that has been imparted to us. It is a strenuous life of obedience to God, and God has given us bodies through which to work out the life and circumstances to react against in order to prove its reality.

(a) Intention

Beware of praying about an intention—act. To pray about what we know we should do is to piously push the whole thing overboard and think no more about it. Every intention must be acted out now, not presently, otherwise it will be stamped out. When the intention of an honest soul is grasped by the Spirit of God that soul will know whether the teaching Jesus gives is of God or not. Am I going to think, and think habitually, and act on what I think, so that the will of God may be performed in me, until I know who Jesus is and that His teaching is the teaching of God? To know that the teaching of Jesus is of God means that it must be obeyed. It may be difficult to begin with, but the difficulty will become a joy.

(b) Intention and Insight

Intentions are born of listening to others. Whenever we obey an intention, insight into either good or bad is sure to follow. If the intention is in agreement with God and we act on it, we get insight into who God is. The discernment of right and wrong intentions depends on how we think. There is a spasmodic type of life that comes from never really think-ing about things; it is at the mercy of every stray intention. Someone makes an appeal for the Hindu or the Chinese, and people say, "Oh yes, I will go and preach the gospel there," and they do it in intention. Then someone else says the best thing is to work in the slums, instantly their intentions are to work there. Then another person says the best thing is to study in a Bible school, and they do that in intention. They are creatures of impulse, there is no real thinking along God's line, no acting on their intentions. If you are sufficiently strong-minded you can generate any number of intentions in people and make them think anything you like; if they are not in the habit of thinking for themselves you can always sway them. The power of an evangelist over men and women who do not think is a dangerous thing. That is why it is so peril-ous to tell people to yield. Don't yield! Keep as stiff a neck as ever you had, and yield to nothing and to no one, unless you know it is the Lord Jesus Christ to whom you are yielding. Once you go on the yielding line, on the surrendering line, and you do not know that it is the Lord Jesus who is calling for the yielding, you will be caught up by supernatural powers that will wield you whether you like it or not. Woe be to you if, when Jesus has asked you to yield to Him, you refuse, but be sure it is Jesus Christ to whom you yield, and His demands are tremendous.

The insight that relates us to God arises from purity of heart not from clearness of intellect. All the education under heaven will never give someone insight into Jesus Christ's teaching—only one thing will, and that is a pure heart, that is, intentions that go along the right line. Education and scholarship may enable someone to put things well but will never give someone insight. Insight only comes from a pure-heartedness in working out the will of God. That is why the subject of divine guidance is so mysterious. "Be transformed by the renewing of your mind," says Paul, (that is what makes the thinker right), "that you may prove what is that good and acceptable and perfect will of God" (Romans 12:2). You cannot teach another what is the will of God. A knowledge of the will of God comes only by insight into God through acting on the right intention.

(c) Intention and Insight into Instruction

Studying our Lord's teaching will not profit us unless we intend to obey what we know is the immediate present duty. As we listen to certain interpretations of Jesus Christ's statements we do not feel warm to them, though we do not know what is wrong. Whenever the Spirit of God works in the conscious life it is like an intuition—I don't know how I know, but I know. The Holy Spirit witnesses only to His own nature, not to our reason. Jesus said, "My sheep hear

My voice" (John 10:27), not because it is argued to them but because they have His Spirit. There are statements of Jesus that mean nothing to us just now because we have not been brought into the place where we need to understand them. When we are brought there, the Holy Spirit will bring back a particular word, and as we intend to obey He gives us the insight into it. The Spirit of God never allows us to face spiritual subjects by spiritual curiosity first. We cannot say, "I am going to study the subject of sanctification or of the Second Coming"; we shall make about as much headway as a steamer in a fog. Insight into the instruction of Jesus depends upon our intention to obey what we know to be the will of God. If we have some doctrine or some end of our own to serve, we shall always find difficulty.

The Weighing of Doctrine

> . . . whether it is from God or whether I speak on My own authority.

(a) Discernment

The reason the Incarnation and the Atonement are not credible to some people is that their dispositions are unregenerated. One may adopt the dogma of the Incarnation and the Atonement upon a basis of authority while one's heart is unchanged, with the result that sooner or later the accumulated pride of unregenerate years will rise in revolt and secretly protest that it is incredible. That was the case with the people to whom Jesus is speaking here, and it is the case of hundreds who accept creeds but refuse to act on their beliefs; the consequence is they fling their creeds overboard and ignore the central test of Christianity, namely, who is Jesus Christ to me?

The atonement of our Lord never contradicts human reason, it contradicts the logic of human intellect that has never partaken of regeneration. The understanding of the Atone-ment depends not on Bible study, not on praying, but on spir-itual growth. As we "grow up in all things into Him" (Ephesians 4:15), we get moral understanding of the mystery of Redemption and understand why Jesus said "Blessed are the pure in heart, for they shall see God" (Matthew 5:8). The Spirit of God brings people to the place where they begin to discern with their hearts, not with their heads.

Jesus says we shall know, that is, discern, whether His teaching is from God or not when we do what we know to be His will. We discern according to our dispositions. There are moments in life when the little thing matters more than any-thing else, times when a critical situation depends upon my attitude of mind to another person. If one is hesitating between obeying and not obeying God, the tiniest thing con-trary to obedience is quite sufficient to swing the pendulum right away from the discernment of Jesus Christ and of God. "If you bring your gift to the altar, and there remember that your brother has something against you . . . first be recon-ciled" (v. 23). Distempers of mind make all the difference in the discernment of Jesus Christ's teaching. Have I a distem-pered view about any man or woman on earth? If I have, there is a great deal of Jesus Christ's teaching I do not want to listen to, then I shall never discern His teaching. Once let me obey God and I shall discern that I have no right to an attitude of mind to anyone, other than His attitude. If I am determined to know the teaching of Jesus Christ at all costs, I must act on the intention that is stirred in me to do God's will, however humiliating it may be, and if I do, I shall discern.

(b) Discernment of Inspiration

Our Lord's teaching is God-breathed. What makes the difference between the attitude of a spiritual Christian to the teaching of Jesus and that of an unspiritual person? An unspiritual person takes the statements of Jesus to pieces as if they were human statements, annulling Jesus, dissolving Him by analysis. A spiritual Christian confesses "that Jesus Christ has come in the flesh" (1 John 4:3). The basis of membership in the early church was discernment of who Jesus is by the revelation of God (see Matthew 16:17–18). All through, the test is, Do I know who Jesus Christ is; do I know that His teaching is of God?

The mystery of the Bible is that its inspiration was direct from God (2 Peter 1:21). To believe our Lord's consciousness about Himself commits me to accept Him as God's last, endless Word. That does not mean that God is not still speaking, but it does mean that God is saying nothing different from the Final Word, Jesus Christ; all God says expounds that Word.

(c) Discernment of Inspiration of Christ's Teaching

Is Jesus Christ's teaching God-breathed to me? There is an intention that seeks God's blessings without obeying Jesus Christ's teaching. We are apt to say, with sanctimonious piety, "Yes, Jesus Christ's teaching is of God," but how do we measure up to it? Do we intend to think about it and act on it? Beware of tampering with the springs of your life when it comes to the teaching of Jesus.

Purity of heart, not subtlety of intellect, is the place of understanding. The Spirit of God alone understands the things of God; let Him indwell, and slowly and surely the great revelation facts of the Atonement begin to be comprehended. The mind of God as revealed in the Incarnation becomes slowly and surely the mind of the spiritual Christian.

Freedom of the Will

Psalm 27:4–6

One thing I have desired of the LORD, that will I seek: that I may dwell in the house of the LORD all the days of my life, to behold the beauty of the LORD, and to inquire in His temple. For in the time of trouble He shall hide me in His pavilion; in the secret place of His tabernacle He shall hide me; He shall set me high upon a rock. And now my head shall be lifted up above my enemies all around me; therefore I will offer sacrifices of joy in His tabernacle; I will sing, yes, I will sing praises to the LORD.

The subject of human free will is apt to be either understated or overstated. No human being has the power to act an act of pure, unadulterated, free will. God is the only Being who can act with absolute free will. The Bible reveals that humankind is free to choose, but it nowhere teaches that humankind is fundamentally free. The freedom humanity has is not that of power but of choice, consequently we are accountable for choosing the course we take. For instance, we can choose whether or not we will accept the proposition of salvation that God puts before us, whether or not we will let God rule our lives, but we have not the power to do exactly what we like. This is easily demonstrated when we think of the number of vows that are made every New Year and so quickly are broken.

People are free to choose insofar as no human force can constrain them against their will. Pope is often misquoted; he did not say, "Convince a man against his will, he is of the same opinion still," but, "Compel a man against his will, he is

165

of the same opinion still." God has so constituted human beings that it is not possible to convince us against our wills; you can compel us and crush us, but you cannot convince us against our wills. Only God could exercise constraint over us that would compel us to do what in the moment of doing it is not our own will—but that God steadily refuses to do.

The reason humans are not free is that within human personality there is a disposition that has been allowed to enslave the will, the disposition of sin. Human destiny is determined by human disposition; we cannot alter the disposition, but we can choose to let God alter it. Jesus said, "Whoever commits sin is a slave of sin" (John 8:34), but He also said, "Therefore, if the Son makes you free, you shall be free indeed" (v. 36), that is, free in essence. We are only free when the Son sets us free, but we are free to choose whether or not we will be made free. In the experience of regeneration one takes the step of choosing to let God alter one's disposition. When the Holy Spirit comes into a person, He brings His own generating will power and makes that person free in will. *Will* simply means the whole nature active, and when the Holy Spirit comes in and energizes a human will, a person is able to do what he or she never could do before, namely, one is able to do God's will (see Philippians 2:13).

The Universe of the Will

> Thus not only our morality but our religion, so far as the latter is deliberate, depend on the effort which we can make. —James

Some propositions are alive to us, and we want to work at them; other propositions are dead, they do not appeal to us at all. We have to be brought out of one universe of the will into another universe where propositions that were dead become alive. You can never tell when a proposition that, up to a certain stage, has been dead may suddenly become of living interest.

(a) The Live Quest of the Will

> One thing I have desired of the LORD, . . . that I may dwell in the house of the LORD all the days of my life. Psalm 27:4

The depths of personality are hidden from our sight; we do not know anything beyond the threshold of consciousness—God is the only One who knows. When we try to go beyond the conscious life into the depths of the personality, we do not know where we are; our only refuge is Psalm 139:23: "Search me, O God, and know my heart." Whatever rouses your will is an indication of the bias of your personality. The Bible reveals that in human personality there is a bias that makes a woman or a man choose not the proposition of godliness but the proposition of ungodliness. This bias is not a matter of deliberate human choice; it is in the personality when a person is born. "Therefore, just as through one man sin entered the world" (Romans 5:12). The proposition that appeals to healthy, once-born people is that of self-realization—"I want to develop myself." If you bring before them the proposition that they should be saved and give up their right to themselves to Jesus Christ, it will be a dead proposition, without meaning for them; but let conviction of sin or disaster or bereavement or any of the great surprises of God touch them, and instantly the proposition takes on a totally new aspect and they will want to act on it. Jesus Christ always puts the emphasis on the effort of obedience, there must be a live quest of the will. If you want to know My doctrine, whether it is from God or on My own authority, do My will, says Jesus (see John 7:17). The truth of God is only revealed to us by obedience.

(b) The Lure of the Voluntary Quest

> . . . to behold the beauty of the Lord . . .

When once the will is roused it always has a definite end in view, an end in the nature of unity. Always distinguish between will and impulse. An impulse has no end in view and must be curbed, not obeyed. Will is the whole effort of someone consciously awake with the definite end of unity in view, which means that body, soul, and spirit are in absolute harmony. This end of satisfaction offers a great fascination. The characteristic of a moral hell is satisfaction, no end in view, perfectly satisfied. Moral sickness is a perilous time, it is the condition to which sin brings us, and it accounts for the unutterable disappointments in life; there is no lure, no aim, no quest, no end in view. The characteristic of the spiritual life is the delight of discerning more and more clearly the end God has in view for us. Jesus did not say that eternal life was satisfaction, but something infinitely grander: "This is eternal life, that they may know You" (John 17:3). The demand for satisfaction is God-given (compare Matthew 5:6), but it must be satisfaction in the highest.

(c) The Liberty to Question

. . . and to inquire in His temple.

When someone has been awakened from sin to salvation, the only propositions that are alive to the will are the propositions of God. There is an insatiable inquiry after God's commands, and to every command there is a desire to act in obedience. Recall your own experience and see how true that is. The things that used to be ends in view have not only ceased to be ends, they have ceased to have any interest for you at all; they have become tasteless. This is the way God enables us to be fundamentally dead to the things of the world while we live amongst them. Jesus Christ's outward life was densely immersed in the things of the world, yet He was inwardly disconnected; the one irresistible purpose of His life was to do the will of His Father.

If I am in right relationship to God there comes this delightful liberty of inquiring in His temple. It is not to be a

Sabbath day spent in a temple, but the whole of the life, every domain of body, soul, and spirit is to be lived there. The dead set of the will is toward one end only: to do the will of God. Jesus said, "My sheep hear My voice" (John 10:27). When Jesus has not spoken there is an unutterable dullness all through, our spirits do not witness to what is being said. When once that fine balance of discernment is tampered with we give an opportunity to Satan, but if it is kept in perfect accord with God's Word, He will guard. Jesus said that the Holy Spirit would bring His word to our remembrance (John 14:26). The Holy Spirit does not bring text after text until we are utterly confused; He simply brings back with the greatest of ease the words that we need in the particular circumstances we are in. Then comes in the use of the will—will I obey the word that has been brought back to my remembrance? The battle comes when we begin to debate instead of obeying. We have to obey and leave all consequences with God.

The Utmost Uses of the Will

> Character exists only in so far as unity and continuity of conscious life exists, and manifests itself in systematic consistency of conduct.
>
> —Stout

Will is the very essence of personality, and in the Bible will is always associated with intelligence and knowledge and desire. The will of a saint is not to be spent in dissipation in spiritual luxuries, but in concentration upon God.

(a) The Quietness of Strength

> For in the time of trouble He shall hide me in His pavilion. Psalm 27:5

God gives us the energy of an impregnable position, the heavenly places in Christ Jesus, and we have to make the effort to be strong from that position. We have not to work up to that position but to work from it with the full energy of will. It is impossible to live according to our Lord's teaching without this secret of position. We do not get to the heavenly places by struggling or aspiring or consecration; God lifts us there, and if we will work from that position, He keeps us in His pavilion. No wonder the life of a saint appears such an unmitigated puzzle to rational human beings without the Spirit of God. It seems so ridiculous and so conceited to say that God almighty is our Father and that He is looking after our affairs, but looked at from the position in which Jesus places us we find it is a marvelous revelation of truth.

(b) The Quarters of Security

He shall set me high upon a rock.

In our spiritual lives God does not provide pinnacles on which we stand like spiritual acrobats; He provides tablelands of easy and delightful security. Recall the conception you had of holiness before you stood, by the grace of God, where you do today; it was the conception of a breathless standing on a pinnacle for a second at a time but never with the thought of being able to live there; but when the Holy Spirit brought you there, you found it was not a pinnacle but a plateau, a broad way, where the provision of strength and peace comes all the time, a much easier place to live than lower down.

The security of the position into which God brings His saints is such that the life is maintained without ecstasy. There is no place for ecstasy and manifestations in a normal, healthy, spiritual life. The emotions that are beyond the control of the will are a sign that there is something not in the secure position, something undisciplined, untrained. When

we are in the quarters of security we have to will our obser-
vation of the things of God and of the way in which He
works. There are things we are obliged to observe, such as
fireworks, but God uses for the training of His children the
things that we have to will to observe, namely, trees and
grass and sparrows.

Never allow the idea of conscious, straining effort when
you think of the exercise of the will spiritually. The straining
effort comes in when we forget the great lines laid down by
God. If you are a worker for God, Satan will try to wear you
out to the last cell, but if you know God's grace you will be
supernaturally recuperated physically. Recall how often you
have been surprised, you thought you would have been
exhausted after certain services, and instead, you became recreated whilst taking them. In this place of security there is no
such thing as weariness without a corresponding recupera-
tion, if we maintain a right relationship with God.

(c) The Quality of Supremacy

And now my head will be lifted up above my enemies all around
me. Psalm 27:6

The supremacy over our old enemies is accounted for by
the fact that God makes them our subjects. What things used
to be your enemies? Stodginess of head, laziness of body or
spirit, the whole vocabulary of "I can'ts." When you live in
the right place these things are made your subjects; the things
that used to hinder your life with God become subject to you
by His power. The very things that used to upset you now
minister to you in an extraordinary way by reason of the
spiritual supremacy God gives you over them. The life of a
saint reveals a quietness at the heart of things, there is something firm and dependable, because the Lord is the strength
of the life.

Habit

In the conduct of life, habits count for more than maxims,
because habit is a living maxim, become flesh and instinct.
To reform one's maxims is nothing; it is but to change the
title of the book. To learn new habits is everything for it is
to reach the substance of life. Life is but a tissue of habits.

—Amiel

Man's Soul the Scene of Habit

Plasticity, then, in the wide sense of the word, means the
possession of a structure weak enough to yield to influences, but strong enough not to yield all at once.

—James

Beware of dividing the human being up into body, soul, and
spirit; people are body, soul, and spirit. Soul has no entity, it
depends entirely upon the body, and yet there is a subtle spiritual element in it. Soul is the rational expression of my personal spirit in my body, the way I reason and think and work.
Habits are formed in the soul, not in the spirit, and they are
formed in the soul by means of the body. Jesus Christ told His
disciples that they must lose their souls, that is, their ways of
reasoning and looking at things, and begin to estimate from an
entirely different standpoint. For a while a born-again soul is
inarticulate, it has no expression; the equilibrium has been
upset by the incoming of a totally new spirit into the human
spirit, and the reasoning faculties are disturbed. "By your
patience possess your souls," says Jesus (Luke 21:19); that is,
the new way of looking at things must be acquired with
patience. On the basis of His redemption Jesus Christ claims

that He can put into my personal spirit His own heredity, the Holy Spirit; then I have to form character on the basis of that new disposition. God will do everything I cannot do, but He will do nothing He has constructed me to do.

"Our virtues are habits as well as our vices." God does not give us our habits, but He holds us responsible, in proportion, for the habits we form. For instance, God does not hold a child born in the slums responsible in the same degree for its habits as He does a child born in a Christian home. The fact remains, however, that we form our own habits. God gives a new disposition, but He gives us nothing in the shape of character. We have to work out what God works in, and the way we work it out is by the mechanical process of habit.

(a) The Mental Phase

Philippians 4:8–9; 2 Corinthians 10:5.

By the mental phase is meant thinking that can be stated in words. There is a great deal of thinking that cannot be expressed in words, such as that which is stirred by suscepti-bility to the beauties of nature or art or music; that is spirit not yet made rational in soul. We are responsible for our habits of thinking, and Paul in these passages is dealing with the phase of mental life in which one can choose one's think-ing and is able to express it in words. The old idea that we cannot help evil thoughts has become so ingrained in our minds that most of us accept it as a fact. But if it is true, then Paul is talking nonsense when he tells us to choose our think-ing, to think only on those things that are true and honorable and just and pure.

> We may take as an example of mental habit that of answering letters on the day on which they are received. Here what is habitual and automatic is not the process of writing the reply, but the writing of the reply on the same day on which the letter was received.
>
> —Stout

Habit   173

The point is that I make a mental decision to do a certain thing, and the habit of doing it grows until it becomes absolutely mechanical. Remember, then, we can and we must choose our thinking, and the whole discipline of our mental lives is to form the habit of right thinking. It is not done by praying, it is done only by strenuous determination, and it is never easy to begin with.

(b) The Moral Phase

Romans 6:11–19; 2 Peter 1:5–8

The Spirit of God through the apostles bases on the mechanism that is alike in every one of us, the mechanism of habit. Paul says, "Present your members as slaves of righteousness" (Romans 6:19); Peter says, "Add to your faith. . . " (2 Peter 1:5). There is something we have to do. The human soul is "weak enough to yield to influences, but strong enough not to yield all at once." The phrase "the freedom of the will" is a catch phrase that has more of error than of truth in it. We are all so made that we can yield to an influence that is brought to bear upon us, and if we keep ourselves long enough under right influences, slowly and surely we shall find that we can form habits that will develop us along the line of those influences.

> The peculiarity of the moral habits, contradistinguishing them from the intellectual acquisitions, is the presence of two hostile powers, one to be gradually raised into the ascendant over the other. It is necessary, above all things, in such a situation, never to lose a battle. Every gain on the wrong side undoes the effect of many conquests on the right.
>
> —Bain

The idea is that of winding up a ball of wool. Let the ball drop, and infinitely more is undone than was wound in the same time. This is true of moral and spiritual habits. If once you allow the victory of a wrong thing in you, it is a long way back again to get readjusted. We talk on the moral and spiritual line as if God were punishing us, but He is not, it is because of the way God has constructed human nature that "the way of the unfaithful is hard" (Proverbs 13:15).

When once we begin the life with God on the moral line we must keep strictly to it. In the beginning, the Holy Spirit will check us in doing a great many things that may be perfectly right for everyone else but not right for us in the stage we are in. We have to narrow ourselves to one line and keep ourselves narrow until our souls have gained the moral habit. The maimed life is always the characteristic to begin with (see Matthew 5:29–30), but our Lord's statements embrace the whole of the spiritual life from beginning to end, and in Matthew 5:48 He says, "Therefore you shall be perfect, just as your Father in heaven is perfect."

Never go contrary to your conscience, no matter how absurd it may be in the eyes of others. Conscience is to be our law in conduct, but Paul says it is not his own conscience but the conscience of his weak brother that is his guide (see 1 Corinthians 8:9–13).

The characteristic of Christians is that we have the right not to insist on our rights. That will mean that I refuse to do certain things because they would cause my brother or sister to stumble. To me the restrictions may be absurd and narrow-minded, I can do the things without any harm; but Paul's argument is that he reserves the right to suffer the loss of all things rather than put an occasion to fall in someone else's way. The Holy Spirit gives us the power to forgo our rights. It is the application of the Sermon on the Mount in practical life; if we are Jesus Christ's disciples we shall always do more than our duty, always do something equivalent to going the second mile. These are some of the moral habits we ought to form.

(c) The Mystical Phase

"Abide in Me." John 15:4

Our Lord did not say, Ask God that you may abide in Me; He said "Abide in Me"; it is something we have to do. Abiding in Jesus embraces physical, mental, and moral phases as well as spiritual. How am I going to acquire the spiritual habit of union with Christ in God's sight? First of all by putting my body into the condition where I can think about it. We are so extraordinarily fussy that we won't give ourselves one minute before God to think, and unless we do we shall never form the habit of abiding. We must get alone in secret and think, screw our minds down and not allow them to woolgather. Difficult? Of course it is difficult to begin with, but if we persevere we shall soon take in all the straying parts of our mental lives, and in a crisis we shall be able to draw on the fact that we are one with Jesus in God's sight.

> One must first learn, unmoved, looking neither to the right nor left, to walk firmly on the strait and narrow path, before one can begin "to make one's self over again." He who every day makes a fresh resolve is like one who, arriving at the edge of the ditch he is to leap, forever stops and returns for a fresh run. Without unbroken advance there is no such thing as accumulation of the ethical forces possible, and to make this possible, and to exercise us and habituate us in it, is the sovereign blessing of regular work.
>
> —Bahnsen

In the mystical life, the majority of us are hopeless woolgatherers, we have never learned to brood on such subjects as abiding in Christ. We have to form the habit of abiding until we come into the relationship with God where we rely on Him almost unconsciously in every particular.

Mechanical Scientific Side of Habit

> Man is born with a tendency to do more things than he
> has ready-made arrangements for in his nerve-centres.
>
> —James

(a) The Physical Side

> Water wears away stones and . . . torrents wash away the soil
> of the earth. Job 14:19

In physical nature there is something akin to habit. Flowing water hollows out for itself a channel that grows broader and deeper, and after having ceased to flow for a time, it will resume again the path traced before. It is never as easy to fold a piece of paper the first time as after, for after the first time it folds naturally. The process of habit runs all through physical nature, and the brain is physical. When once we understand the bodily machine with which we have to work out what God works in, we find that the body becomes the greatest ally of the spiritual life. The difference between a sentimental Christian and a sanctified saint is just here. The sanctified saint is one who has disciplined the body into perfect obedience to the dictates of the Spirit of God, consequently the body does with the greatest of ease whatever God wants the saint to do. The sentimental type of Christian is the sighing, tear-flowing, beginning-over-again Christian who always has to go to prayer meetings, always has to be stirred up or to be soothed and put in bandages, because he or she has never formed the habit of obedience to the Spirit of God. The spiritual life does not grow in spite of the body but because of the body. "Of the earth, made of dust" (1 Corinthians 15:47), is humanity's glory, not its shame; and it is in the "earth, made of dust" that the full regenerating work of Jesus Christ has its ultimate reach.

(b) The Physiological Side

> He asked his father, "How long has this been happening to him?"
>
> And he said, "From childhood." Mark 9:21

Every nervous affection makes a groove in the brain. Dr. Carpenter, the great physiologist, suffered from habitual neuralgia all the days of his life; the only time he was free from it was when he was lecturing. He said himself it was simply because the nerves had got into the habit. What a medical practitioner aims at in the case of nervous affections is to forcibly cut short the attacks so as to give the other physical forces possession of the field. Nervous trouble can be cured by sudden calamity, by something that stops the whole nervous system and starts it again in another way, and it can be cured suddenly by the power of God. In the case of the demoniac boy our Lord did not deal with him on the medical line but on the supernatural line. There was no gradual, "take a little holiday," but a sudden and emphatic breaking off, simply because our Lord recognized the way God has made the nervous system. No power on earth can touch a nervous trouble if I have submitted to it for a long time, but God can touch it if I will let Him. I may pray forever for it to be altered, but it never will be until I am willing to obey. The arresting may be terrific, a tremendous break and upset, but if I will let God have His way He will deal with it.

(c) The Psychical Side

> Work out your own salvation with fear and trembling; for it is God who works in you. Philippians 2:12–13

"Man is born with a tendency to do more things than he has ready-made arrangements for in his nerve centres." For instance, we are not born with a ready-made habit of dressing ourselves, we have to form that habit. Apply that spiritually;

when we are born again, God does not give us a fully fledged series of holy habits, we have to make those habits. It is the application of the theological statement that we have to transform innocence into holiness by a series of moral choices. Ask yourself how much time you have taken up asking God that you may not do the things you do. He will never answer, you have simply not to do them. Every time God speaks, there is something we must obey. We would do well to revise what we pray about. Some of the things we pray about are as absurd as if we prayed, "O Lord, take me out of this room," and then refused to go. We have to revise and see whether we intelligently understand what God has done for us; if He has given us the Holy Spirit, then we can do everything He asks us to do. If our bodies have been the slaves of wrong habits physically, mentally, and morally, we must get hold of a power big enough to remake our habits, and that power lies in the word *regeneration*. "If anyone is in Christ, he is a new creation" (2 Corinthians 5:17); that means this marvelous thing— that I may be loosened from every wrong habit I have formed if only I will obey the Spirit of God. As soon as I do obey, I find I can begin to form new habits in accordance with God's commands and prove physically, mentally, and morally that I am a new creation. That is why it is so necessary to receive the Holy Spirit, then when God gives a command it is sufficient to know He has told me to do it and I find I can do it. Frequently God has to say to us, Say no more to Me on this matter; don't everlastingly cry to Me about this thing, do it yourself, keep your forces together and go forward. God is for you, the Spirit of God is in you, and every place that the sole of your foot shall tread on shall be yours.

Beware of the luxury of spiritual emotions unless you are prepared to work them out. God does the unseen, but we have to do the seen.

N.B.—All divisions of the human personality are arbitrary.

Dust and Divinity

Genesis 2:7

> And the LORD God formed man of the dust of the ground, and
> breathed into his nostrils the breath of life; and man became a
> living being.

Genesis 2:7 reveals that human beings are made up of dust
and divinity. This means that in practical psychology we
must always make allowance for the incalculable. You cannot
exhaust human nature by examining its dust qualities nor by
describing it in terms of poetic sentiment, for after you have
described as much as you can, there is always an incalculable
element to be taken into account. There is more than we
know, therefore we cannot deal with ourselves as machines.
One part of the self must be dealt with as a machine, and the
more we deal with it as a machine the better; but to try and
sum up a person as a machine only is to miss out on the bigger part, or to say that humans are altogether spiritual beings
without anything mechanical in them is to miss out on the
incalculable element that cannot be summed up. These two
things, dust and divinity, make up human beings. That we are
made of the dust is our human glory, not our shame; our dust
has been the scene of human shame, but it was designed to be
human glory.

A certain type of mind gets impatient when you talk
about the incalculable element in humankind and says it is

nonsense to talk of people being spiritual personalities, we are nothing more than animals. That outlook is prevalent today, it is called healthy-mindedness; it is rather blatant ignorance. We all say what is obvious until we are plunged into the deeps, but when we are profoundly moved we instantly find ourselves beyond the reach of help or comfort from the obvious. The obvious becomes trivial, it is not what our hearts want. What we need is something that can minister to the incalculable element. When once real thought begins to trouble the mind, the disturbance goes on throughout the whole personality until the right center is gained for thought. In the spiritual domain, when you are convicted of sin, you realize that there are deeper depths in yourself than you have ever known, and the things that can be clearly explained become utterly shallow, there is no guidance whatever in them. We begin by thinking we know all about ourselves, but when we get a dose of the plague of our own hearts, it upsets all our thinking. As soon as we begin to examine ourselves, we find we are inscrutable; there are possibilities below the threshold of our lives that no one knows but God.

The Explorer of the Will

Work out your own salvation with fear and trembling.
Philippians 2:12

Psalm 139 is the classic in all literature concerning human personality. In this psalm the tendency in human beings that makes us want to examine ourselves takes the form of prayer, O Lord, explore me. The psalmist implies: You are the God of the early mornings and late at nights, the God of the mountains and the fathomless deep; but, my God, my soul has farther horizons than the early mornings, deeper darkness than the nights of earth, higher heights than any mountain peaks, greater depths than any sea in nature; search me out, and see if there be any way of grief in me. The psalmist realized that God knew all about the vast universe outside him, but there was something more mysterious to him than the universe outside, and that was the mystery of his own heart, and he asks the great Creator to come and search him. God does not search people unless they know it, and it is a marvelous moment in someone's life when she or he is explored by the Spirit of God. The great, mystic work of the Holy Spirit is in the dim regions of human personality where we cannot go. God Himself is the explorer of human will, and this is how He searches us.

> It is God who works in you both to will and to do for His good pleasure. Philippians 2:13

"Will" is not a faculty; will is the whole person active, and the springs of will go deeper down than we can go. Paul says it is God who works in us to enable us to will, that is, the Holy Spirit, who is the expression of God, will come into our spirits and energize our wills so that we have power to actively will to do according to the standards of Jesus Christ. The Holy Spirit does not become my spirit; He invades my spirit and lifts my personality into a right relationship with God, and that means I can begin now to work out what God has worked in. The Holy Spirit enables me to fulfill all the commands of God, and I am without excuse for not fulfilling them. Absolute, almighty ability is packed into my spirit, and to say "can't," if I have received the Holy Spirit, is unconscious blasphemy. We have not sufficiently realized the practical moral aspect of the Atonement in our lives. "If we walk in the light as He is in the light"—then comes the amazing revelation, that "the blood of Jesus Christ His Son cleanses us from all sin" (1 John 1:7). Cleansing from all sin does not mean conscious deliverance from sin only, it means infinitely more than we are conscious of. The part we are conscious of is walking in the light; cleansing from all sin means something infinitely profounder, it means cleansing from all sin in the sight of God. God never bases any of His work on our consciousness.

"Do you mean to tell me that God can search me to the inmost recesses of my dreams, my inmost motives, and find nothing to blame? That God almighty can bring the winnowing fan of His Spirit and search out my thoughts and imaginations and find nothing to blame?" Who can stand before God and say, "My hands are clean, my heart is pure"? Who can climb that hill of the Lord? (see Psalm 24:3–4). No one under heaven, saving the one who has been readjusted at the cross of Christ. That one can stand before the scrutiny of God and know with a knowledge that passes knowledge that the work of God's Son in her or in him passes the scrutiny of God. No soul ever gets there except by the sovereign grace of God through the Atonement.

The Expression of the Conscience

I myself always strive to have a conscience without offense toward God and men. Acts 24:16

Conscience is that faculty in human beings that attaches itself to the highest they know and tells them what the highest they know demands that they do. Never be caught away with the phrase that conscience is the voice of God. If it were, it would be the most contradictory voice human ears ever listened to. Conscience is the eye of the soul and it looks out either toward God or toward what it regards as the highest, and the way conscience records is dependent entirely upon the light thrown on God (compare Acts 26:9 and 24:16).

Take the case if you have had a great spiritual crisis and have entered into the experience of sanctification; your conscience is now looking toward God in the light that Jesus

Christ throws upon God—what have you to do? You have to walk in that light and begin to get your bodily machine into harmony with what your conscience records, that is, you have to walk now not in the light of your convictions but in a purer, sterner light, the light of the Lord. It is something you alone can do; God cannot do it for you. Supposing we say we believe God can give us the Holy Spirit and can energize our wills "to do for His good pleasure," as soon as we see that, conscience records that we must obey. Any deflection in obedience to God is a sin. We have been used to doing things in these bodies in accordance with the old disposition—my right to myself, my self-interest; now we have to be regulated from a different standpoint. You did use the body as a slave to the wrong disposition, says Paul, see that you use it now as a slave to the right disposition (see Romans 6:19). It is never done suddenly. Salvation is sudden, but the working out of salvation in the life is never sudden. It is moment by moment, here a little and there a little. The Holy Spirit educates us down to the smallest detail.

Paul says he exercised himself to have "a conscience without offense toward God and men." We have to endeavor to obey our consciences in the life of faith before God and in the life of fact before other people. That does not mean we must not do things people will not like. Your conduct with them is measured by the way God has dealt with you, not by what they think of you. Your conscience will show you how God has dealt with you, "forgiving one another, even as God in Christ forgave you" (Ephesians 4:32). That is the standard that is without offense toward God and toward other people. Many of us are feeble Christians because we do not heed this standard. God works in the great incalculable element of our personalities; we have to work out what He works in and bring it out into expression in our bodily lives. It has not sufficiently entered into us that in our practical lives we must do what God says we must do—not try to do it, but do it—and the reason we can do it is that it is God who works in us to will.

The Expectation of the Heart

He will strengthen your heart. Psalm 27:14

Hope in God. 42:5

Heart is simply another term for "personality." The Bible never speaks of the heart as the seat of the affections. *Heart* is best understood if we simply say "me" (compare Romans 10:10). When once expectation is killed out of the heart, we can scarcely walk, the feet become as lead, the very life and power goes, the nerves and everything begin to fall into decay. The true nature of a human heart, according to the Bible, is that of expectation and hope. It is the heart that is strengthened by God (compare Psalm 73:26), and Jesus Christ said that He came to "heal the brokenhearted" (Luke 4:18). The marvel of the indwelling Spirit of God is that He can give heart to despairing people. There is a difference between the human sympathy we give to a discouraged or brokenhearted individual and what the Holy Spirit will do for him or for her. We may sit down beside brokenhearted people and pour out a flow of sympathy and say how sorry we are for them and tell them of other people with broken hearts, but all that only makes them more submissive to being brokenhearted. When our Lord sympathizes with the heart broken by sin or sorrow, He binds it up and makes it a new heart, and the expectation of that heart ever after is from God.

The great discipline of our lives spiritually is to bring other people into the realm of shadows. When God has brought other people into the realm of shadows, He can bring us into the relationship we need to be in toward Him.

The expectation of the heart must be based on this certainty: "in all the world there is none but Thee, my God, there is none but Thee." Until the human heart rests there, every other relationship in life is precarious and will end in heart-break. There is only one Being who can satisfy the last aching abyss of the human heart, and that is the Lord Jesus Christ. The whole history of envy and cruelty in human relationships is summed up in the demand for infinite satisfaction from human hearts; we will never get it, and we are apt to become cruel, vindictive, bitter, and often criminal. When once the heart is right with God and the real center of the life satisfied, we never expect or demand infinite satisfaction from a finite heart; we become absolutely kind to all other hearts and never become snares. If our hearts are not rightly related to Jesus Christ, danger and disillusionment are on our track wherever we go, because other lives are not being led to God; they stick at us, they cannot get any further and they become enervated. But once the heart is established in expectation on God, I defy other hearts to stick at you, they may try to, but all the time they are being led on to God Himself.

The Exhortation of the Mind

Bringing every thought into obedience to Christ. 2 Corinthians 10:5

Before a human spirit forms a mind it must express itself in words; as soon as it expresses itself in words, it becomes a spirit of mind. In the natural man, it is a spirit of mind according to the flesh, but when the Holy Spirit energizes some-one's spirit, the words the person expresses give him or her a mind according to the spirit. When once the Spirit of God energizes our spirits, we are responsible for forming the mind of Christ. God gives us the disposition of Jesus Christ, but He does not give us His mind; we have to form that, and we form it by the way we react on external things. "Let this mind be in you which was also in Christ Jesus" (Philippians 2:5). Most of us balk forming the mind of Christ; we do not object to being delivered from sin and hell, but we do object to giving up the energy of our minds to form the mind of Christ. The Holy Spirit represents the actual working of God in a person, and He enables us to form the mind of Christ if we will. We construct the mind of Christ in the same way as we construct the natural mind, namely, by the way our dispositions react when we come in contact with external things.

The mind is closely affiliated with its physical machine, the brain, and we are responsible for getting that machine into right habits. Glean your thinking, says Paul (see Philippians 4:8). Never submit to the tyrannous idea that you cannot look after your mind; you can. If one leaves one's garden alone it very soon ceases to be a garden, and if a saint leaves his or her mind alone it will soon become a rubbish heap for Satan to make use of. Read the terrible things the New Testament says will grow in the mind of a saint if the saint does not look after that mind. We have to rouse ourselves up to think, to bring "every thought into captivity to the obedience of Christ" (2 Corinthians 10:5). Never pray about evil thoughts, it will fix them in the mind. Quit—that is the only thing to do with anything that is wrong—to ruthlessly grip it on the threshold of your mind and allow it no more way. If you have received the Holy Spirit, you will find that you have the power to bring "every thought into captivity to the obedience of Christ."

Behavior

1 Thessalonians 2:10

You are witnesses, and God also, how devoutly and justly and blamelessly we behaved ourselves among you who believe.

The Fundamental Resources of Personality

Behavior means in its widest application every possible kind of reaction to the circumstances into which you may be brought.

There are resources of personality known only to God. Psalm 139 is the prayer of a man asking God to explore him where he cannot go, and to garrison him. In 1 Thessalonians 2:10, Paul is alluding to the working out of what God works in. The majority of us keep taking in and forget altogether that somehow we must work out what we take in; we cannot elude our destiny, which is practical. The profound nature of each one of us is created by God, but our perceptions of God depend entirely upon our own determined efforts to understand what we come in contact with, and the perception is always colored by the ruling disposition. If my ruling disposition is self-interest, I perceive that everything that happens to me is always for or against my self-interest; if, on the other hand, my ruling disposition is obedience to God, I perceive Him to be at work for my perfecting in everything that happens to me.

When my thought has been stirred by the Spirit of God, and I understand what God wants me to be, and I experience the thrill that comes through the vision, I have to use my body to work out the vision. The first great psychological law to be grasped is that the brain and the body are pure mechanisms, there is nothing spiritual about them; they are the machines we use to express our personalities. We are meant to use our brains to express our thoughts in words and then to behave according to the way we have thought. A human spirit only expresses itself as soul by means of words; the brain does not deal with pure thought. No thought is ours until it can be expressed in words. As soon as a thought is expressed in words, it returns to the brain as an idea upon which we can work. The type of life called the intellectual life is apt to deal only with these ideas, consequently there is a divorce from the practical life. The tyranny of intellect is that we see everything in the light of one principle, and when there is a gap, as there is in the moral development of human-ity, the intellect has to ignore it and say these things are mere upsets. The Bible supplies the facts for the gap that the intel-lect will not accept. The intellect simply works on a process of logic along one line. Life is never a process of logic, life is the most illogical thing we know. The facts of life are illogi-cal, they cannot be traced easily. Intellect is secondary, not primary. An intellectualist never pushes an issue of will.

We are not meant to spend our lives in the domain of intellectual thinking. A Christian's thinking ought never to be in reflection but in activities. The philosopher says, "I must isolate myself and think things out"; such a person is like a spider who spins its web and only catches flies. We come to right discernment in activities; thinking is meant to regulate the doing. Our destiny as spiritual men and women is the same as our destiny as natural men and women, namely, practical, from which destiny there is no escape.

Memory is a quality of personality; it does not exist in the brain but in the heart. The brain recalls more or less clearly what the heart remembers, and whether we can recall readily depends upon the state of our physical health. We take in through the words of others conceptions that are not ours as yet; we take them in through our ears and eyes, and they disappear into the unconscious mind and become incorporated into our thinking. We say that the things we hear and read slip away from memory; they do not really, they pass into the unconscious mind. We may say at the time, "I don't agree with that," but if what we hear is of the nature of reality we will agree with it sooner or later. A truth may be of no use to us just now, but when the circumstances arise in which that truth is needed, the Holy Spirit will bring it back to our remembrance. This accounts for the curious way in which the statements of Jesus emerge; we say, "I wonder where that word came from?" It came from the unconscious mind; the point is, are we going to obey it?

The matter of behavior is ours, not God's. God does not make the character; character is formed by the reaction of the inner disposition to outer things through the nervous system. God does what we cannot do: He alters the mainspring and plants in a soul a totally new disposition; then begins our work, we must work out what God works in. The practicing is ours, not God's. We have to bring the mechanism of body and brain into line by habit and make it a strong ally of the grace of God. We all know that it is never the grace of God that fails in a crisis; it is we who fail because we have not been practicing. To refuse to form mental habits is a crime against the way we are made. It is no use praying, "O Lord, give me mental habits." God won't; He has made us so that we can make our own mental habits, if we will. When we are regenerated, God does not give us other bodies—we have the same bodies, and we have to get the bodily mechanism into working order according to His teaching. Think of the time we waste in talking to God and in longing to be what He has already made us, instead of doing what He has told us to do!

"Be renewed in the spirit of your mind" (Ephesians 4:23). The expression of the mind comes through the mechanism of the brain, and the marvelous emancipation that comes slowly and surely is that we have the power to do what God wants us to do. There is nothing that a man or a woman energized by the Spirit of God cannot do. All the commandments of God are enablings. "If you love Me, keep My commandments," said Jesus (John 14:15); that is the practical, simple test. Our Lord did not say, If a man obeys Me, he will keep My commandments; but, "If you love Me, keep My commandments." In the early stages of Christian experience we are inclined to hunt with a surplus of zeal for commands of our Lord to obey, but as we mature in the life of God, conscious obedience becomes so assimilated into our makeup that we begin to obey the commands of God unconsciously, until in the maturest stage of all we are simply children of God through whom God does His will for the most part unconsciously. Many of us are on the borders of consciousness—consciously serving, consciously devoted to God; all that is immature, it is not the life yet. The first stages of spiritual life are passed in conscientious carefulness; the mature life is lived in unconscious consecration. The term *obey* would be better expressed by the word *use*. For instance, scientists, strictly speaking, "use" the laws of nature; that is, they more than obey them, they cause them to fulfill their destiny in scientific work. That is exactly what happens in saints' lives: they use the commands of the Lord, and the commands fulfill God's destiny in the saints' lives. The fundamental resources of personality will always stand true to God and to the way God has made us.

The Facile Receptivity of Personality

There are endless powers of reception in the deeper realms of personality where we cannot go, and it is these realms that God guards and garrisons. Personality is built to receive, it simply absorbs and absorbs, and education gives us the facility of expressing what we have received. We are designed with a great capacity for God, and the nature of personality is that it always wants more and more. Education is the drawing out of what is in, for the purpose of expression, and we have to fit ourselves by acquired habits of conduct to express what we have received. What is the difference between educated and uneducated persons? Educated people are those whose memories are so stored with abstract conceptions that whenever they are put into new circumstances, their memories instantly come to their aid and they know how to conduct themselves. Uneducated people are nonplussed in new circumstances because they have nothing to come to their aid, whereas educated people are able to extricate themselves by means of examples with which their memories are stored and by the abstract conceptions they have formed of circumstances in which they have never been placed.

Apply it spiritually: Suppose you are asked to speak in the open air—"Oh, I can't!"; to take a Sunday school class—"Oh, I can't!"; to write an essay—"Oh, I can't!"; to expound a particular passage—"Oh, I can't!" What is the matter? You have not been educated on the right line. Some of us do not know what to do in certain circumstances spiritually because we have never stored our memories with the counsels of God, never watched the way God's servants conduct themselves. If we have been storing our minds with the Word of God, we are never taken unawares in new circumstances because the Holy Spirit brings back these things to our remembrance and we know what we should do; but the Holy Spirit cannot bring back to our minds what we have never troubled to put there. "My people do not consider," God says (Isaiah 1:3); they live on baby food spiritually, go to church on Sunday, and expect to live in the strength of it all the week without doing anything. We should be so in the habit of obeying the Holy Spirit as He interprets the Word of God to us that wherever we are placed, we extricate ourselves in a holy and just and unblameable manner.

These things will always come to the rescue in the nick of time to the educated mind—the memory of how we have seen others act in the same circumstances and the conceptions we form as we study God's Word. We do not become educated all at once, nor do we form habits all at once; it is done bit by bit, and we have to take ourselves strongly in hand. The one thing that keeps us back from forming habits is laziness. The lazy person in the natural world is always captious, and the lazy person spiritually is captious with God—"I haven't had a decent chance." Never let the limitation of natural ability come in. We must get to the place where we are not afraid to face our lives before God and then begin to work out deliberately what God has worked in. That is the way the habits that will show themselves in holy and just and unblameable behavior are formed.

The Fit Reactions of Personality

There is no reception without a reaction and no impression without a corresponding expression. The great law regarding impressions and emotions is that if an emotion is not carried out on its own level, it will react on a lower level. The only test as to whether to allow an impression or emotion is to ask, What will this emotion lead to if I let it have its way? Push it to its logical conclusion, and if the outcome is something God would condemn, grip it on the threshold of your mind as in a vice and allow it no more way. But if it is an emotion kindled by the Spirit of God, at the peril of your soul you refuse to act it out, because if you do not let that emotion have its right issue in your life, it will react on a lower level; whereas if you act an emotion out on its right level, you lift your whole life on to God's platform. Paul mentions gross immorality in close connection with sanctification because every devotional emotion not worked out on its own level will react on an immoral level secretly. This accounts for the fact that women and men whose private lives are exceedingly wrong often show an amazing liking for devotional literature, for the writings of the saints, for the stirring of abstruse emotions. That is the way sentimentalists are made. Every emotion must express itself, and if it is not expressed on the right level, it will react on a lower level, and the higher the emotion, the more degraded the level on which it will react.

A saint is a bundle of specially qualified reactions. For every possible circumstance in life there is a line of behavior marked out in advance for us; it is not stated in black and white, we have to be so familiar with God's Book that when we come to a crisis the Spirit of God brings back to our memories the things we had read but never understood, and we see what we should do. God is making characters, not mechanisms. We have to get our bodily mechanisms into line with what God has worked in. The mighty work of God is done by His sovereign grace, then we have to work it out in our behavior.

"You are witnesses, and God also, how devoutly and justly and blamelessly we behaved ourselves among you who believe." "Blamelessly" does not mean faultless, it means a blameless disposition, undeserving of censure; that is, undeserving of censure in the sight of God who sees everything. "Now to Him who is able to keep you from stumbling, and to present you faultless before the presence of His glory with exceeding joy" (Jude 24).

Attention

1 Timothy 4:11–16

Attention is never possible without conscious effort; interest frequently is—we can take up a book and our interest is riveted at once. Naturally we never attend to anything, we are like children, and children do not attend until they are taught to. We all have certain native interests in which we are absorbed, but attention is always an effort of will. We are held responsible by God for the culture of attention.

The Capacity to Attend

These things command and teach. 1 Timothy 4:11

Interest is natural; attention must be by effort, and the great secret of a Christian's life is the attention to realities. Reality is only possible where person comes in contact with person, all the rest is a shadow of reality. That is why Jesus said, "I am the truth" (John 14:6). When Saint Paul told Timothy to command and teach, he was building his counsel on this capacity to attend, which must be by effort. We are always more willing to get ideas from books and from other people, which is simply an indication that we are not willing to attend but prefer to have our natural interest awakened. We scoop other people's brains either in books or in conversation in order to avoid attending ourselves. One of our greatest needs is to have a place where we deliberately attend; that is the real meaning of prayer. "Go into your room, and when you have shut your door, pray to your Father who is in the secret place" (Matthew 6:6). Prayer that is not an effort of the will is unrecognized by God. "If you abide in Me, and My words abide in you, you will ask what you desire, and it shall be done for you," said Jesus (John 15:7). That does not mean ask anything you like, but ask what you will. What are you actively willing? Ask for that. We shall find that we ask very few things. The tendency in prayer to leave ourselves all abroad to the influence of a meeting or of a special season is not scriptural. Prayer is an effort of will, and Jesus Christ instructs us by using the word "ask." "Everyone who asks receives" (Matthew 7:8; Luke 11:10). These words are an amazing revelation of the simplicity with which God would have us pray. The other domains of prayer, the intercession of the Holy Spirit and the intercession of Christ, have nothing to do with us; the effort of our wills is to do with us.

The Contemporary Attention

Let no one despise your youth, but be an example to the believers. 1 Timothy 4:12

Today people's attention is being focused along scientific lines; that is where the effort is being made. Think of the sweat and labor that a scientific student will expend in order to attain his or her end; where do we find men and women concentrating with the same intensity on spiritual realities? The majority of us are totally ignorant of the one abiding reality that demands our attention, namely, our relationship to God, which should exhibit itself in a life in accordance with that relationship. The essence of sin is the refusal to recognize that we are accountable to God at all. The relationship to God must be recognized and lived up to, from the crown of the head to the soles of the feet; nothing is unimportant in this relationship.

"Let no one despise your youth," Paul said to Timothy. Youth is a thing to be despised, a person up to thirty ought to be shut up in a box and not allowed to speak. Paul is not saying, Stand up for your rights; not, "Let no one despise your youth," because you are as good as anybody else, but by being an example in word, in conduct, in love, in spirit, in faith, and in purity to all who believe the realities that you believe; don't be caught up by contemporary attentions. It is so easy to attend to the thing everyone else is attending to, but it is difficult to attend to what no one is attending to. Paul did not say, Pay attention to the Greek philosopher, to the history of your people, to the thousand and one things that were contemporary in his day; he said, Focus your attention with all your effort on the one reality, your relationship to God, and be an example in that all through.

The Commiserating Attention

Give attention to reading. verse 13

How many of us spend our time expecting that we will be something we are not! "Oh, the time is coming when I am going to be so and so." It never will come; the time is always now. The amazing thing about the salvation in our Lord is that He brings us into contact with the reality that is, until we are just like children, continually seeing the wonder and beauty of things around us. The characteristic of young men and young women of today is an affected tiredness of everything, nothing interests them. The salvation in Jesus is not a divine anticipation, it is an absolute fact. People talk about the magnificent ideals that are yet to be, but the marvel of being born from above is that the reality is infinitely more wonderful than all we have imagined. Our Lord taught us to look at such things as grass and trees and birds; grass is not ideal, it is real; flowers are not ideal, they are real; sunrises and sunsets are not ideal, they are real. These things are all round about us, almost pressing themselves into our eyes and ears, and yet we never look at them. Jesus Christ drew all His illustrations from His Father's handiwork, from sparrows and flowers, things that none of us dream of noticing; we take our illustrations from things that compel attention. When we are born from above, the Spirit of God does not give us new ideals, we begin to see how ideal the real is, and as we pay attention to the things near at hand, we find them to be the gate of heaven for our souls. The reality of the salvation of Jesus Christ is that He makes us pay attention to realities, not appearances.

The Soul's Awakening

> Do not neglect the gift that is in you. verse 14

There is a difference between such books as Trine's *In Tune with the Infinite* and the reality of life. It is possible to go dreaming through life till we are struck not by an ideal but by a sudden reality, and all we have ever pictured of what a man or a woman should be pales before the reality we see. That is what happened when people saw Jesus Christ in the days of His flesh. The Spirit of God saves us from the absurd futility of useless tears, when the near objects have become far, by making us open our eyes to what is near. We weep around the graves of people and things because we have never realized that we have to pay attention to the reality that is at hand. Take a lad who has become impatient with his home, he is sick of it, he cannot stand his parents, his sisters are prosaic, and he leaves—the best thing for him. Let him come in contact with other people's fathers and mothers and sisters—oh, yes, he much prefers them; but he will soon come to realize that the ones he has left are infinitely better. Naturally we much prefer the friends we make to our God-made relations, because we can be noble with our friends—we have no past history with them.

This principle works all through. We long for something that is not and shut our eyes to the thing that is. When the Lord Jesus awakens us to reality by new birth and brings us in contact with Himself, He does not give us new fathers and mothers and new friends; He gives us new sight, that is, we focus our eyes on the things that are near and they become wonderfully distant. "Put thy distance on the near." This craving to go somewhere else, to see the things that are distant, arises from a refusal to attend to what is near.

Have I ever realized that the most wonderful thing in the world is the thing that is nearest to me, namely, my body? Who made it? Almighty God. Do I pay the remotest attention to my body as being the temple of the Holy Spirit? Remember our Lord lived in a body like our bodies. The next reality that I come in contact with by my body is other people's bodies. All our relationships in life, all the joys and all the miseries, all the hells and all the heavens are based on bodies, and the reality of Jesus Christ's salvation brings us down to the Mother Earth we live on and makes us see by the regenerating power of God's grace how amazingly precious are the ordinary things that are always with us. Master that, and you have mastered everything. We imagine that our bodies are a hindrance to our development, whereas it is only through our bodies that we develop. One cannot express a character without a body.

This is also true of nature. We do not get at God through nature, as the poets say; we get at nature through God when once we are rightly related to Him, and nature becomes a sacrament of His presence. Such books as Trine's start at the wrong end, they try to bring us from the ideal to the real; it is by coming in contact with the real that we find the ideal.

"Do not neglect the gift that is in you." We have to be careful not to neglect the spiritual reality planted in us by God. The first thing that contact with reality does is to enable us to diagnose our moods. It is a great moment when we realize that we have the power to trample on certain moods. Moods never go by praying, moods go by kicking. A mood nearly always has its seat in the physical condition, not in the moral, and it is a continual effort to refuse to listen to those moods that arise from a physical condition; we must not submit to them for a second. It is a great thing to have something to neglect in your life, a great thing for your moral character to have something to snub. "The expulsive power of a new affection"—that is what Christianity supplies. The Spirit of God on the basis of Redemption gives us something else to think about. Are we going to think about it?

By heeding the reality of God's grace within us we are never bothered again by the fact that we do not understand ourselves or that other people do not understand us. If anyone understood me, he or she would be my god. The only Being who understands me is the Being who made me and who redeems me, and He will never expound me to myself; He will only bring me to the place of reality, namely, into contact with Himself, and the heart is at leisure from itself forever afterwards.

The first things Christians are emancipated from are the tyranny of moods and the tyranny of feeling that they are not understood. These things are the most fruitful sources of misery. Half the misery in the world comes because one person demands of another a complete understanding, which is absolutely impossible. The only Being who understands us is the Being who made us. It is a tremendous emancipation to get rid of every kind of self-consideration and learn to heed only one thing, the relationship between God and me. "In all the world there is none but Thee, my God, there is none but Thee." Once we get there, other people become shadows, beautiful shadows, but shadows under God's control.

The Scriptural Attitude

> Meditate on these things; give yourself entirely to them, that
> your progress may be evident to all. verse 15

Meditation means getting to the middle of a thing, pinning yourself down to a certain thing and concentratedly brooding on it. The majority of us attend only to the muddle of things, consequently we get spiritual indigestion, the counterpart of physical indigestion, a desperately gloomy state of affairs. We cannot see anything rightly, and all we do see is stars. "Faith is . . . the evidence of things not seen" (Hebrews 11:1). Suppose Jesus suddenly lifted the veil from our eyes and let us see angels ministering to us, His own presence with us, the Holy Spirit in us, and the Father around us— how amazed we would be! We have lived in the muddle of things instead of in the middle of things. Faith gets us into the middle, which is God and God's purpose. Elisha prayed for his servant, "LORD, I pray, open his eyes that he may see" (2 Kings 6:17), and when his eyes were opened he saw the hosts of God and nothing else.

We have to learn to pay attention to reality; one soul attending to reality is an emancipation to hundreds more. We are impertinently inquisitive about everything except that one thing. Through inattention to our own true capacities we live as in a dream, when all around us and in us are the eternal realities. Attend to these duties, let them absorb you, "that your progress may be evident to all." We are apt to be busy about everything but that which concerns our spiritual progress, and at the end of a profitless day we snatch up a Bible or Daily Light and read a few verses, and it does us good for precisely three-quarters of a second. We have to take time to be diligent. Meditation is not being like a pebble in a brook, allowing the waters of thought to flow over us; that is reverie. Meditation is the most intense spiritual act, it brings every part of body and mind into harness. To be spiritual by effort is a sure sign of a false relationship to God; to be obedient by effort in the initial stages is a sure sign that we are determined to obey God at all costs. Take time. Remember we have all the time there is. The majority of us waste time and want to encroach on eternity. "Oh, well, I will think about these things when I have time." The only time you will have is the day after you are dead, and that will be eternity. An hour or half an hour of daily attention to and meditation on our own spiritual lives is the secret of progress.

The Sacred Attention

Take heed to yourself. 1 Timothy 4:16

If we have been living in unrealities, we shall find ourselves faced with a great impatience when we do endeavor to face reality, and we are apt to behave like caged wild beasts. We have to take a grip of ourselves when we come to the true center of things, and it means discipline and discipline, until we face nothing but realities. We have to exert a tremendous effort, and God is pleased to see us exert it. If you try and settle down before God in prayer when you have been dwelling in unrealities, you will recognize instantly the condition of things. As soon as you get down to pray you remember a letter you ought to write or something else that needs to be done, a thousand and one little impertinences come in and claim your attention. When we suspend our own activities and get down at the foot of the Cross and meditate there, God brings His thoughts to us by the Holy Spirit and interprets them to us. The only mind that understands the things of God is the child mind (see Matthew 11:25); our Lord continually mentioned this simplicity (see Matthew 18:3). It is the simplicity of God, not of an imbecile—a fundamental simplicity of relationship. God has not the remotest opportunity of coming to some of us, our minds are packed full with our own thoughts and conceptions, until suddenly He comes in like the wind and blows all our thoughts right away, and thoughts come sauntering in from the Word of God. We can never get those thoughts for ourselves. They are the free gift of God for anyone and everyone who is learning to pay attention to Him.

Natural Growth in Supernatural Grace

1 Peter 2:7–12

Our Lord's maxims:

Consider the lilies of the field, how they grow. Matthew 6:28

Look at the birds of the air. verse 26

Become as little children. 18:3

Our Lord did not point out wonderful sights to His disciples all the time; He pointed out things that were apparently insignificant—lilies and grass and sparrows. God does not deal with the things that interest us naturally and compel our attention; He deals with things that we have to will to observe. The illustrations Jesus Christ used were all taken from His Father's handiwork because they express exactly how the life of God will develop in us. We draw our illustrations from human works, consequently we get into a hustling condition and forget our Lord's maxims.

"Consider the lilies of the field, how they grow"—in the dark! We are apt to consider a lily when it is in the sunshine only, but for the greater part of the year it is buried in the ground, and we imagine that we are to be always above ground, shedding perfume and looking beautiful, or continually being cut and put into God's showroom to be admired, forgetting altogether that we cannot be as lilies unless we have spent time in the dark, totally ignored. As a disciple, Jesus says, consider your hidden life with God. When we breathe fresh air we are not consciously, exhilaratingly different all the time, but if we continue to take in fresh air, it makes a profound difference. This is true of the life in Christ. If we receive the Holy Spirit and obey Him, He makes a profound difference, and it will be manifested one day as a great surprise. It is not done in a minute, as far as consciousness is concerned, but when we come to a crisis we find to our astonishment that we are not upset or perplexed, as we might have expected, but we realize that our whole outlook has been altered. The Spirit of God awaits His own time to bring the crisis; we are apt to say, "I want the crisis now." We shall never see God's point of view as long as we bring our own ideas to Him and dictate to God what we expect Him to do. We must become as little children, be essentially simple, keep our minds brooding on what God tells us to brood on, and let God do as He likes. The difficulties come because we will not be simple enough to take God at His Word.

Our natural reactions are not wrong, although they may be used to express wrong dispositions. God never contradicts our natural reactions; He wants them to be made spiritual. When we are saved God does not alter the construction of the bodily life, but He does expect us to manifest in that bodily life the alteration He has made. We express ourselves naturally through our bodies, and we express the supernatural life of God in the same way, but it can only be done by the sacrifice of the natural. How many of us are spiritual in eating and drinking and sleeping? Those acts were spiritual in our Lord; His relationship to the Father was such that all His natural life was obedient to Him, and when He saw that His Father's will was for Him not to obey a natural reaction, He instantly obeyed His Father (see Matthew 4: 1–4). If our Lord had been fanatical He would have said, I have been so long without food, I will never eat again. That would have been to obey a principle instead of God. When God is educating us along the line of turning the natural into the spiritual, we are apt to become fanatical. Because by God's grace things have been done that are miraculous, we become devoted to the miracles and forget God, then when difficulties come we say it is the antagonism of the devil. The fact is we are grossly ignorant of the way God has made us. All that we need is a little of what we understand by instinct in the natural world put into the spiritual. Don't let your body get on top and say there is nothing after all in what God said. Stand up to the difficulty, and all that you ever believed about the transforming grace of God will be proved in your bodily life.

Curiosity

To you who believe, He is precious. 1 Peter 2:7

Curiosity is the desire to come to a full knowledge and understanding of a thing; it is a natural reaction. Imagine a child without curiosity! Children cannot sit and listen to a lecture, but let them see something bright and instantly they are curious and want to get hold of it, whether it is the moon or a ball. The reaction is based not so much on the desire to have it for themselves as on the desire to know more about it. As men and women we are curious about intellectual or philosophic or scientific things, and when a particular quality is presented the curiosity is aroused—"I want to know more about this matter, can anyone explain it to me satisfactorily?" It is the natural reaction of the way we are made, and to ignore it is fanatical. The instinct of curiosity can be used in the wrong way (see Genesis 3:6), but that does not mean that the reaction itself is wrong; it depends upon the motive. A point that is frequently missed in dealing with the questions of children is that they ask them from disinterested motives; a teacher can always appeal to the disinterested curiosity of a child. A child's questions are at the very heart of things, questions that scarcely occur to a philosopher.

In natural life we grow by means of curiosity, and spiritually we grow by the same power. The Spirit of God uses the natural reaction of curiosity to enable us to know more about the One who is precious. The instinct is not denied but lifted onto a different platform and turned toward knowing Jesus Christ. As saints our curiosity must not be all abroad; we become insatiably curious about Jesus Christ— He is the One who rivets our attention. Think of the avidity with which you devour anything that has to do with expounding the Lord Jesus Christ: "Therefore, to you who believe, He is precious."

Imitation

You are a chosen generation . . . that you may proclaim the praises of Him who called you out of darkness. 1 Peter 2:9

Imitation is one of the first reactions of a child; it is not sinful. We come to a right knowledge of ourselves by imitating others. The instinct that makes us afraid of being odd is not a cowardly instinct, it is the only power of self-preservation we have. If you live much by yourself you become an oddity, you never see the quirks in yourself. Some people won't live with others spiritually, they live in holes and corners by themselves. The New Testament warns of those who separate themselves (see Hebrews 10:25). By the grace of God we are taken out of the fashion we were in and we become more or less oddities. As soon as you introduce a standard of imitation that the set to which you belong does not recognize, you will experience what Peter says: "They think it strange that you do not run with them in the same flood of dissipation" (1 Peter 4:4).

The Spirit of God lifts the natural reaction of imitation into another domain and by God's grace we begin to imitate our Lord and show forth His praises. It is the natural instinct of a child to imitate its mother, and when we are born again the Holy Spirit lifts this instinct into the spiritual domain and it becomes the most supernaturally natural thing for us to imitate our Lord. We grow in grace naturally, not artificially. Mimicking is the counterfeit of imitation and produces "pi" persons, those who try their level best to be what they are not. When you are good you never try to be. It is natural to be like the one we live with most; then if we spend most of our time with Jesus Christ, we shall begin to be like Him, by the way we are built naturally and by the Spirit God puts in.

Emulation

> You are a chosen generation, a royal priesthood, a holy nation,
> His own special people. 1 Peter 2:9

Emulation is the instinct to imitate what you see another doing, in order not to appear inferior. Children who accept the place of inferiority are either lazy or are becoming heart-broken; they have no right to sit down and submit to being inferior, they are not built that way naturally. A child always admires anyone with skill, and the teacher who says, "Do this and that," has no influence over a child compared with the one who says, "Come and do this with me." When a child has seen the teacher do a thing and is asked to do it, instantly the instinct of emulation is at work.

Our Lord builds His deepest teaching on the instinct of emulation. When His Spirit comes in He makes me desire not to be inferior to Him who called me. Our example is not a good man or a good woman, not even a good Christian man or woman, but God Himself. By the grace of God I have to emulate my Father in heaven. "Therefore you shall be perfect, just as your Father in heaven is perfect" (Matthew 5:48). The most natural instinct of the supernatural life of God within me is to be worthy of my Father. To say that the doctrine of sanctification is unnatural is not true, it is based on the way God has made us. When we are born again we become natural for the first time; as long as we are in sin we are abnormal, because sin is not normal. When we are restored by the grace of God it becomes the most natural thing to be holy, we are not forcing ourselves to be unnatural. When we are rightly related to God, all our natural instincts help us to obey Him and become the greatest allies of the Holy Spirit. We disobey whenever we become independent. Independence is not strength but unrealized weakness and is the very essence of sin. There was no independence in our Lord; the great characteristic of His life was submission to His Father.

Emulation and imitation both center around whatever is our ideal. When once we see Jesus, it is good-bye to all ideals; we cannot have them back again, nor do we want them back again if we are true to Him. We have to keep the one Lodestar, the Lord Jesus Christ, in front and be absorbingly taken up with Him; consequently we have to put ourselves through discipline and fast from every other type of emulation.

Ambition

> Beloved, I beg you as sojourners and pilgrims, abstain from fleshly lusts which war against the soul. 1 Peter 2:11

Ambition is a mixture of pugnacity and pride, a reaction of unwillingness to be beaten by any difficulty. It is a natural reaction. Think of a child without the instinct to fight! The reaction that makes one child punch another is not bad, although the disposition behind it may be. The natural reaction of ambition in people saved by God's grace is that they will not be beaten by anything the world, the flesh, or the devil can put in the way of their fulfilling God's idea for them. By the grace of God we get to the place where we do not punch other people, but punch the devil clean out of the arena. "Resist the devil" (James 4:7). How can we resist the devil unless we are ambitious not to be beaten by him! When we become spiritual the reaction of pugnacity is lifted onto another plane and we say to our bodies, "It can be done and it shall be done" (compare 1 Corinthians 9:27). Most of us are devoid of spiritual pluck. Many who are naturally plucky lose all their pluck when they get a smattering of grace and become sentimental and pathetic; every tiny ache that they would have ignored altogether before they were saved is of the devil! God does not tell us to leave the natural life entirely alone; the natural life has to be turned into the spiritual, and it is because we do not realize this that we become whining people spiritually where we would have scorned to whine naturally.

When we are born into the kingdom of God, we realize that we are not fighting against flesh and blood but against spiritual enemies, "against spiritual hosts of wickedness in the heavenly places" (Ephesians 6:12). The book of the Revelation is based on the reaction to overcome. "To him who overcomes" (2:7 and following). You cannot overcome if there is nothing to overcome. In natural education everything is built up on difficulty, there is always something to overcome. And this is true in the spiritual world. If the world, the flesh, and the devil have knocked you out once, get up and face them again and again, until you are done with them. That is how character is made in the spiritual domain as well as in the natural. Our prayers for God's help are often nothing but incarnate laziness, and God has to say, Speak no more to Me of this matter; get up!

The pugnacious element is a natural reaction, and as Christian teachers we have to recognize it. Ambition in the spiritual domain is the reaction that refuses to bow its neck to any yoke but the yoke of the Lord Jesus Christ. Nothing awakens scorn amongst society more than a quitter, one who funks in a game. Weakness or imbecility do not awaken contempt as much as one sign of the white feather, a refusal to face the music, the tiniest sign of the lack of pugnacity. The law of antagonism runs all through life, physical, moral, mental, and spiritual. I am only healthy according to the fighting corpuscles in my blood; when the fighting millions inside get low, I become diseased, and after a while I shall be snuffed out. Morally it is the same; we are not born moral, we are born innocent and ignorant; morality is the outcome of fight. As soon as I am lazy in moral matters, I become immoral. Spiritually it is the same. "In the world you shall have tribulation"—everything that is not spiritual makes for our undoing—"but be of good cheer, I have overcome the world" (John 16:33). Why did not our Lord say that He would help us to overcome? Because we have to imitate Him through the power He has put in us. Think of sitting in a corner before the Almighty and saying, "But my difficulties are so enormous." Thank God they are! The bigger the difficulty, the more amazing is your profit to Jesus Christ as you draw on His supernatural grace.

Ownership

> Beloved, I beg you as sojourners and pilgrims, abstain from fleshly lusts . . . , having your conduct honorable among the Gentiles, that . . . they may, by your good works which they observe, glorify God in the day of visitation. 1 Peter 2:11–12

The instinct of ownership is seen from the first of life to the last. As soon as an infant tongue can say anything, it will say "me" and "mine."

"Is this mine?"

"Yes"—then expect to see it smashed. Children wish you to understand that they can do what they like with their own. It is only the discipline of life that teaches us to keep things. The instinct of ownership is a right one, though the disposition expressed through it may be wrong. In a saint the idea of ownership is that we have the power to glorify God by good works (see Matthew 5:16). What we own is the honor of Jesus Christ. Have I ever realized that His honor is at stake in my bodily life? "Or do you not know that your body is the temple of the Holy Spirit who is in you?" (1 Corinthians 6:19). Do I own my body for that one purpose? Do I own my brain to think God's thoughts after Him? We have to be intensely and personally God's.

The Spirit of God brings us into the realization of our ownership, and the instinct of ownership becomes a tremendous wealth in the life. "All things are yours" (1 Corinthians 3:21), and Paul prays that the eyes of our understanding may be enlightened that we may know what is ours in Christ Jesus.

No personality, from a tiny child to almighty God, is without this sense of ownership. How wonderfully sprightly a dog looks when he is owned! How weary and hang-dog we become when we are convicted of sin; but when we experience God's salvation, we straighten up immediately, everything is altered, we can fling our heads back and look the world in the face because the Lord Jesus Christ is ours and we are His. A dominant ownership, such as the ownership of the Lord, means that we own everything He owns. "Blessed are the meek, for they shall inherit the earth" (Matthew 5:5).

The Way of a Soul

Ephesians 5:14–18

The Way of the Awakening of the Soul

Awake you who sleep, arise from the dead. Ephesians 5:14

What Is Possible in the Way of Habits. A good many of us are in the condition that Saint Augustine described himself to be in, the condition of a half-awakened man who does not wish to be awakened—"a little more sleep." God smote Saint Augustine with the words, "not in chambering and wantonness" (Romans 13:13 KJV). When the Spirit of God brings a word of God to us, are we going to wake up and lay hold of it or remain in the condition Saint Augustine was in: "a little more worldliness; a little less intensity"? If God tells us to awake, we must get into the habit of awakening. We have to wake up physically before we can wake up spiritually. When God tells us to do a thing He empowers us to do it, only we must do the doing. Think of the number of times we say, "Oh, I can't." For the good of your own soul, say "I won't." To say "I can't" enervates the whole life. If we really cannot, God has misled us. Jesus said, "All authority has been given to Me" (Matthew 28:18); if He tells us to do something and we cannot, this is simply not true.

We talk about attacks of the devil: "I cannot concentrate my mind, the devil hinders me." The reason we cannot concentrate is that we are culpably ignorant about ourselves. The devil does not need to bother about us as long as we remain ignorant of the way God has made us and refuse to discipline ourselves; inattention and our own slovenliness will soon run away with every power we have. Watch the care students take in other domains of life, and then think of our own laziness and the way we continually fall back and say, "It can't be done." All we need is grit and gumption and reliance on the Holy Spirit. We must bring the same determined energy to the revelations in God's Book as we bring to earthly professions. Most of us leave the sweat of brain outside when we come to deal with the Bible.

Anything and everything is possible in the way of habits. Habits form pathways in the material stuff of the brain. We cannot form a habit without thinking about it, but when once the pathway in the brain is formed we can do a thing easily without thinking about it. For instance, we were not born with the ready-made habit of dressing ourselves, we had to form that habit. If we persist in using our bodies in a certain way, alterations will take place in the makeup of the brain. Spiritually we have to learn to form habits on the basis of the grace of God. What happens at new birth is that the incoming of a totally new life breaks all the old habits, they are completely dislodged by the "expulsive power of a new affection." Most of us do not realize this and we continue to obey habits when there is no need to. The incoming of the Spirit of God from without forms a disassociation physically, and new habits can be formed. Never dispute for a second when God speaks; if you debate, you give an opportunity to the old habits to reassert themselves. Launch yourself with as strong an initiative as possible on the line of obedience; it is difficult at first, but as soon as you start to obey, you find you can do it. The danger is to say "I can't," or, "I will do it presently." When in your soul's vision you see clearly what God wants, let me advise you to do something physical immediately. If you accompany a moral or spiritual decision with a physical effort, you give the necessary initiative to form the new habit. A physical exertion is imperative in spiritual transactions, otherwise it is in danger of passing into thin air. When God tells you to do a thing, never wait for a fitting opportunity, do it now. You may dream endlessly about doing it; the only thing to do is to launch out at once and make things inevitable, make it impossible to go back on the decision.

Beware of divorcing the physical and the spiritual. Habits are physical, and every command of God has a physical basis. "He that has an ear, let him hear" (Revelation 2:7 and following). You cannot hear with your heart if you do not listen with your physical ears. Does God find me quick in the uptake to discern what He says? Am I awake enough to hear? God always locates His spiritual revelations in a physical body. The great God became incarnate in flesh and blood; the great thoughts of God became crystallized in words. When the Spirit of God touches us, we are responsible for forming the mind of Christ. God does the wonderful indwelling part, but we have to do the expressing (see Philippians 2:12–13), and when once we understand how God has made us, it becomes not at all difficult to do it. The Spirit of God knocks and says, "Wake up, form this habit," and if you try, you find you can because you find you have a wealth of power within. It is only when we are willing to be identified with the death of Jesus that the full power of His life is able to work, and we find a new page of consciousness open in our lives. There are new forces in us and we are able now to do what we never could before; we are free from the old bondage and limitations. The gateway into this life is through the death of Jesus Christ.

Be a saint physically.

The Way of the Apprehension of the Soul

Understand what the will of the Lord is. Ephesians 5:17.

What Is Possible in the Way of Intelligence. Have we begun to form the habit of thinking? Thinking is the habit of expressing what moves our spirits. In order to think we must concentrate. Thinking is a purely physical process. No one can tell us how to begin to think, all anyone can do is to tell us what happens when we do think. In the gray matter of the brain are multitudes of blood vessels, distributed equally all over the brain, and when we think, the blood gathers to the one part of the brain we are using. This is called concentration. Dissipated thinking means that the blood goes back to the other parts of the brain and wakes up associated ideas. When one focuses one's will around certain thoughts, the blood converges to that particular part of the brain; if we can hold our wills fixed there for five minutes, we have done a tremendous thing—we have begun to form the habit of mental concentration. The majority of us allow our brains to woolgather, we never concentrate on any particular line. Concentration is physical, not spiritual. The brain must be brought into order by concentration, then when the Spirit of God brings a spontaneous illumination of a particular theme, instantly the brain is at the disposal of God. If one has not learned to concentrate, the brain cannot focus itself anywhere, it fusses all round and woolgathers. No one is responsible for that but we ourselves.

This is true in ordinary thinking, and the same brain is used by the Holy Spirit. We have to learn to bring "every thought into captivity to the obedience of Christ" (2 Corinthians 10:5), to stay our imaginations on God. This can only be done by concentration, by fixing our thoughts and our imaginations deliberately on God. The majority of us are unable to fix our thoughts in prayer, we lie all abroad before God and do not rouse ourselves up to lay hold of Him, consequently we have wandering thoughts continually. God will not bring every thought and imagination into captivity; we have to do it, and that is the test of spiritual concentration. The inattentive, slovenly way we drift into the presence of God is an indication that we are not bothering to think about Him. Whenever our Lord spoke of prayer, He said, "ask." It is impossible to ask if you do not concentrate. The marvel of the goodness of God is that He does so much for us; if we would only meet with physical obedience what God does for us spiritually, the whole of our bodies would be under such control that we would apprehend His meaning when He speaks. It is not a question of learning a thing outside but of determination inside. God gives us the Holy Spirit not only for holy living but for holy thinking, and we are held responsible if we do not think concentratedly along the right lines. To concentrate with our minds fixed on one trend of things is never easy to begin with. There never is a time when we cannot begin to concentrate.

"Do not be not unwise, but understand what the will of the Lord is" (Ephesians 5:17). We have to use the same power of concentration spiritually as we do naturally. How are we going to find out the will of God? "God will communicate it to us." He will not. His will is there all the time, but we have to discover it by being renewed in our minds, by taking heed to His Word and obeying it. If we are not going to "be conformed to this world, but be transformed," we must use our brains. God does the spiritual, powerful part we cannot do; but we have to work it out, and, as we do the obeying, we prove, that is, make out, "what is that good and acceptable and perfect will of God" (Romans 12:2).

I need to make my human nature the ally of the Spirit of God. The grace of God never fails us, but we often fail the grace of God because we do not practice. If we do not practice when there is no need, we shall never do it when there is a need. When people say, "I cannot think, I have not the gift," they mean that they have never used their brains. We all have bodies and brains. When we use our brains in concentration in a way we have never done before, we will have growing pains; a headache after thinking is a sign we have brains. The more we work and get beyond the conscious stage of doing things, the more easily will we do them. We all have unconscious mental methods. Never imitate to stick to what you imitate; imitate only in order to provoke your mind to know its own mechanism.

An artist is one who not only sees, but is prepared to pay the price of acquiring the technical knowledge to express what she or he sees. Artistic people are those who have not enough art in them to make them work at the technique of art whereby they can express themselves, they indulge in moods and tones and impressions; consequently there are more artistic people than there are artists. The same is true of poetry; there are many people with poetic notions, but very few poets. It is not enough for people to feel the divine flame burning in them; unless they go into the concentrated, slogging business of learning the technique of expression, their geniuses will be of no use to anyone. Apply these illustrations spiritually: if we have not enough of the life of God in us to overcome the difficulty of expressing it in our bodies, then we are living impoverished spiritual lives. Think of the illuminations the Spirit of God has given you; He expected you to bring your physical body, that He made, into obedience to the vision, and you never attempted to, but let it drift, and when the crisis came and God looked for you to be His mouthpiece, you crumpled all to pieces. You had not formed the habit of apprehending; your physical machine was not under control. It is a terrible thing to sit down to anything.

Beware of being sidetracked by the idea that you can develop a spiritual life apart from physical accompaniments. It is a desperately dangerous thing to allow the spiritual vision to go ahead of physical obedience.

Do some practical obeying.

The Way of Appreciation by the Soul

Be filled with the Spirit. Ephesians 5:18

What Is Possible in the Way of Inspiration. There are two ways of inspiration possible—being drunk with wine and being filled with the Spirit. We have no business to be non-descript, drunk neither one way nor the other. Someone may be sober and incapable as well as drunk and incapable. Watch human nature; we are so built that if we do not get thrilled in the right way, we will get thrilled in the wrong. If we are without the thrill of communion with God, we will try to get thrilled by the devil or by some concoction of human ingenuity. Don't be inspired with wine, the counterfeit of the Spirit, says Paul, but be filled with the Spirit. Enthusiasm is the idea—intoxicated with the life of God. Paul puts it as a command, "Be being filled." When our Lord talked to the woman of Samaria, He said, "The water that I shall give him will become in him a fountain of water springing up into everlasting life" (John 4:14). Profoundly speaking, there is no refilling; "a fountain of water" is there all the time. The picture is not that of a channel but of a fountain, a continual infilling and overflowing of the inspiration of God.

In the matter of inspiration, the first thing to watch is the temper of our own souls. A blameworthy temper of mind about another soul will end in the spirit of the devil. We cannot approach God in a wrong temper of mind, it will put a shutter down between and we shall not see Him. God introduces us to people who conduct themselves to us as we have conducted ourselves to Him, and if we do not recognize what He is doing we will ride a moral hobby horse: "I will not be treated like that." There is no further inspiration possible from the Spirit of God until that temper of mind is gone.

"Take heed to your spirit, that you do not deal treacherously" (Malachi 2:16). Our Lord always puts His finger unerringly on the thing that is wrong. "First be reconciled" (Matthew 5:24). The next thing we have to watch is our private relationship with God. Are we determined to prove that God must do what we have said He must? If so, our intercession becomes frenzied fanaticism. Or are we only concerned about being brought into an understanding of God, which is the real meaning of prayer? The greatest barrier to intercession is that we take ourselves so seriously and come to the conclusion that God is reserved with us; He is not. God has to ignore things we take so seriously until the relationship to Him is exactly that of a child. If we are watching the temper of our minds toward other people and toward God, there will be the continual incoming and outflowing of the inspiration of God, a fresh anointing of the Holy Spirit all the time. Imagine Jesus being jaded in the life of God! There was never anything jaded about Him. When we are jaded there is always a reason, and it is either the temper of our minds toward others or toward God. We have no business to be half dead spiritually, to hang like clogs on God's plan; we should be filled with a radiant intensity of life, living at the highest pitch all the time without any reaction. "I have come that they may have life, and that they may have it more abundantly" (John 10:10).

Be being filled with the life Jesus came to give.

What to Think About

Philippians 4:8

Never run away with the idea that it does not matter much what we believe or think; it does. What we think and believe, we are—not what we say we think and believe, but what we really do think and believe, we are; there is no divorce at all. To *believe*, in the sense our Lord used the word, is never an intellectual act but a moral act. The following quotation from Dr. Arnold of Rugby explains the way fanatics are made and also points out the incongruity of those Christians who are sanctified and yet show an unconscionable bigotry and narrow-mindedness in the mental outlook:

> I am quite sure that it is a most solemn duty to cultivate our understandings to the uttermost, for I have seen the evil moral consequences of fanaticism to a greater degree than I ever expected to see them realised; and I am satisfied that a neglected intellect is far oftener the cause of mischief to a man than a perverted or overvalued one. Men retain their natural quickness and cleverness while their reason and judgment are allowed to go to ruin, and thus they do work their minds and gain influence, and are pleased at gaining it; but it is the undisciplined mind which they are exercising, instead of one wisely disciplined.

The Freedom of Christian Thinking

> Whatever things are true, whatever things are noble, whatever things are just, whatever things are pure, whatever things are lovely, whatever things are of good report, . . . meditate on these things. Philippians 4:8

It is more painful to think about these things than to think about what we know, about what is old in the experience, because as soon as we begin to think God's thoughts after Him we have to bring concentration to bear, and that takes time and discipline. When once the mind begins to think, the horizon is continually broadening and widening, there is a general unsettlement, and the danger is to go back to the old, confined way and become fanatical and obstinate. This explains why some people who really are God's children have such an inveterate dislike of study. They do not quite call it the devil, but they come pretty near it. To give time to soak in God's truth, time to find out how to think along God's line, appears to them a snare and delusion. All the insubordination and difficulties and upsets come from the people who will not think. Glean your thinking, says Paul, and we must do it by will. What are we doing with our brains now that we have entered into the sanctified life? The Holy Spirit energizes the will to a complete mastery of the brain; then don't be a woolgatherer mentally. If we are saved and sanctified by God's grace, it is unadulterated mental laziness on our parts not to rouse ourselves up to think. It is not a question of the opportunities of learning but of the determination to be continually renewed in the spirit of our minds.

(a) The Things of Truth

The things of truth are things that are in keeping with the person of Truth, the Lord Jesus Christ: "I am the truth" (John 14:6). Truth therefore means not only accuracy, but accuracy about something that corresponds with God. We must distinguish between an accurate fact and a truthful fact. The devil, sin, disease, spiritualism are all accurate facts, but they are not truthful facts. Christian Science makes the blunder of saying that because sin is not of the nature of truth, therefore it is not a fact. But sin is a fact. The accuracy of facts and the accuracy of the facts of truth are two different things. Never say that things that are not of the truth are nonexistent. There are many facts that are not of the truth, that is, they do not correspond with God. Paul says, Limit your thinking to the things that are true.

Have you begun to discipline your mind in that way? If you have, people may pour bucket-loads of the devil's garbage over your head, but it will have no more effect on you than dirt has on a crystal. Our minds are apt to be all abroad, like an octopus with its tentacles out to catch everything that comes along—newspaper garbage, spiritualistic garbage, advertisement garbage—we let them all come and make dumping grounds of our heads and then sigh and mourn and say we cannot think right thoughts. Beware of saying you cannot help your thoughts; you can—you have all the almighty power of God to help you. We have to learn to bring every thought into captivity to the obedience of Christ, and it takes time. We want to reach it in a moment, like a rocket, but it can only be done by a gradual moral discipline, and we do not like discipline, we want to do it all at once.

(b) The Things of Nobility

The word "noble"—honest, honorable, reverend—has come down in the world; it means something massive, awe-inspiring and grand that awakens our reverence and inspires sublime thoughts, as a cathedral does. Noble things make a human character sublime, and Paul counsels us to think on these things. See that there is a correspondence between a sublime piece of architecture and your character. Anything that awakens the sense of the sublime is an honorable thing. In the natural realm, a sunset, a sunrise, mountain scenery, music, or poetry will awaken a sense of the sublime. In the moral world, truthfulness in action will awaken it. Truthfulness in action is different from truthfulness in speech. Truth-speaking people are an annoyance—they spank children for having imagination; they are sticklers for exact accuracy of speech and would have everyone say the same thing, like gramophone records; they drag down the meaning of truth out of its sphere. So we mean truthfulness in action, a true act all through.

Another thing that awakens the sense of the sublime is suffering that arises from the misunderstanding by those whom one esteems highest. Jesus Christ brought this suffering to the white heat of perfection; He let those He esteemed misunderstand Him foully and never once vindicated Himself but was meek toward all His Father's dispensations for Him. That is moral sublimity. In the spiritual world, the sense of the sublime is awakened by such a life as that of Abraham or of the apostle Paul or of anyone going through the trial of his or her faith. "Though He slay me, yet will I trust Him" (Job 13:15). That is the most sublime utterance of faith in the Old Testament.

We are accustomed to think of noble things in connection with the spiritual world, but there are noble things in the natural world and in the moral world as well. We have the idea that God has only to do with the spiritual, and if the devil can succeed in keeping us with that idea, he will have a great deal of his own way; but Paul pushes the battleline into every domain: "whatever things are noble, . . . meditate on these things," because behind them all is God.

(c) The Things of Justice

"Just" means right with God; nothing is just until it is adjusted to God. The justice of a law court is superficial exactitude between human beings. That is why we often rebel against the verdict of a law court, although its justice can be proved to the hilt. Paul is not referring to justice between people but to the very essence of justice, and he knows no justice where God is ignored. The great exhibition of justice is Jesus Christ; there was no superficial exactitude in His life because He was perfectly at one with God. The standard all through the Sermon on the Mount is that of conduct arising from a right relationship to God. We say: "Oh, well, I certainly would show a forgiving spirit to her if she would be right with me." Jesus said, "If you do not forgive men their trespasses, neither will your Father forgive your trespasses" (Matthew 6:15). Take any of the teaching of the Sermon on the Mount and you will find it is never put on the ground that because a person is right with me, therefore I will be the same to her or to him, but always on the ground of a right relationship to Jesus Christ first, and then the showing of that same relationship to others. To look for justice from other people is a sign of deflection from devotion to Jesus Christ. Never look for justice, but never cease to give it. We think of justice in the most absurd connections—because people tread on our little notions, our sense of what is right, we call that injustice. When once we realize how we have behaved toward God all the days of our lives until we became adjusted to Him through the Atonement, our attitude to our other people will be that of absolute humility (compare Ephesians 4:32).

(d) The Things of Purity

Purity is not innocence; it is much more. Purity means stainlessness, an unblemishedness that has stood the test. Purity is learned in private, never in public. Jesus Christ demands purity of mind and imagination, chastity of bodily and mental habits. The only men and women it is safe to trust are those who have been tried and have stood the test; purity is the outcome of conflict, not of necessity. You cannot trust innocence or natural goodness; you cannot trust possibilities. This explains Jesus Christ's attitude. Our Lord trusted no one (see John 2:24–25), yet He was never suspicious, never bitter; His confidence in what God's grace could do for people was so perfect that He never despaired of anyone. If our trust is placed in people, we will end in despairing of everyone. But when we limit our thinking to the things of purity, we shall think only of what God's grace has done in others and put our confidence in that and in nothing else. Look back over your life and see how many times you have been pierced through with wounds, and all you can say when God deals with you is, "Well, it serves me right; over and over again God taught me not to trust in myself, not to put confidence in human beings, and yet I have persisted in doing it." God holds us responsible for being ignorant in these matters, and the cure for ignorance is to think along the lines Paul indicates here. It will mean that we shall never stand up for our own honor or for the honor of others; we shall stand only for the honor and the dignity of the Lord Jesus Christ. Our temperamental outlook is altered by thinking, and when God alters the disposition, temperament begins to take its tone from the new disposition. These things are not done suddenly, they are only done gradually, by the stern discipline of the life under the teaching of the Spirit of God.

(e) The Things of Loveliness

The things that are lovely means things that are morally agreeable and pleasant. The word "lovely" has the meaning of juicy and delicious. That is the definition given by Calvin, and he is supposed to be a moloch of severity! We have the idea that duty must always be disagreeable, and we make any number of duties out of diseased sensibilities. If our duties are disagreeable, it is a sign that we are in disjointed relationship to God. If God gave some people a fully sweet cup, they would go carefully into a churchyard and turn the cup upside down and empty it and say, "No, that could never be meant for me." The idea has become incorporated into their makeup that their lot must always be miserable. Once we become rightly related to God, duty will never be a disagreeable thing of which we have to say with a sigh, "Oh, well, I must do my duty." Duty is the daughter of God. Never take your estimate of duty after a sleepless night or after a dose of indigestion; take your sense of duty from the Spirit of God and the word of Jesus. There are people whose lives are diseased and twisted by a sense of duty that God never inspired, but once let them begin to think about the things of loveliness, and the healing forces that will come into their lives will be amazing. The very essence of godliness is in the things of loveliness; think about these things, says Paul.

(f) The Things of Good Report

The things of good report are, literally, the things that have a fine face, a winning and attractive tone about them. What would we be like after a year of thinking on these things? We might not be fatter, but I am certain we would look pleasanter! When we do think about the things of good report we shall be astonished to realize where they are to be found; they are found where we only expected to find the opposite. When our eyes are fixed on Jesus Christ, we begin to see qualities blossoming in the lives of others that we never saw there before. We see people whom we have tabooed and put on the other side exhibiting qualities we have never exhibited, although we call ourselves saved and sanctified. Never look for other people to be holy; it is a cruel thing to do, it distorts your view of yourself and of others. Could anyone have had a sterner view of sin than Jesus had, and yet had anyone a more loving, tender patience with the worst of humankind than He had? The difference in the attitude is that Jesus Christ never expected people to be holy—He knew they could not be; He came to make us holy.

All He asks of us is that we acknowledge we are not right, then He will do all the rest: "Blessed are the poor in spirit" (Matthew 5:3). It comes back to the central message of Jesus Christ: "I, if I am lifted up" (John 12:32). If we preach anything other than "Jesus Christ and Him crucified" (1 Corinthians 2:2), we make our doctrines god and ourselves the judges of others. Think of the times we have hindered the Spirit of God by trying to help others when only God could help them, because we have forgotten to discipline our own minds. It is the familiar truth that we have to be stern in proclaiming God's Word—let it come out in all its rugged bluntness, unwatered down and unrefined; but when we deal with others we have to remember that we are sinners saved by grace. The tendency today is to do exactly the opposite; we make all kinds of excuses for God's Word—"Oh, God does not expect us to be perfect," and when we deal with people personally we are amazingly hard.

All these things lead us back to Jesus Christ—He is the truth; He is the noble; He is the just; He is the pure; He is the altogether lovely; He is the only One of good report. No matter where we start from, we will always come back to Jesus Christ.

The Frontiers of Christian Thinking

If there is any virtue and if there is anything praiseworthy—meditate on these things.

Paul seems to come to the conclusion that he has not made the area of thinking wide enough yet, so he says, If there is any morally excellent thing, anything whatever to praise, anything recommendable, take account of it. We are apt to discard the virtues of those who do not know Jesus Christ and call them pagan virtues. Paul counsels, If there is any virtue anywhere in the world, think about it, because the natural virtues are remnants of God's handiwork and will always lead to the one central Source, Jesus Christ. We have to form the habit of keeping the mental life on the line of the great and beautiful things Paul mentions. It is not a prescribed ground. It is we who make limitations and then blame God for them. Many of us behave like ostriches, we put our heads in the sand and forget altogether about the world outside: "I have had this and that experience and I am not going to think of anything else." After awhile we have aches and pains in the greater part of ourselves, which is outside our heads, and then we find that God sanctifies every bit of us, spirit, soul, and body. God grant we may get out into the larger horizons of God's Book.

Always keep in contact with those books and those people that enlarge your horizon and make it possible for you to stretch yourself mentally. The Spirit of God is always the Spirit of liberty; the spirit that is not of God is the spirit of bondage, the spirit of oppression and depression. The Spirit of God convicts vividly and tensely, but He is always the Spirit of liberty. God who made the birds never made birdcages; it is people who make birdcages, and after a while we become cramped and can do nothing but chirp and stand on one leg. When we get out into God's great, free life, we discover that that is the way God means us to live "the glorious liberty of the children of God" (Romans 8:21).

Thinking Godliness

Philippians 4:5–8; 3:7–14

In physical life we do best those things we have habitually learned to do, and the same is true in mental and spiritual life. We do not come into the world knowing how to do anything; all we do we have acquired by habit. Remember, habit is purely mechanical.

Thinking Habits

> Let your gentleness be known to all men. The Lord is at hand.
> Philippians 4:5

Our thinking processes are largely subject to the law of habit. "Let your gentleness," that is, self-control, "be known to all men." Self-control is nothing more than a mental habit that controls the body and mind by a dominant relationship, namely, the immediate presence of the Lord—for "the Lord is at hand." The danger in spiritual matters is that we do not think godliness; we let ideas and conceptions of godliness lift us up at times, but we do not form the habit of godly thinking. Thinking godliness cannot be done in spurts, it is a steady, habitual trend. God does not give us our physical habits or our mental habits; He gives us the power to form any kind of habits we like, and in the spiritual domain we have to form the habit of godly thinking.

To children, the universe is a great, confusing, amazing "outsideness"; when children grow to adulthood, they have the same nervous systems and brains, but the will has come in and determined their tendencies and impulses. It is natural for a child to be impulsive, but it is a disgraceful thing for a man or a woman to be guided by impulse. To be creatures of impulse is the ruin of mental life. The one thing our Lord checked and disciplined in the disciples was impulse; the determining factor was to be their relationship to Him.

We are so made that our physical lives give us an affinity with every material thing; our thinking lives give us affinity with everything in the mental realm, and it is the same with our moral and spiritual lives. We are held responsible by God for the way we deal with the great mass of things that come into our lives. We all have susceptibilities in every direction; everyone is made in the same way as everyone else; consequently it is not true to say we cannot understand why some people like to devote themselves to pleasure, to races and dancing, and so on. If we do not understand it, it is because part of our human natures has become atrophied. Whatever one person can do, either in the way of good or bad, any person can do. There are things we must deny, but the negation that is the outcome of ignorance is of no value whatever to the character; the denial by will is of enormous value. "If your right eye causes you to sin, pluck it out and cast it from you" (Matthew 5:29); determine to select those elements of your conscious life that are going to tell for the characteristic of godliness.

Trending Habitually

> Be anxious for nothing, but in everything by prayer and supplication, with thanksgiving, let your requests be made known to God. Philippians 4:6

We have to watch the trend of things. The trend of our conscious lives is determined by us, not by God, and Paul makes the determining factor in the conscious life of a godly person the determination to pray. Prayer is not an emotion, not a sincere desire; prayer is the most stupendous effort of the will. "Let your requests be made known to God; and the peace of God, which surpasses all understanding, will guard your hearts and minds through Christ Jesus" (vv. 6–7), the poising power of the peace of God will enable you to steer your course in the mix-up of ordinary life. We talk about circumstances over which we have no control. None of us have control over our circumstances, but we are responsible for the way we pilot ourselves in the midst of things as they are. Two boats can sail in opposite directions in the same wind, according to the skill of the pilots. The pilot who conducts one vessel on to the rocks says it could not be helped, the wind was in that direction; the pilot who took the other vessel into the harbor had the same wind but knew how to trim the sails so that the wind conducted the boat in the direction the pilot wanted. Never allow to yourself that you could not help this or that, and never say you reach anywhere in spite of circumstances; we all attain because of circumstances and no other way.

> Let us not always say
> "Spite of this flesh today
> I strove, made head, gained ground upon the whole!"
> —Robert Browning

Touching Habitual Fundaments

Whatever things are true, whatever things are noble, whatever things are just, whatever things are pure, whatever things are lovely, whatever things are of good report, if there is any virtue and if there is anything praiseworthy—meditate on these things. Philippians 4:8

There is a difference between thinking and grinding. Such subjects as languages or mathematics require grinding, and it is no use saying we have not the mental power to grind—we have; and the more we grind the more the mechanical part of our natures will come to our aid if we keep at it uninterruptedly. When it comes to matters of imagination, different faculties are needed. Some minds are more easily put on the grind than others, and some are more easily taught on the imaginative line than others. We have to discipline ourselves along both lines. *Insubordination* is another name for mental laziness. Watch the difference between listening to a language lesson and to a sermon or lecture; you will be worn out in no time by the former unless you have learned to grind; but with the latter, after a few sentences, your mind is kindled through the connection of previous thinking. It is not that we are gifted in this way but that we are created in this way. Paul insists on this very law: "whatever things are true, . . . think on these things." Glean your thinking; don't allow your mind to be a harborage for every kind of vagabond sentiment; resolutely get into the way of disciplining your impulses and stray thinking. The law of attention controls the mind and keeps it from shifting hither and thither. The forming of a new habit is difficult until you get into the way of doing the thing, then everything you meet with aids you in developing along the right line. It is good practice to sit down for five minutes and do nothing; in that way you will soon discover how little control you have over yourself. In forming a new habit it is vitally important to insist on bringing the body under control first. Paul says, "I maul and master my body, in case, after preaching to other people, I am disqualified myself" (1 Corinthians 9:27 MOFFATT). The natural man is created by God as well as the new man in Christ, and the new man has to be manifested by the natural man in the mortal flesh. Paul puts it very practically in Romans 6:19: "You presented your members as slaves of uncleanness, and of lawlessness. . . . now present your members as slaves of righteousness for holiness." In 1 Corinthians 10:31 he puts it still more practically: "Therefore, whether you eat or drink, or whatever you do, do all to the glory of God." It is difficult to begin with, but as you go on you find it becomes easier, until you are able not only to practice the presence of God in your spirit, but are able to prove by the habits of your actual life that your body is the temple of the Holy Spirit.

Native and Acquired Interests

What things were gain to me, these I have counted loss for Christ. Philippians 3:7

There are some subjects that are natively interesting and other subjects for which we have to acquire an interest. A child's mind is only natively interested; an adult mind if it is well formed has voluntarily acquired an interest in other subjects. We imagine that a native interest will develop into an acquired interest all at once, but it won't. It will only become a dominant interest when it has come into the very makeup of our beings. Think of the things you are interested in today, the things that are really forming your mind, you can remember the time when you had no affinity with them at all, they awakened no interest in you. What has happened? The Spirit of God by the engineering of God's providence has brought some word of His and connected it with your circumstances in such a way that the whole of your outlook is altered. "Old things have passed away; behold, all things have become new" (2 Corinthians 5:17). God alters the thing that matters.

The interests of children are altogether in the senses, and in teaching them you must begin by interesting them. The teacher who succeeds best with children is the one who does things before them; it is no use teaching children abstract stuff. That is why it is necessary in teaching a young life, whether young in years of the flesh or the spirit, for teachers to attend more to what they do than to what they say. The crystallizing point of our Lord's teaching lies here, and the reason our Lord condemned the Pharisees was that "they say, and do not do" (Matthew 23:3). Everyone has a perfect right to come and ask those of us who teach whether we practice what we teach. The influence of our teaching is in exact proportion to our practical doing.

In Philippians 3:7–8, Paul states that he has flung overboard the things that were natively interesting to him in order to acquire other interests that at one time were of no value to him, and now the whole of his attention is set on Jesus Christ's idea for him: "I press on, that I may lay hold of that for which Christ Jesus has also laid hold of me" (Philippians 3:12). Someone can go through any drudgery under heaven to attain the object he or she has in view. Paul's object was to win Christ, and "what things were gain to me, these I have counted loss for Christ. . . . I have suffered the loss of all things, and count them but rubbish," to attain his object.

Nurturing Appreciation

That I may know Him and the power of His resurrection, and the fellowship of His sufferings, being conformed to His death.
Philippians 3:10

These words never fail to awaken a thrill of emotion in the heart of every Christian, but the question arises: "How can I become interested in these matters to the degree that the apostle was interested in them?" The only way in which a truth can become of vital interest to me is when I am brought into the place where that truth is needed. Paul calls the people to whom the gospel is not vitally interesting "dead," but when once they are brought under conviction of sin, the one thing they will listen to is the thing they despised before, namely, the gospel. There is a difference between the way we try to appreciate the things of God and the way in which the Spirit of God teaches. We begin by trying to get fundamental conceptions of the creation and the world; why the devil is allowed; why sin exists. When the Spirit of God comes in He does not begin by expounding any of these subjects; He begins by giving us a dose of the plague of our own hearts, He begins where our vital interests lie—in the salvation of our souls. In every Christian life spiritual sentiment is at times carried to the white heat of devotion, but the point is how can we so attend to these things that the devotion is there all the time. In spiritual life most of us progress like frogs; we jump well at times, but at other times we stay a long while in one place, until God in His providence tumbles up our circumstances. The apostle Paul's life was not a frog-jumping business, not a spasmodic life kept going by conventions and meetings, but an abiding, steadfast, attending life. If we are alive spiritually, the Spirit of God will continually prod us to attend to new phases of our salvation, and if we sit down, we sit on something that hurts. There will be always something that "bids nor sit nor stand but go!" The people who are of absolutely no use to God are those who have sat down and have become overgrown with spiritual mildew; all they can do is to refer to experiences they had twenty or thirty years ago. That is of no use whatever; we must be vitally at it all the time. With Paul it was never an experience I once had but "the life which I now live" (Galatians 2:20).

Negotiating Associations

Not that I have already attained, or am already perfected; but I press on, that I may lay hold of that for which Christ Jesus has also laid hold of me. Brethren, I do not count myself to have apprehended, but one thing I do, forgetting those things which are behind and reaching forward to those things which are ahead, I press toward the goal for the prize of the upward call of God in Christ Jesus. Philippians 3:12–14

We have to build up useful associations in our minds, to learn to associate things for ourselves, and it can only be done by determination. There are ideas associated in each mind that are not associated in the mind of anyone else, and this accounts for the difference in individuals. For instance, learn to associate the chair you sit in with nothing else but study; associate a selected secret place with nothing but prayer. We do not sufficiently realize the power we have to infect the places in which we live and work by our prevailing habits in those places.

The law of associated ideas applied spiritually means that we must drill our minds in godly connections. How many of us have learned to associate our summer holidays with God's divine purposes? To associate the early dawn with the early dawn on the Sea of Galilee after the Resurrection? If we learn to associate ideas that are worthy of God with all that happens in nature, our imaginations will never be at the mercy of our impulses. Spiritually, it is not a different law that works but the same law. When once we have become accustomed to connecting these things, every ordinary occurrence will serve to fructify our minds in godly thinking because we have developed our minds along the lines laid down by the Spirit of God. It is not done once for always; it is only done always. Never imagine that the difficulty of doing these things belongs peculiarly to you, it belongs to everyone. The character of a person is nothing more than the habitual form of his or her associations.

Learn to beware of marginal preoccupations that continually provoke other associations. For instance, there are people who cultivate the margin of vision; they look at you, but out of the margin of the eye they are really occupied with something else all the time; and in the mental realm there are people who never pay attention to the subject immediately at hand but only to the marginal subjects round about. Spiritually there is the same danger. Jesus Christ wants us to come to the place where we see things from His standpoint and are identified with His interests only. "My one thought is, by forgetting what lies behind me and straining to what lies before me, to press on to the goal" (MOFFATT).

Concentration is the law of life mentally, morally, and spiritually.

The Mind of Christ

Philippians 2:5–8

Let this mind be in you which was also in Christ Jesus.
Philippians 2:5

We are apt to forget that the mind of Christ is supernatural, His mind is not a human mind at all. Never run away with the idea that because you have the Spirit of Christ, therefore you have His mind. God gives us the Spirit of Jesus, but He does not give us His mind; we have to construct the mind of Christ, and it can only be done as we work out in the habits of a holy life the things that were familiar in the life of our Lord. We cannot form the mind of Christ once for always; we have to form it always, that is, all the time and in everything. "By your patience possess your souls" (Luke 21:19), that is, by patience acquire a new way of looking at things, and learn never to say fail! When God re-creates us in Christ Jesus He does not patch us up; He makes a new creation. Every power of our beings is no longer to be used at the dictates of our right to ourselves but to be subordinated to the Spirit of God in us, who will enable us to form the mind of Christ.

The type of mind Paul urges us to form is prescribed clearly—the mind of true humility, the mind "which was also in Christ Jesus" when He was on this earth, utterly self-effaced and self-emptied—not the mind of Christ when He was in glory. Humility is the exhibition of the Spirit of Jesus Christ and is the touchstone of saintliness.

His Deity and Our Dependence

> . . . who, being in the form of God, did not consider it robbery
> to be equal with God. Philippians 2:6

Paul precludes the idea that Jesus thought nothing of Himself; our Lord thought truly about Himself. There was no assertion in any shape or form, and no presumption. It was along this line that Satan tempted Him: "Remember who You are: You are the Son of God; then assert the prerogative of Sonship—command that these stones become bread; do something supernatural—cast Yourself down from hence" (see Matthew 4:1–11).

It was a temptation to the fulfillment of the Incarnation by a shortcut. Each time the temptation came, our Lord blunted it: I did not come here to assert Myself; I came for God's will to be done through Me in His own way (see Matthew 4:4, 7, 10). Paul connects the two things: though it was not robbery for Christ to be equal with God, He took the form of a bondservant. Our Lord never once asserted His dignity, He never presumed on it.

When we are sanctified, the same temptation comes to us: "You are a child of God, saved and sanctified—presume on it, think it something to be asserted." As long as our thoughts are fixed on the experience instead of on the God who gave us the experience, the habit of making nothing of ourselves is an impossibility. If we think only along the line of our experiences we become censorious, not humble. Sanctification is the gateway to a sanctified life, not to boasting about an experience. The habit of forming the mind of Christ will always make us obey our Lord and Master as He obeyed His Father, and there are whole domains of natural life to be brought under the control of this habit. It is not sinful to have a body and a natural life; if it were, it would be untrue to say that Jesus Christ was sinless, because He had a body and was placed in a natural life; but He continually sacrificed His natural life to the word and the will of His Father and made it a spiritual life, and we have to form the same habit. It is the discipline of a lifetime; we cannot do it all at once. We are absolutely dependent, and yet, strange to say, the last thing we learn spiritually is to make nothing of ourselves.

But made Himself of no reputation . . . Philippians 2:7

Jesus Christ effaced the Godhead in Himself so effectually that people without the Spirit of God despised Him. No one without the Spirit of God, or apart from a sudden revelation from God, ever saw the true Self of Jesus while He was on earth. He was "as a root out of dry ground" (Isaiah 53:2), thoroughly disadvantaged in the eyes of everyone not convicted of sin. The reference in 2 Corinthians 8:9 is not to a wealthy individual becoming poor but to a wealthy God becoming poor for human beings: "For you know the grace of our Lord Jesus Christ, that though He was rich, yet for your sakes He became poor, that you through His poverty might become rich." Our Lord is the time-representation of a self-disglorified God. The purpose of the Incarnation was not to reveal the beauty and nobility of human nature but to remove sin from human nature. To those who seek after wisdom, the preaching of Christ crucified is foolishness; but when people know that their lives are twisted, that the mainspring is wrong, they are in the state of heart and mind to understand why it was necessary for God to become incarnate. The doctrine of the self-limitation of Jesus is clear to our hearts first, not to our heads. We cannot form the mind of Christ unless we have His Spirit, nor can we understand our Lord's teaching apart from His Spirit. We cannot see through it; but when once we receive His Spirit we know implicitly what He means. Things that to the intellect may be hopelessly bewildering are lustrously clear to the heart of the humble saint (see Matthew 11:25).

Taking the form of a bondservant . . .

Our Lord took upon Him habitually the part of a slave: "I am among you as the One who serves" (Luke 22:27); consequently He could be put upon to any extent, unless His Father prevented it (compare John 19:11) or His Father's honor was at stake (compare Mark 11:15–19). It was our Lord's right to be "in the form of God," but He renounced that right and took "the form of a bondservant," not the form of a noble but of a slave. Our Lord crowned the words that the powers of this world detest: *servant, obedience, humility, service.*

Coming in the likeness of men . . .

That is, in "the likeness of sinful flesh." The assimilation was as complete as our Lord's sinlessness would permit and gave Him so truly human a life that by His fulfilling all righteousness in the face of temptation, He "condemned sin in the flesh" (Romans 8:3).

> The nature was sinless in Him because He was sinless in it, not vice versa. . . . Jesus Christ does not stand for an originally holy human nature, but a sanctified or made-holy human nature.
>
> —Du Bose

The First Adam came in the flesh, not in sinful flesh; Jesus Christ, the Last Adam, came on the plane of the First Adam; He partook of human nature but not of human sin. By His mighty atonement He can lift us into the kingdom in which He lived while He was on this earth, so that we may be able to live a life freed from sin. That is the practical point the apostle Paul is making.

> And being found in appearance as a man, He humbled Himself and became obedient to the point of death, even the death of the cross. Philippians 2:8

Right at the threshold of adulthood our Lord took upon Him His vocation, which was to bear away the sin of the world—by identification, not by sympathy (John 1:29). Our Lord's object in becoming Deity Incarnate was to redeem humankind, and Satan's final onslaught in the Garden of Gethsemane was against our Lord as Son of Man, namely, that the purpose of His incarnation would fail. The profundity of His agony has to do with the fulfilling of His destiny. The Cross is a triumph for the Son of Man; any and every human being has freedom of access straight to the throne of God by right of what our Lord accomplished through His death on the Cross. "Though He was a Son, yet He learned obedience [as a Savior] by the things which He suffered, and having been perfected, He became the author of eternal salvation to all who obey Him" (Hebrews 5:8–9).

"He was crucified through weakness" (2 Corinthians 13:4). Jesus Christ represents God limiting His own power for one purpose: He died for the weak, for the ungodly, for sinners, and for no one else. "I did not come to call the righteous, but sinners, to repentance" (Matthew 9:13). No chain is stronger than its weakest link. In one aspect Jesus Christ became identified with the weakest thing in His own creation, a baby; in another aspect He went to the depths of a bad man's hell, consequently from the babe to the vilest criminal Jesus Christ's substitution tells for salvation, nothing can prevail against Him.

The first thing the Spirit of God does in us is to efface the things we rely upon naturally. Paul argues this out in Philippians 3; he catalogues who he is and the things in which he might have confidence, "but," he says, "I deliberately renounce all these things that I may gain Christ" (see vv. 7–11). The continual demand to consecrate our gifts to God is the devil's counterfeit for sanctification. We have a way of saying—"What a wonderful power that man or that woman would be in God's service." Reasoning on broken human virtues makes us fix on the wrong thing. The only way one can ever be of service to God is when one is willing to renounce all one's natural excellencies and determine to be weak in Him: "I am here for one thing only, for Jesus Christ to manifest Himself in me." That is to be the steadfast habit of a Christian's life. Whenever we think we are of use to God, we hinder Him. We have to form the habit of letting God carry on His work through us without let or hindrance, as He did through Jesus, and He will use us in ways He dare not let us see. We have to efface every other thought but that of Jesus Christ. It is not done once for all; we have to be always doing it. If once you have seen that Jesus Christ is All in all, make the habit of letting Him be All in all. It will mean that you not only have implicit faith that He is All in all, but that you go through the trial of your faith and prove that He is. After sanctification God delights to put us into places where He can make us wealthy. Jesus Christ counts as service not what we do for Him but what we are to Him, and the inner secret of that is identity with Him in person. "That I may know Him."

His Dedication and Our Discipline

And for their sakes I sanctify Myself. John 17:19

How does that statement of our Lord fit in with our idea of sanctification? Sanctification must never be made synonymous with purification; Jesus Christ had no need of purification, and yet He used the word "sanctify." In the words, "I sanctify Myself," Jesus gives the key to the saint's life. Self is not sinful; if it were, how could Jesus say "I sanctify Myself"? Jesus Christ had no sin to deny, no wrong self to deny; He had only a holy self. It was that self He denied all the time, and it was that self that Satan tried to make Him obey. What could be holier than the will of the holy Son of God? And yet all through He said, "not as I will, but as You will" (Matthew 26:39). It was the denying of His holy self that made the marvelous beauty of our Lord's life.

If we have entered into the experience of sanctification, what are we doing with our holy selves? Do I, every morning I wake, thank God that we have a self to give to Him, a self that He has purified and adjusted and baptized with the Holy Spirit so that I might sacrifice it to Him? Sacrifice, in its essence, is the exuberant, passionate love-gift of the best I have to the One I love best. The best gift the Son of God had was His holy humanity, and He gave that as a love-gift to God that He might use it as an atonement for the world. He poured out His soul to death, and that is to be the character-istic of our lives. God is at perfect liberty to waste us if He chooses. We are sanctified for one purpose only, that we might sanctify our sanctification and give it to God.

One of the dangers of present-day teaching is that it makes us turn our eyes off Jesus Christ onto ourselves, off the Source of our salvation onto salvation itself. The effect of that is morbid, hypersensitive lives, totally unlike our Lord's life; they have not the passion of abandon that characterized Him. The New Testament never allows for a moment the idea that continually crops up in modern spiritual teaching: "I have to remember that I am a specimen of what God can do." That is inspired by the devil, never by the Spirit of God. We are not here to be specimens of what God can do but to have our lives so hid with Christ in God that our Lord's words will be true of us, that people, beholding our good works, will glorify our Father in heaven. There was no "show busi-ness" in the life of the Son of God, and there is to be no show business in the life of the saint. Concentrate on God, let Him engineer circumstances as He will, and wherever He places you, He is healing the brokenhearted through you, setting at liberty the captives through you, doing His mighty soul-sav-ing work through you, as you keep rightly related to Him.

Self-conscious service is killed, self-conscious devotion is gone; only one thing remains: "witnesses to Me" (Acts 1:8)— Jesus Christ first, second, and third.

The Father who dwells in Me does the works. John 14:10

Our Lord habitually submitted His will to His Father, that is, He engineered nothing, but left room for God. The modern trend is dead against this submission; we do engineer—and engineer with all the sanctified ingenuity we have, and when God suddenly bursts in in an expected way, we are taken unawares. It is easier to engineer things than determinedly to submit all our powers to God. We say we must do all we can: Jesus says we must let God do all He can.

As My Father taught Me, I speak these things. John 8:28

The secret of our Lord's holy speech was that He habitually submitted His intelligence to His Father. Whenever problems pressed on the human side, as they did in the Temptation, our Lord had within Himself the Divine remembrance that every problem had been solved in counsel with His Father before He became incarnate (compare Revelation 13:8) and that therefore the one thing for Him was to do the will of His Father and to do it in His Father's way. Satan tried to hasten Him, tried to make Him face the problems as a human being and do God's will in His own way: "The Son can do nothing of Himself, but what He sees the Father do" (John 5:19).

Are we intellectually insubordinate, spiritually stiff-necked, dictating to God in pious phraseology what we intend to let Him make us, hunting through the Bible to back up our pet theories? Or have we learned the secret of submitting our intelligence and our reasoning to Jesus Christ's word and will, as He submitted His mind to His Father?

The danger with us is that we will only submit our minds to New Testament teaching where the light of our experience shines. "If we walk in the light"—as our experience is in the light? No, "if we walk in the light as He is in the light" (1 John 1:7). We have to keep in the light that God is in, not in the rays of the light of our experience. There are phases of God's truth that cannot be experienced, and as long as we stay in the narrow grooves of experience we shall never become Godlike, but specialists of certain doctrines—Christian oddities. We have to be specialists in devotion to Jesus Christ and in nothing else. If we want to know Jesus Christ's idea of a saint and to find out what holiness means, we must not only read pamphlets about sanctification, we must face ourselves with Jesus Christ, and as we do so He will make us face ourselves with God. "Therefore you shall be perfect, just as your Father in heaven is perfect" (Matthew 5:48). When once the truth lays hold of us that we have to be Godlike, it is the deathblow forever to attempting things in our own strength. The reason we do attempt things in our own strength is that we have never had the vision of what Jesus Christ wants us to be. We have to be Godlike, not good men and good women. There are any number of good men and good women who are not Christians.

The life of sanctification, of service, and of sacrifice is the threefold working out in our bodies of the life of Jesus, until the supernatural life is the only life. These are truths that cannot be learned; they can only be habitually lived.

Our Lord on How to Think

Matthew 6:19–24

We so readily look upon our Lord as Savior in the fundamental way that we are apt to forget He is much more than Savior, He is Teacher as well. In the same way we are familiar with the fact that all Christians have the Spirit of Christ, but not all Christians have the mind of Christ. We balk this because we do not care to go into the laboriousness of forming His mind. We all have times of inspiration and ecstasy, but in these verses our Lord is not talking of times of ecstasy but of the deliberate set of the life all through. God does His great sovereign works of grace in us, and He expects us to bring all the powers under our control into harmony with what He has done. It is an arduous and difficult task, it is not done easily; and remember, God does not do it for us. We have to transform into real thinking possession for ourselves all that the Spirit of God puts into our spirits. The last reach of spirituality is the thinking power, that is, the power to express what moves our spirits.

The Depository of Thought

> Do not lay up for yourselves treasures on earth, . . . but lay up for yourselves treasures in heaven. Matthew 6:19–20

We have to lay up treasure for ourselves, it is not laid up for us; and we have to lay it up in heaven, not on earth. To begin with, we do lay up the treasure of Jesus Christ's salvation on earth, we lay it up in our bodily lives, in our circumstances; and the curse spiritually is to lay up treasure in experience. Whatever we possess in the way of treasure on earth is liable to be consumed by moth and rust. Our Lord's counsel is to lay up treasure that never can be touched, and the place where it is laid up cannot be touched. "And made us to sit together in the heavenly places in Christ Jesus" (Ephesians 2:6). No moth nor rust in the heavenly places, no possibility of thieves breaking through there. When we lay up treasure on earth it may go at any moment, but when we learn to lay up treasure in heaven, nothing can touch it: "Therefore we will not fear, even though the earth be removed" (Psalm 46:2); it is perfectly secure.

Our Lord kept all His treasure of heart and mind and spirit in His oneness with the Father; He laid up treasure in heaven, not on earth. Our Lord never possessed anything for Himself (compare 2 Corinthians 8:9). The temptation of Satan was to get Him to lay up things in the earthly treasury, namely, in His own body, and to draw from that source: "You are the Son of God, command these stones to be made bread. . . . Throw Yourself down. For 'He shall give His angels charge over You' " (Matthew 4:3, 6). Our Lord never drew power from Himself, He drew it always from without Himself, that is, from His Father. "The Son can do nothing of Himself, but what He sees the Father do" (John 5:19). The one great inter-est in our Lord's life was God, and He was never deflected from that center by other considerations, not even by the devil himself, however subtly he came. "I and my Father are one" (John 10:30). It was a oneness not of union but of iden-tity. It was impossible to distinguish between the Father and the Son, and the same is to be true of the saint and the Savior: "that they may be one just as We are one" (John 17:22).

Examine your own experience as a saint and see where your treasure is: is it in the Lord, or in His blessings? In the degree that we possess anything for ourselves we are sepa-rated from Jesus. So many of us are caught up in the shows of things, not in the way of property and possessions but of blessings, and all our efforts to persuade ourselves that our treasure is in heaven is a sure sign that it is not. If our treasure is in heaven we do not need to persuade ourselves that it is, we prove it is by the way we deal with matters of earth. The religion of Jesus Christ is a religion of personal relationship to God and has nothing to do with possessions. A sense of possessions is sufficient to render us spiritually dense because what we possess often possesses us. Whenever our Lord spoke of "life" He meant the kind of life He lived, and He says, "you have no life in you" (John 6:53). Are we living the kind of life Jesus lived, with the skylights always open toward God, the windows of the ground floor open toward other people, and the trapdoor open toward sin and Satan and hell? Nothing was hidden from Jesus, all was faced with fearless courage because of His oneness with the Father.

> For where your treasure is, there your heart will be also. Matthew 6:21

The Bible term "heart" is best understood if we simply say "me"—it is the central citadel of human personality. The heart is the altar of which the physical body is the outer court, and whatever is offered on the altar of the heart will tell ultimately through the extremities of the body. "Keep your heart with all diligence, for out of it spring the issues of life" (Proverbs 4:23).

Where do we make our depository of thinking? What do we brood on most—the blessings of God, or God Himself? Look back over your life as a saint and you will see how the weaning has gone on from the blessing to the Blesser, from sanctification to the Sanctifier. When we no longer seek God for His blessings, we have time to seek Him for Himself.

The Division of Thinking

> The lamp of the body is the eye. If therefore your eye is good, your whole body will be full of light. Matthew 6:22

The eye records exactly what it looks at, and conscience may be called the eye of the soul. A good eye is essential to correct understanding spiritually. If the spirit is illumined by a conscience that has been rightly adjusted, then, says Jesus, the whole body is full of light because body, soul, and spirit are united in a single identity with Him. Beware of mistaking domination for identity. Identity is a oneness between two distinct persons in which neither person dominates, but the oneness dominates both. The only way this can be realized is along the line of our Lord's own life. Jesus Christ's first obedience was to the will of His Father, and our first obedience is to be to Him. The thing that detects where we live spiritually is the word *obey*. The natural human heart hates the word, and that hatred is the essence of the disposition that will not let Jesus Christ rule. The characteristic of our Lord's life was submission to His Father—not the crushing down of His own will to His Father's but the love-agreement of His will with His Father's: I am here for one thing only, to do Your will, and I delight to do it. When the Holy Spirit comes into us, the first thing He does is to make us women and men with a single motive, a good eye for the glory of God. The essential element in the life of a saint is simplicity: "your whole body will be full of light."

> But if your eye is bad, your whole body will be full of darkness.
> Matthew 6:23

What is a bad eye? Thinking that springs from our own point of view. "Is your eye evil because I am good?" (Matthew 20:15). Jesus says that if the eye is bad, we shall misjudge what He does. If our spirits are untouched by God's Spirit, unillumined by God, the very light we have will become darkness. The disposition of the natural man, my claim to my right to myself, banks on things of which our Lord makes nothing—for example, possessions, rights, self-realization; and if that disposition rules, it will cause the whole body to be full of darkness. Darkness in this connection is our own point of view; light is God's point of view (compare 1 John 1:7).

We deal much too lightly with sin; we deal with sin only in its gross actual form and rarely deal with it in its possessing form. "I would not have known sin except through the law. For I would not have known covetousness unless the law had said, 'You shall not covet' " (Romans 7:7). This inheritance of covetousness is the very essence of sin, and the only thing that can touch it is the atonement of our Lord Jesus Christ. It is an aspect of sin that is not familiar to us. We must never lay the flattering unction to our souls that because we are not covetous of money or worldly possessions we are not covetous of anything. Whatever we possess for ourselves is of the nature of sin. The fuss and distress of owning anything is the last remnant of the disposition of sin; whatever we own as Christians apart from Jesus Christ is a chance for the devil.

The Decisions of the Thinker

> No one can serve two masters. . . . You cannot serve God and mammon. Matthew 6:24.

Have we allowed these inexorable decisions of our Lord to have their powerful way in our thinking? The line of detachment runs all through our Lord's teaching: You cannot be good and bad at the same time, you cannot serve God and make your own out of the service; you cannot make "honesty is the best policy" a motive, because as soon as you do, you cease to be honest. There is to be only one consideration—a right relationship with God—and we must see that that relationship is never dimmed. Never compromise with the spirit of mammon. It is easy to associate mammon only with sordid things; mammon is the system of civilized life that organizes itself without any consideration of God (compare Luke 16:15).

To be detached from our possessions is the greatest evidence that we are beginning to form the mind of Christ. If it is possible to conceive being caused sore distress through the withdrawal of any particular form of blessing, it is a sure sign that we are still trying to serve two masters. For instance, can we say not with our lips but with our whole souls: "For I could wish that I myself were accursed from Christ for my brethren" (Romans 9:3)? Have we for one second gotten hold of the spirit that was in Paul when he said that, the very spirit of Jesus? Neither fear of hell nor hope of heaven has anything to do with our personal relationship to Jesus Christ, it is a life hidden with Christ in God, stripped of all possessions except the knowledge of Him. The great Lodestar of the life is Jesus Himself, not anything He does for us.

This kind of thinking is impossible until we are spiritual, and when we become spiritual we realize how completely our thinking has been reconstructed. Watch God's method of teaching us to think along the lines He has taken our spirits by His grace. In the initial stages we learn that we cannot serve two masters by recognizing the disposition that Paul calls "the carnal mind" and are only too passionately grateful to come to the place where we know that that disposition is identified with the death of Jesus (see Romans 6:6). No wonder Paul says "the carnal mind is enmity against God" (Romans 8:7); he does not say it is "at enmity," it is enmity against God. The carnal mind is the kin of the devil; it is all right until you bring it in contact with Jesus, but as soon as you do it is a chip off the old block, it hates with an intense vehemence everything to do with Jesus Christ and His Spirit. My right to myself is the carnal mind in essence, and we need a clear-thinking view of what it means to be delivered from this disposition. It means that just as our personalities used to exhibit ruling dispositions identical with the prince of this world, so the same personalities can now exhibit identity with the Lord Jesus Christ. Sanctification means that and nothing less. Sanctification is not once for all but once for always. Sanctification is an instantaneous, continuous work of grace. If we think of sanctification as an experience once for all, there is an element of finality about it; we begin the hop, skip, and jump testimony, "Bless God, I am saved and sanctified," and from that second we begin to get "sanctified." Sanctification means we have the glorious opportunity of proving daily, hourly, momentarily this identity with Jesus Christ, and the life bears an unmistakable likeness to Him. The religion of Jesus Christ makes a person united; we are never meant to develop one part of our beings at the cost of another part. When someone is united with Jesus He garrisons every part, "and the wicked one does not touch him" (1 John 5:18).

Another way by which we learn that we cannot serve two masters is by putting away the aim of successful service forever. When the Seventy returned with joy, our Lord said, in effect, "Don't rejoice that the demons are subject to you, that is My authority through you; but rejoice that you are rightly related to Me" (see Luke 10:20). It is sadly true that after an experience of sanctification many do try to serve two masters, they go into the joy of successful service, and slowly the eye becomes fixed on the sanctified "show business" instead of on Jesus Himself. The only illustrations our Lord used of service were those of the vine (John 15:1–6) and the rivers of living water (John 7:37–39). It is inconceivable to think of the vine delighting in its own grapes; all that the vine is conscious of is the vinedresser's pruning knife. All that the one out of whom rivers of living water are flowing is conscious of is belief in Jesus and maintaining a right relationship to Him. Are we bringing forth fruit? We certainly are if we are identified with the Lord—luscious bunches of grapes for the Vinedresser to do what He likes with. Pay attention to the Source, believe in Jesus, and God will look after the outflow. God grant we may let the Holy Spirit work out His passion for souls through us. We have not to imitate Jesus by having a passion for souls like His but to let the Holy Spirit so identify us with Jesus that His mind is expressed through us as He expressed the mind of God.

Do we recognize Jesus Christ as our Teacher, or are we being led by vague spiritual impulses of our own? We have to learn to bring into captivity every thought to the obedience of Christ and never be intellectually insubordinate. The teaching of Jesus Christ fits every point of a saint's life, but no point of the life of a natural man. If we apply these statements: "Seek first the kingdom of God and His righteousness" (Matthew 6:33); "Do not worry about your life" (v. 25)—to the life of a natural man, they are open to ridicule. We reverse God's order when we put Jesus as a Teacher first instead of Savior; but when we are rightly related to God on the basis of the Atonement and begin to put Jesus Christ's teaching into practice, the marvel of marvels is we find it can be worked out. If we as saints are strenuously seeking first the kingdom of God and His righteousness, His "in-the-rightness," all the time, we shall find not only the divine unreason of things, but the divine reason of things working out beyond all our calculations: "and all these things shall be added to you" (v. 33), "For your heavenly Father knows that you need all these things" (v. 32).

Never allow anything to fuss your relationship to Jesus Christ, neither Christian work nor Christian blessing nor Christian anything. Jesus Christ first, second, and third, and God Himself, by the great indwelling power of the Spirit within, will meet the strenuous effort on your part, and slowly and surely you will form the mind of Christ and become one with Him as He was one with the Father. The practical test is: "Is Jesus Christ being manifested in my bodily life?"

Education in Holy Habit

Psalm 86:11; 143:10

Educative Evangelism versus Emotional Evangelism

After a great crisis, such as an experience of salvation or sanctification, the danger is that we fix ourselves there and become spiritual prigs. A spiritual prig is one who has had an experience from God and has closed down on it, there is no further progress, no manifestation of the graces of the Spirit. The world pours contempt on that kind of Christian; he or she seems to have very little conscience, no judgment, and little will. We have to remember that unless we are energized by the Spirit of God, the margins of our spirits retain the damage done by the Fall.

By the Fall, human beings not only died from God but fell into disunion within themselves; that means it became possible for people to live in one of the three parts of human nature. What happens at new birth is that a soul is not only introduced into a relationship to God but into union with itself. The one thing that is essential to the new life is obedience to the Spirit of God who energizes our spirits, and that obedience must be complete in body, soul, and spirit. It is not done suddenly. Salvation is sudden, but the working out of it in our lives is never sudden. It is moment by moment, here a little and there a little. God educates us down to the smallest detail. The area of the conscious life gradually gets broader and broader, and we begin to bring into line with the new life things we never thought of before.

We have to remember that we have a bodily machine that we must regulate—God does not regulate it for us. Until we learn to bring the bodily machine into harmony with God's will, there will be friction, and the friction is a warning that part of the machine is not in working order. As we bring the bodily life into line bit by bit, we shall find that we have God's marvelous grace on the inside enabling us to work out what He has worked in.

The Habit of a Refined Conscience

Teach me Your way, O Lord. Psalm 86:11

Conscience is that power in a person's soul that fixes on what she or he regards as the highest. Never call conscience the voice of God. If it were, it would be the most contradictory voice humanity ever listened to. For instance, Saul of Tarsus obeyed his conscience when he hounded men and women to death for worshiping Jesus Christ, and he also obeyed his conscience when later on in his life he acted in exactly the opposite way (see John 16:2; Acts 26:9).

(a) Regulated after Sin

I thank Christ Jesus our Lord, . . . because He counted me faithful, putting me into the ministry, although I was formerly a blasphemer, a persecutor, and an insolent man. . . . And the grace of our Lord was exceedingly abundant. 1 Timothy 1:12–15

After the disposition of sin is removed there is the need for conscience to be regulated. The Spirit of God always begins by repairing the damage after sin. The apostle Paul argues in Romans 6, "You did use your members as slaves of the wrong disposition, now use them as slaves of the right disposition" (v. 19, paraphrase). It is a long way to go and many of us faint in the way. After a great spiritual crisis one's conscience looks out toward God in a new light, the light that Jesus Christ throws upon God, and one has to walk in that light and bring one's bodily life into harmony with what one's conscience records.

Sin is the disposition of my right to myself, and it is also independence of God. These two aspects of sin are strikingly brought out in the Bible. Sin has to be dealt with from the ethical and intellectual aspect as well as from the spiritual aspect. The way sin works in connection with the life of the soul is in independence of God. Many people are never guilty of gross sins, they are not brought up in that way, they are too refined, have too much good taste; but that does not mean that the disposition to sin is not there. The essence of sin is my claim to my right to myself. I may prefer to live morally because it is better for me; I am responsible to no one, my conscience is my god. That is the very essence of sin. The true characteristic of sin is seen when we compare ourselves with Jesus Christ. We may feel quite happy and contented as long as we compare ourselves with other people, because we are all pretty much the same, but when we stand before Jesus Christ we realize what He meant when He said, "If I had not come. . . they would have no sin, . . . but now they have no excuse for their sin" (John 15:22).

There is a difference between a refined conscience toward God and the fussy conscience of a hyperconscientious person without the Spirit of God. Hyperconscientious people are an absolute plague to live with, they are morally and spiritually nervous, always in terror expecting something to happen, always expecting trials—and trials always come. Jesus Christ was never morally or spiritually nervous any more than He was physically nervous. The refinement of conscience in a Christian means learning to walk in accordance with the life of the Lord Jesus, drawing from God as He did. It is a life of absolute largeness and freedom.

(b) Restored after Prejudice

> My manner of life from my youth . . . all the Jews know. . . . I
> lived a Pharisee. Acts 26:4–5

Prejudice means a foreclosed judgment without sufficiently weighing the evidence. When first we get right with
God we are all prejudiced, ugly, and distorted. When we
come up against a prejudice we are stubborn and obstinate,
and God leaves us alone; then the prejudice comes up again,
and God waits, until at last we say, "I see," and we learn how
to be restored after our prejudices. Wherever there is a prejudice, the grace of God is hammering at it to break it down.
The havoc in lives that are going on with God is accounted
for because they are being restored after prejudice. Wherever you find a prejudice in yourself, take it to Jesus Christ.
Our Lord is the only standard for prejudice, as He is the only
standard for sin. Our Lord never worked from prejudice,
never foreclosed His judgment without weighing the evidence. Are we letting God restore us after prejudice, or are
we tied up in compartments?

"I have always worshiped God in this way and I always
intend to." Be careful!

"I have always believed this and that, and I always shall."
Be careful!

It is easier to be true to convictions formed in a vivid religious experience than to be true to Jesus Christ, because if
we are going to be true to Jesus Christ our convictions have
to be altered. Unless our experiences lead us on to a life, they
will turn us into fossils; we will become mummified gramo-
phones of convictions instead of "witnesses to Me" (Acts
1:8). Some of us are no good unless we are placed in the circumstances in which our convictions were formed, but God
continually stirs up our circumstances and flings us out, to
make us know that the only simplicity is not the simplicity of

a logical belief but of a maintained relationship with Jesus Christ, and that is never altered in any circumstances. We must keep in unbroken touch with God by faith and see that we give other souls the same freedom and liberty that God gives us. The duty of every Christian—and it is the last lesson we learn—is to make room for God to deal with other people direct; we will try and limit others and make them into our molds.

(c) Roused after Compromise

> You are witnesses, and God also, how devoutly and justly and blamelessly we behaved ourselves among you . . . as we exhorted, and comforted, and charged every one of you . . . that you would walk worthy of God. 1 Thessalonians 2:10–12.

In the temptation of our Lord the compromise for good ends is pictured, "Don't be so stern against sin; compromise judiciously with evil and You will easily win Your kingship of humanity." When we become rightly related to God our intellects are apt to say exactly the same thing, "Don't be narrow; don't be so pronounced against worldliness, you will upset your friends." Well, upset them, but never upset the main thing that God is after. There is always the tendency to compromise, and we have to be roused up to recognize it. We have to walk in very narrow paths before God can trust us to walk in the wide ones. We have to be limited before we can be unlimited.

The Bible nowhere teaches us to be uncompromising in our opinions. Jesus did not say, Leap for joy when people separate you from their company for the sake of your convictions; He said, "Blessed are you when men hate you, and when they exclude you, and revile you, and cast out your name as evil, for the Son of Man's sake. Rejoice in that day and leap for joy!" (Luke 6:22–23). I may be such a pigheaded crosspatch and have such determined notions of my own that no one can live with me. That is not suffering for the Son of Man's sake, it is suffering for my own sake. Never compromise with anything that would detract from the honor of the Lord. Remember that the honor of Jesus is at stake in your bodily life and rouse yourself up to act accordingly.

The Habit of Reliable Judgment

Teach me to do Your will. Psalm 143:10

Our consciences may be right toward God, and yet we may err in judgment. When the disposition has been perfectly adjusted toward God, it does not mean we have perfectly adjusted bodies and brains; we have the same bodies and brains as before and we have to bring them into line until we form the judgment that is according to Jesus Christ. Many of us are impulsive spiritually, and we live to be sorry for it. We have to form the habit of reliable judgment. God never gives someone reliable judgment; He gives a disposition that leads to perfect judgment if one will work out that disposition.

(a) The Disciplined Imagination

Bringing every thought into captivity to the obedience of Christ. 2 Corinthians 10:5

We have to practice the submitting of our intelligence to Jesus Christ in His Word. The imagination of a saint too often is vague and intractable. We have to learn to bring every thought and imagination into captivity to the obedience of Christ. An undisciplined imagination will destroy reliable judgment more quickly even than sin. Mental and spiritual insubordination is the mark of today. Jesus Christ submitted His intelligence to His Father. Do I submit my intelligence to Jesus Christ and His Word?

(b) The Illuminated Judgment

> Judge nothing before the time, until the Lord comes.
> 1 Corinthians 4:5

We have to learn to see things from Jesus Christ's standpoint. Our judgment is warped in every particular in which we do not allow it to be illuminated by Jesus Christ. For instance, if we listen to what our Lord says about money we shall see how we disbelieve Him. We quietly ignore all He says, He is so unpractical, so utterly stupid, from the modern standpoint. "Seek first the kingdom of God and His righteousness, and all these things shall be added to you" (Matthew 6:33). Which one of us believes that? If we are the children of God He will bring us into circumstances where we will be tested on every line to see whether we will form the habit of reliable judgment.

We have to learn to see things from Jesus Christ's standpoint. He says, "All authority has been given to Me" (Matthew 28:18). The illumination of judgment comes personally when we recognize that the evil and wrong in our spheres of life is there not by accident but in order that the power of God may come in contact with it as His power has come into us. When we come into contact with objectionable people, the first natural impulse of the heart is to ask God to save them because they are trials to us; He will never do it for that reason. But when we come to see those lives from Jesus Christ's standpoint and realize that He loves them as He loves us, we have a different relationship to them, and God can have His way in their lives in answer to our prayers.

(c) The Resourcefulness of Tact

> I have made myself a servant to all. . . . I have become all things
> to all men . . . for the gospel's sake. 1 Corinthians 9:19–23

It is instructive to notice the way our Lord dealt with different people. In every case where He did not find bigotry He won them immediately. When we first become rightly related to God we have the idea that we have to talk to everyone, until we get one or two well-deserved snubs, then our Lord takes us aside and teaches us His way of dealing with them. How impatient we are in dealing with others! Our attitudes imply that we think God is asleep. When we begin to reason and work in God's way, He reminds us, first of all, how long it took Him to get us where we are, and we realize His amazing patience and we learn to come on other lives from above. As we learn to rely on the Spirit of God He gives us the resourcefulness of Jesus.

The Habit of a Rectified Will

Unite my heart to fear Your name. Psalm 86:11

Never look upon the will as something you possess as you do a watch. Will is the whole human being active. Education in holy habit is along this line: at first we pray "Teach me Your way, O LORD" (v. 11), then we pray, "Teach me to do Your will" (Psalm 143:10), and step by step God teaches us what is His will; then comes a great burst of joy, "I delight to do Your will" (Psalm 40:8)! There is nothing on earth I delight in more than in Your will. When we become rightly related to God we are the will of God in disposition, and we have to work out God's will; it is the freest, most natural life imaginable. Worldly people imagine that the saints must find it difficult to live with so many restrictions, but the bondage is with the world not with the saints. There is no such thing as freedom in the world, and the higher we go in the social life the more bondage there is. True liberty exists only where the soul has the holy scorn of the Holy Spirit—I will bow my neck to no yoke but the yoke of the Lord Jesus Christ; there is only one law, and that is the law of God.

(a) The Joy of Jesus

> These things I have spoken to you, that My joy may remain in
> you, and that your joy may be full. John 15:11

The joy of Jesus lay in knowing that every power of His
nature was in such harmony with His Father that He did His
Father's will with delight. Some of us are slow to do God's
will; we do it as if our shoes were iron and lead; we do it
with a great sigh and with the corners of our mouths down,
as if His will were the most arduous thing on earth. But
when our wills are rectified and brought into harmony with
God, it is a delight, a superabounding joy, to do God's will.
Talk to saints about suffering and they look at you in amazement—"Suffering? Where does it come in?" It comes in on
God's side along the line of interpretation; on the side of the
saint it is an overwhelming delight in God—not delight in
suffering, but if God's will should lead through suffering,
there is delight in His will.

(b) The Bent of Obedience

> You are My friends if you do whatever I command you. John
> 15:14

Each one of us has to rule, to exercise some authority.
When we have learned the obedience to God that was manifested in our Lord, we shall govern the world. Self-chosen
authority is an impertinence. Jesus said that the great ones in
this world exercise authority but that in His kingdom it is
not so; no one exercises authority over another because in
His kingdom the King is Servant of all (see Luke 22:24–27).
If a saint tries to exercise authority it is a proof that she or he
is not rightly related to Jesus Christ. The characteristic of a
saint's life is this bent of obedience, no notion of authority
anywhere about it. If we begin to say "I have been put in this
position and I have to exercise authority," God will soon

remove us. When there is steadfast obedience to Jesus, it is the authority of God that comes through, and other souls obey at once.

(c) The Stage of Rare Fruition

> I am the vine, you are the branches. He who abides in Me, and I in him, bears much fruit; for without Me you can do nothing. . . . By this My Father is glorified, that you bear much fruit; so you will be My disciples. John 15:5, 8

These verses refer to the stage of fruition—bringing forth fruit and the fruit remaining—that is what glorifies God and blesses others. If we as preachers or teachers are rightly related to God in obedience, God is continually pouring through us. When we stop obeying Him, everything becomes as hard and dry as a ditch in midsummer. When we are placed in a position by God and we keep rightly related to Him, He will see to the supply. Personally, whenever there is dryness I know that it is because I am forgetting some particular point in relation to my own life with God; when that is put right the flow is unhindered, and I believe this is true in every phase of work for God. If you are called to preach, preach; if you are called to teach, teach. Keep obedient to God on that line. The proof that you are on God's line is that other people never credit you with what comes through you. Jesus said, "Let your light so shine before men, that they may see your good works, and glorify your Father in heaven" (Matthew 5:16). Go on doing God's will, and you will be recreated while you do it.

The Philosophy of Sin

The Philosophy of Sin

Departure from God's love is the common nature of all sin; and
when the departure from this love was associated with a desire
to progress in the direction of a selfishly appointed end, rather
than of the end divinely appointed, this was the common nature
of the primal sin of the world-spirit and of humanity.

The Bible is the only Book that tells us anything about the
originator of sin. There is a difference between an experimental knowledge of sin and an intellectual understanding of
what sin is. We seem to be built on the following plan: at
first we experience a need, then we hunt for the satisfaction
of that need; when the need is supplied we turn the whole
nature in the direction of an explanation of how the need
was supplied. When we are convicted of sin, we are convicted of the need of a Savior, and we seek for the Savior
intellectually and in various other ways till we meet with our
Lord by the power of His Spirit and experience salvation;
then comes the great need we are trying to insist on in these
talks, the need of turning the whole nature to understand
how God supplied the need. That is what Christians are
neglecting; they have the experience but they have left their
minds to stagnate, they have not turned back again and tried
to find out what God reveals about sin, about salvation, and
about the whole human life. According to the Bible, God is
only manifested at the last point; when someone is driven by
personal experience to the last limit, he or she is apt to meet
God. The same thing is true in thinking; we can do very well
without God in thinking as long as we think only as splendid
animals. As long as we are not at the last place, not facing our

problems at all, but simply pleased to be in existence, pleased to be healthy and happy, we will never find God—we do not see any need for Him. But when we are driven in thinking to the last limit, then we begin to find that God manifests Himself there. To people who are satisfied on too shallow a level the Bible is a book of impertinences, but whenever human nature is driven to the end of things, then the Bible becomes the only Book and God the only Being in the world.

The Masked Origin of Satan's Primal Sin

Isaiah 14:12–15

We are dealing not so much with the experience of sin as with the light God's Word throws on how sin began; we must have a basis for thinking. If we have been delivered from sin by the power of God within us, thank God for it; but there is something more than that—we have now to allow God to illuminate our darkness by His revelation.

We take this passage in Isaiah as the early Christian fathers did, as an exposition of Satan behind his material puppets. One of the significant things the Bible reveals about Satan is that he rarely works without being incarnated (see Genesis 3:15 and Matthew 16:23). God's Spirit and our Lord trace Satan behind men and women who are really time-manifestations of Satan. That is the region in which we are to look for the obscure origin of sin; it does not look as if sin came in that way at all. Only when we are driven to extremes do we realize that the Bible is the only Book that gives us any indication of the true nature of sin and where it came from.

(a) Marvelous Originator of Sin

> How are you fallen from heaven, O Lucifer, son of the morning!
> Isaiah 14:12

An angel next in power to God is revealed to be the originator of sin.

(b) Mystic Order of Revolt

> You have said in your heart: "I will ascend into heaven, I will exalt my throne above the stars of God." verse 13

In this verse the mystic order of Satan's revolt is revealed, it was a purely spiritual revolt against God.

(c) Mad Outrival of God

> I will ascend above the heights of the clouds, I will be like the Most High. verse 14

This verse shows a determination to rival God.

These three points are nonsense unless we are driven to the last limit. The fact that people ridicule the belief in Satan and sin is simply an indication of the principle we have laid down, that we do not see God till we get to the last point, and His Word has no meaning for us until we get there, but when the human soul is driven to the last lap of trying to find out things, then the Bible becomes the only Book there is, and this "theory," as people call it, is seen to be the revelation of God about the origin of sin. Sin is that factor in human nature which has a supernatural originator who stands next to God in power. The sin of Satan is revealed only dimly, but the dim outline indicates that it was the summit of all sin, full, free, conscious, spiritual sin; he was not entrapped into it, he was not ensnared into it, he sinned with the full clear under-standing of what he was doing. We know that much; so far the veil is transparent.

The Masked Outguards of Satan's Primal Snare

Genesis 3:6–7

Satan guards the main body of his purpose; neither Eve nor Adam had the slightest notion who he was; he was as far removed in his first snare from his real body of intent as could possibly be. We have to remember that God created

Adam "a son of God," and God required Adam to develop himself by obeying Him; that obedience necessarily involved the sacrifice of the natural life to transform it into spiritual life, and this was to be done by a series of moral choices. Satan lays his first snare there, the first outguard of his snare is away altogether from the main body of his purpose, he does not reveal what he is after in the beginning.

(a) Soul Stained by Natural Interest

> When the woman saw that the tree was good for food, that it was pleasant to the eyes, and a tree desirable to make one wise, she took of its fruit and ate. Genesis 3:6

Verse 6 reveals that Satan was part of God's natural creation, he spoke to the woman first, who represented all we understand by the affinities of a human soul for the natural life, unsuspecting, unsuspicious, sympathetic and curious. In looking at sin in its beginnings, we find its true nature in all its working. Our Lord spoke about people as sheep; sheep have no set, conscious purpose to go wrong, they simply wander, and our Lord used the illustration for people; the majority of people wander like sheep, without any conscious bad intent at all. That is the first outwork or outguard of Satan, he gets us all here like silly, stupid sheep; he has never altered his way of working, and although it is written clearly in God's Book, we never seem to be forewarned that the soul is stained through natural interest.

(b) Soul Snared by Natural Intimacy

> The woman saw that the tree was good for food. . . . She took of its fruit and ate. She also gave to her husband with her, and he ate.

The two intimacies indicated in verse 6 are, first, intimacy with the object desired, and, second, intimacy with the closest vital relationship; when Eve saw the food was good she fetched her husband. To sin alone is never possible. In writing of Eve, Paul says that Satan deceived her, meaning by that that there was no clear understanding on her part of the wrong she had done; but "Adam was not deceived" (1 Timothy 2:14). "He ate." Adam's sin was the perfect, conscious realization of what he was doing.

(c) Soul Sin by Natural Influence

> The eyes of both of them were opened, and they knew that they were naked; and they sewed fig leaves together and made themselves coverings. Genesis 3:7

Adam was required by God to take part in his own development, that is, he had to transform the life of nature into the spiritual life by obeying God. The life of nature is neither moral nor immoral; our bodies are neither moral nor immoral, we make them moral or immoral. Our Lord had a body, and we read that He hungered; it was not a sin for Him to be hungry, but it would have been a sin for Him to have eaten during the forty days in the wilderness, because His Father's word at that time was that He should not eat. It is not a sin to have a body, to have natural appetites, but it is a sin to refuse to sacrifice them at the word of God. Satan's first fundamental outguards are in the innocence of nature. We say, "But it cannot be wrong to have a little sympathy here, a little curiosity there"; the Bible lifts the veil just enough to show there is a great supernatural force behind that entices for one purpose, to get us away from obeying God's voice.

The Masked Overset of Spiritual Surrender

Genesis 3:1–7

Satan succeeded in putting his outguards so far away from the main body of his purpose that no one but God Himself knew what he was doing. Unsuspecting Eve was as far removed from understanding what Satan was doing as we are when we sin, but where both are culpable in every respect is in the refusal to obey God, and whenever there is a refusal to obey God, instantly Satan's first snare is entered into. When once the first snare has caught us, we are done for, the rest is as easy as can be; once let the principle of refusing to sacrifice the life of nature to the will of God have way, and all the rest happens easily.

(a) Infused Suspicion of the Innermost

Has God indeed said, 'You shall not eat of every tree of the garden'? Genesis 3:1

It was the internal region of being, the innermost, that yielded first, bodily action was last; the first thing that yielded was the mind. The Bible reveals that human nature possesses an incurable suspicion of God. Its origin is explained in the Bible; two great primal creatures of God, the angel who became Satan, and Adam, negotiated a relationship that God never sanctioned. That was how sin was introduced into the world. As long as we live on the surface of things merely as splendid animals, we shall find the Bible nonsense. We are reverent over the Bible simply because our fathers and mothers taught us to be reverent, but we find no practical reason for reverence until we get to the last lap, until we are pressed out of the outer court into the inner, then we find there is no human mind that has ever penned words that are sufficient for us there; we begin to find that the only Book there is the Bible. When we get to the last point the only exact counterpart for the natural life is this Book.

When the Bible touches the question of sin, it always comes right down to this incurable suspicion of God that never can be altered apart from the Atonement because it is connected with a great supernatural power behind. Paul talks about it and calls it the "carnal mind"; he does not say it is at enmity with God, because that might mean it could be cured; he says it "is enmity against God" (Romans 8:7). Remember the summit of all sin was a conscious, red-handed revolt against God. Adam's sin was not a conscious revolt against God; it worked out ultimately through the race as a revolt against God, but Adam's sin, instead of being at the summit of all sin, is at the foundation of all sin. Consequently whatever sin you take, you will get the characteristics that were in this first sin, namely, the principle and the disposition of this infused suspicion, "Has God indeed said." Absolute devastation awaits the soul that allows suspicion to creep in. Suspicion of God is like a gap in a dike: the flood rushes through, nothing can stop it. The first thing you will do is to accept slanders against God. Because it is peculiar to you? No, because it is according to the stock that runs right straight through the human race, from this first sin of infused suspicion in the intelligence, in the innermost part of humankind.

The majority of us prefer to trust our innocence rather than the statements of Jesus. It is always risky to trust your innocence when the statements of Jesus are contrary to it. Jesus says that "from within, out of the heart of men, proceed . . ." (Mark 7:21), then comes the awful catalogue. You say, "Why, that is nonsense, I never had any of those things in my heart, I am innocent." Someday you will come up against a set of circumstances that will prove that your innocence was a figment and that what Jesus said about the human heart was perfectly true.

(b) Irresistible Sensuality of the Inner

You will be like God. Genesis 3:5

Once allow suspicion of God and of His goodness and justice to enter into a person's mind and the floodgates of sensuality are opened. We mean by *sensuality* the life that draws its sustenance from natural surroundings, guided by a selfishly appointed purpose. We used to mean by *sensuality* gross awful and shocking sins; the word means that but a great deal more. Sensuality may be refined down to the thinness of a cloud. It is quite possible to be grossly sensual and spiritual. It is possible to say, "I have one desire in being good, in being saved and sanctified, a particular end of my own"; that is sensuality. Once suspicion of God is allowed to come in, there is no limit to the flood of sensuality. *Lust*, too, is a word that the Bible uses in a different way. We use the word *lust* for the gross abominable sins of the flesh only, but the Bible uses it for a great deal more than that. Lust simply means, "I must have this at once"; it may be a bodily appetite or a spiritual possession. The principle lust works on is, "I must have it at once, I cannot wait for God's time, God is too indifferent," that is the way lust works. Watch how our Lord faced people, He always faced this disposition of sin, He never summed people up by their external conduct. He was not driven into panics by immorality and fleshly sordidness— that sort of sin never seemed to bother Him half as much as the respectable pride of men and women who never were guilty of those things. The mainspring of such lives is a wise, judicious working that keeps all outward circumstances in harmony with the one ruling desire. The soul, remember, is simply the spirit of a person expressing itself. The spirit of a child can rarely express itself, the soul has not become articulate. *Soul* in the Bible nearly always refers to the fleshly nature, it is the only power one has for expressing one's true spirit. "God is always manifested in the ultimates" (Goethe). That is what we mean by saying that God is only revealed at the last point. If we are only living on the surface of things, the Bible line will appear stupid, but if we have had a dose of the plague of our own hearts and realize what God has delivered us from, we know much too much ever to accept a human definition of sin, we know that there is no other

explanation than the Bible one, and nothing but pity is awakened when we hear people trying to explain sin apart from
the Bible.

(c) Iniquitous Succumbing of the Individual

Then the eyes of both of them were opened. verse 7

Iniquitous means an unjust and unequal twisting, and *individual* means here the whole person going out in a definite
act. Suspicion first, sensuality next, and manifest ruin last. If
sin is a radical twist with a supernatural originator, salvation
is a radical readjustment with a supernatural Originator. To
present salvation as less than that is deplorable. If all Jesus
Christ can do is to run a parallel counteraction with what
Satan can do, His right name is Culture, not Savior; but His
revealed nature was stated by the angel to Mary and
repeated over and over again, "You shall call His name Jesus,
for He will save His people from their sins" (Matthew 1:21).
The slight views of salvation, the sympathetic drifty views
that all Jesus Christ can do is to put in us a principle that
counteracts another principle, will cause anyone who has got
to the last limit to blaspheme God for a thing like that. It all
comes from a flimsy, wrong view of sin. If that is all He can
do, what is the good of calling Him Savior? No one who has
ever faced sin in its reality would ever give one cent for that
kind of salvation, it is nothing but the exalting of education;
culture will do that, or cunning. When you come to the New
Testament and to your own experience you find that salvation is as radical as sin, and if God has not radically altered
your heredity, thank God you may know He can by the
power of Jesus Christ's atonement. It is only the right view
of sin and right thinking about sin that ever will explain Jesus
Christ's life and death and resurrection. It is sin that He came
to cope with; He did not come to cope with the poor little

mistakes of women and of men—they cope with their own mistakes; He came to give them a totally new stock of heredity, that is, He came to implant into them His own nature, so that Satan's power in the soul is absolutely destroyed, not counteracted.

When God has put His Spirit in you and identified you with Jesus Christ, what is to be your attitude to your bodily life? You have the same body, the same appetites, and the same nature as before, your members used to be slaves of sin; but Jesus Christ is your example now. He sacrificed Himself to His Father's will—see that you do the same as a saint. He submitted His intelligence to His Father's will—see that you do the same as a saint. He submitted His will to His Father—see that you as a saint do the same. Jesus Christ did all that Adam failed to do. Satan met our Lord with his masked outguards exactly as he met Adam, and the Spirit of God drove Jesus into the wilderness to meet these outguards of Satan. "If You are the Son of God . . ." (see Matthew 4:4–11). Satan tried to insinuate the first suspicion, but it would not work, Jesus refused to be suspicious of God. He overcame by obeying the word of His Father, that is, He transformed His natural life into a spiritual life by obeying the voice of God, and as saints we have to obey Jesus Christ and sacrifice the life of nature to His will.

Educative Insight
into Redemption

How much more shall the blood of Christ, who through the eternal Spirit offered Himself without spot to God, cleanse your conscience from dead works to serve the living God? Hebrews 9:14

True to the Cross

As we go on with God, the Holy Spirit brings us back more and more to the one absorbing theme of the New Testament, namely, the death of the Lord Jesus Christ and its meaning from His standpoint. Our right to ourselves in every shape and form was destroyed once and forever by the death of Jesus, and we have to be educated into the realization of what this means in all its fullness. We have to come to a relationship to the Cross in thought as well as in life.

How much more . . .

How much more is there to know, for instance, after sanctification? Everything! Before sanctification we know nothing, we are simply put in the place of knowing; that is, we are led up to the Cross; in sanctification we are led through the Cross—for what purpose? For a life of outpouring service to God. The characteristic of saints after identification with the death of Jesus is that they are brought down from the ineffable glory of the heavenly places into the valley, to be crushed and broken in service for God. We are here with no right to ourselves, for no spiritual blessing for ourselves; we are here for one purpose only—to be made servants of God, as Jesus was. Have we as saints allowed ourselves to be brought face-to-face with this great truth? The death of Jesus not only gives us remission from our sins, it enables us to assimilate the very nature of Jesus, until in every detail of our lives we are like Him. "How much more" does the death of Jesus mean to us today than it ever has before? Are we beginning to be lost in wonder, love and praise at the marvelous loosening from sin, and are we so assimilating the nature of Jesus that we bear a strong family likeness to Him?

shall the blood of Christ . . .

It was not the blood of a martyr, not the blood of goats and calves, that was shed, but "the blood of Christ." The very life of God was shed for the world: "the church of God which He purchased with His own blood" (Acts 20:28). All the perfections of the essential nature of God were in that blood; all the holiest attainments of humanity were in that blood. The death of Jesus reaches away down underneath the deepest sin human nature ever committed. This aspect of the death of Jesus takes us into a spiritual domain beyond the threshold of the thinking of the majority of us. The cry on the Cross, "My God, My God, why have You forsaken Me?" (Matthew 27:46; Mark 15:34) is unfathomable to us. The only ones—and I want to say this very deliberately—the only ones who come near the threshold of understanding the cry of Jesus are not the martyrs—they knew that God had not forsaken them, His presence was so wonderful; not the lonely missionaries who are killed or forsaken—they experience exultant joy, for God is with them when people forsake them; the only ones who come near the threshold of understanding the experience of God-forsakenness are people like Cain: "My punishment is greater than I can bear!" (Genesis 4:13); people like Esau: "He cried with an exceedingly great and bitter cry" (27:34); people like Judas. Jesus Christ knew and tasted to a fuller depth than any human being could ever taste what it is to be separated from God by sin. If Jesus Christ was a martyr, our salvation is a myth. We have followed cunningly devised fables if Jesus Christ is not all that this cry represents Him to be—the Incarnate God becoming identified with sin in order to save people from hell and damnation. The depth of this cry of Jesus is deeper than anyone can go because it is a cry from the heart of God. The height and depth of our salvation are only measured by God almighty on His throne and Jesus Christ in the heart of hell. The most devout among us are too flippant about this great subject of the death of Jesus Christ. When we stand before the Cross, is every commonplace pious mood stripped off, or do we get caught up by the modern spirit and think of the Cross only as delivering us from sin or as a type of sanctification? Thank God for salvation through the Cross, for sanctification through the Cross, but thank God also for insight into what it cost God to make that salvation and sanctification possible. God grant that the pulsing power of identification with the death of Jesus may come again into our testimonies and make them glow with devotion to Him for His unspeakable salvation.

Who through the eternal Spirit . . .

The life of Jesus portrays the handiwork of the Holy Spirit; we know what the Holy Spirit will be in us if we let Him have His way. The underlying consciousness of Jesus was the eternal God Himself; the eternal Spirit was behind all He did. It is not so with us. There is a fundamental difference as well as a similarity between the Spirit in Jesus and the Spirit in us. The eternal Spirit was incarnated in Jesus; He never is in us. By regeneration and sanctification He energizes our spirits and brings us into oneness with Jesus Christ, so that the underlying consciousness is "hidden with Christ in God" (Colossians 3:3). We are only made acceptable to God by relying on the eternal Spirit who was incarnated absolutely in Jesus Christ. The Spirit in us will never allow us to forget that the death of Jesus was the death of God Incarnate. "God was in Christ reconciling the world to Himself" (2 Corinthians 5:19).

offered Himself without spot to God . . .

Who offered Himself? The Son of God. He was immaculate, without spot, yet He was crucified. This rules out once and forever the conception that Jesus died the death of a martyr; He died a death no martyr could touch. He died the death not of a good person but of a bad person, with the vicarious pain of almighty God in His heart.

Our hearts are wrung with pathos when we read of the offering of Isaac and the sacrifice of Jephthah's daughter, for they are unbearably pathetic. The offering of Jesus is not pathetic in the tiniest degree—it is beyond all pathos. There is something infinitely profounder than pathos in the death of Jesus—there is a mystery we cannot begin to touch. The death of Jesus is the death of God, at the hands of human beings inspired by the devil. He gathered round Him the raging hate of humanity and was crucified. He offered Himself through the eternal Spirit—He died in the Spirit in which He lived.

Are we being true to the Cross in our preaching, putting first the holiness of God that makes people know that they are sinners? When we preach the love of God there is a danger of forgetting that the Bible reveals not first the love of God but the intense, blazing holiness of God, with His love as the center of that holiness. When the holiness of God is preached, people are convicted of sin; it is not the love of God that first appeals but His holiness. The awful nature of the conviction of sin that the Holy Spirit brings makes us realize that God cannot, dare not, must not forgive sin; if God forgave sin without atoning for it, our sense of justice would be greater than His.

True to Conscience

cleanse your conscience . . .

How does all the profound thought underlying the death of Jesus touch us? The writer to the Hebrews instantly con-nects it with conscience: "How much more shall the blood of Christ . . . cleanse your conscience from dead works to serve the living God?" Has conscience the place in our salvation and sanctification that it ought to have? Hyperconscientious people blind themselves to the realization of what the death of Jesus means by saying, "No, I have wronged this person and I must put the thing right." It springs from the panging remorse that we experience when we realize we have wronged another. "All you say about the Cross may be true, but I have been so mean and so wrong that there are things I must put right first." It sounds noble to talk like that, but it is the essence of the pride that put Jesus Christ to death. The only thing to do is to cast the whole thing aside: "My God, this thing in me is worthy only of death, the awful death of crucifixion to the last strand of life. Lord, it is my sin, my wrong, not Jesus Christ, that ought to be on that cross." When we get there and abandon the whole thing, the blood of Christ cleanses our consciences and the freedom is ineffa-ble and amazing.

The greatest problems of conscience are not the wrong things we have done but wrong relationships. We may have become born again, but what about those we have wronged? It is of no use to sit down and say, "It is irreparable now, I cannot alter it." Thank God He can alter it! We may try to repair the damage in our own way, by apologizing, by writ-ing letters; but it is not a simple, easy matter of something to apologize for. Behind the veil of human lives God begins to reveal the tragedies of hell. Or we may say, "I have been atoned for, therefore I do not need to think about the past." If we are conscientious, the Holy Spirit will make us think about the past, and it is just here that the tyranny of nerves and the bondage of Satan comes in. The shores of life are strewn with ruined friendships, irreparable severances through our own blame or others, and when the Holy Spirit begins to reveal the tremendous twist, then comes the strange distress, "How can we repair it?" Many a sensitive soul has been driven into insanity through anguish of mind because he or she has never realized what Jesus Christ came to do, and all the asylums in the world will never touch these people in the way of healing; the only thing that will is the realization of what the death of Jesus means, namely, that the damage we have done may be repaired through the efficacy of His cross, Jesus Christ has atoned for all, and He can make it good in us, not only as a gift but by a participation on our parts. The miracle of the grace of God is that He can make the past as though it had never been; He can "restore to you the years that the swarming locust has eaten, the crawling locust, the consuming locust, and the chewing locust" (Joel 2:25).

How Jesus Christ does cleanse the conscience! It is freedom not only from sin and the damage sin has done, but emancipation from the impairing left by sin, from all the distortions left in mind and imagination. Then when the conscience has been purged from dead works, Jesus Christ gives the marvelously healing ministry of intercession as "a clearinghouse for conscience." Not only is all sense of past guilt removed, but we are given the very secret heart of God for the purpose of vicarious intercession (see Romans 8:26–27).

from dead works . . .

What are dead works? Everything done apart from God. All prayer, all preaching, all testifying, all kind, sacrificial deeds done apart from God are dead works that clog the life. Never forget for one moment that you are what you are by the grace of God. If you are not what you are by the grace of God, then may God have mercy on you! Everything we are that is not through the grace of God will be a dead clog on us. Oh, believe me, the curse of the saints is our goodness! Let the whole thing go, be true to the Cross, and let Jesus Christ cleanse your conscience from dead works. Many saints misunderstand what happens to the natural virtues after sanctification. The natural virtues are not promises of what we are going to be but remnants of what God created us to be. We have the idea that we can bank on our natural patience and truthfulness and conscientiousness; we can bank on nothing in heaven above or earth beneath but what the grace of God has wrought in us. Everything we possess in the way of moral property, of noble spiritual property, severs us from God; all must go. "Nothing in my hands I bring." As soon as we abandon like that, we experience what Paul says in Galatians 2:20: "I have been crucified with Christ," and the reconstruction of our lives proves that God has purged us from all dead works.

. . . to serve the living God.

This means a life laid down for Jesus, a life of narrowed interests, a life that deliberately allows itself to be swamped by a crowd of paltry things. It is not fanaticism, it is the steadfast, flintlike attitude of heart and mind and body for one purpose—spoiled for everything except as we can be used to win souls for Jesus. It is not a passion for souls, but something infinitely profounder than that—it is the passion of the Holy Spirit for Jesus Christ. There are things that are too humanly tender for this kind of service. There are lives prevented by claims that are not God's, prevented by the tender, passionate love of others who have come in between. Oh, the amount of wasted service for God, the agonies of weeping and self-pity, the margins of mourning over wasted opportunities! Jesus Christ never spent one moment of His life mourning in that way. The kind of things we grieve over is the evidence of where our lives are hidden. Some of us have social consciences, we are shocked at moral crime; some of us have religious consciences, we are shocked at the things that go against our creeds. The conscience formed in us by the Holy Spirit makes us amazingly sensitive to the things that tell against the honor of God.

I am convinced that what is needed in spiritual matters is reckless abandonment to the Lord Jesus Christ, reckless and uncalculating abandonment, with no reserve anywhere about it; not sad—you cannot be sad if you are abandoned absolutely. Are you thankful to God for your salvation and sanctification, thankful He has purged your conscience from dead works? Then go a step further; let Jesus Christ take you straight through into identification with His death until there is nothing left but the light at the foot of the Cross, and the whole sphere of the life is hidden with Christ in God.

Lacey

Lacie

beautiful spirit

Restless &

Unbending

acey

Salvation

You who have escaped the sword, [go] away, do not stand still!
Remember the LORD afar off, and let Jerusalem come to your
mind. Jeremiah 51:50

Salvation is the biggest, gladdest word in the world; it cannot
mean pretense in any shape or form, therefore suppression is
no element of the word, neither is counteraction. Salvation is
God's grace to sinful people, and it takes a lifetime to say the
word properly. Most of us restrict the meaning of salvation,
we use it to mean new birth only, or something limited. We
are dealing with the subject here practically, not theologically.

The Element of Destruction in Salvation

You who have escaped the sword . . .

Jeremiah 51 almost burns the page, it is so full of strong
and intense destruction; but it gives the keynote to the purpose of God in destruction, namely, the deliverance of the
good. You will never find in the Bible that things are
destroyed for the sake of destruction. Human beings destroy
for the sake of destruction, and so does the devil; God never
does, He destroys the wrong and the evil for one purpose
only, the deliverance of the good.

(a) The Purpose of the Sword

The purpose of the sword is to destroy everything that
hinders a person from being delivered. The first thing in salvation is the element of destruction, and it is this that people
object to. With this thought in mind, recall what our Lord

287

said about His own mission: "Do not think that I came to bring peace on earth. I did not come to bring peace but a sword" (Matthew 10:34). Our Lord reveals Himself as the destroyer of all peace and happiness and of ignorance, wherever these are the excuse for sin (compare Matthew 3:10). It sounds startling and amazing to say that Jesus did not come to bring peace, but He said He did not. The one thing Jesus Christ is after is the destruction of everything that would hinder the emancipation of men and women. The fact that people are happy and peaceful and prosperous is no sign that they are free from the sword of God. If their happiness and peace and well-being and complacency rest on undelivered lives, they will meet the sword before long, and all their peace and rest and joy will be destroyed.

(b) The Peril of the Sword

To say that God loves the sinner but hates the sin sounds all right, but it is a dangerous statement, because it means that God is far too loving ever to punish the sinner. Jesus Christ came to save us so that there should be no "sinner" left in us. The phrase, "a sinner saved by grace," means that one is no longer a sinner; if someone is, she or he is not saved. If I refuse to let God destroy my sin, there is only one possible result—I must be destroyed with my sin. The light of the Lord's presence convicts of sin (see John 15:22–24). Sin is never imputed unless it is conscious. These verses reveal the very essence of the destructive element of salvation. I can easily say I am not convicted of sin, but as soon as I stand face-to-face with Jesus Christ I know the difference between Him and me; I have no excuse, and if I refuse to allow the Lord to deliver me from all that He reveals, I shall be destroyed with the thing He came to destroy. "For this purpose the Son of God was manifested, that He might destroy the works of the devil" (1 John 3:8).

(c) The Power of the Sword

An ancient legend tells of a blacksmith who became famous for the magnificent swords he made; he claimed that they could cut a coat of armor in two with one sweep. The king, hearing of this boast, summoned the blacksmith to his presence and told him to cut through his coat of armor and if he could not do it, he would be put to death for his boasting. The blacksmith swung his sword round and put it back in its sheath; the king was about to challenge him when the blacksmith said, "Shake yourself, Your Majesty"; the king shook himself—and fell in two. The legend is an illustration of the tremendous power of the sword in God's hands, "the sword of the Spirit, which is the word of God" (Ephesians 6:17). "The word of God is . . . sharper than any two-edged sword" (Hebrews 4:12), and it deals effectually with the sin in us; for a while we may not be conscious that anything has happened, then suddenly God brings about a crisis and we realize that something has been profoundly altered. No one is ever the same after listening to the Word of God—you cannot be; you may imagine you have paid no attention to it, and yet months after maybe a crisis arises and suddenly the Word of God comes and grips you by the throat, so to speak, and awakens all the terrors of hell in your life, and you say, "Wherever did that word come from?" Years ago, months ago, weeks ago, it sank straight into your unconscious mind, God knew it was there though you did not, and it did its damaging work, and now it has suddenly come to light. The question is will you allow yourself to escape the edge of the sword, or will you be destroyed with the thing the sword has pierced?

Look back over your own life and examine the points of view you have now and the points of view you once had. At one time you were violently opposed to the views you now hold; what has altered you? You cannot honestly say it was conscious study. God says that His word shall not return to Him void (Isaiah 55:11)—the abiding success of the Word of God! The Word of God is never without power, and as a servant of God you have nothing whatever to do with whether people dislike and reject the Word of God or purr over it. So you preach it no matter what they think of you—that is a matter of absolute indifference; sooner or later the effect of that word will be manifested. The great snare is to seek acceptance with the people we talk to, to give people only what they want; we have no business to wish to be acceptable to the people we teach. "Be diligent to present yourself approved"—to the saints? No, "to God" (2 Timothy 2:15). I have never known a woman or a man who taught God's Word to be always acceptable to other people. As a worker for God truths are all the time coming into your own life that you would never have seen for yourself, and as you give other people truths they never saw before, they will say: "I don't agree with that." It is foolish to begin to argue—if it is God's truth leave it alone; let mistakes correct themselves. When a crisis comes that shakes the life, one will find the old, dominating power is not there at all. What has happened? The destruction by God has gone on. Then comes the critical moment—will I go with the thing that is destroyed, or will I stay by the hand that holds the sword?

> The best measure of the profundity of any religious doctrine is given by its conception of sin and its cure of sin.

Do I believe that sin needs to be corrected, or killed? If sin only needed to be corrected, the symbol would have been a lash not a sword; but God uses the symbol for killing. Beware of getting into your mind ideas that never came from God's Word—the idea, for instance, that we sin a little less each day; if we do, the salvation of Jesus Christ has never touched us. If we grow in grace a little more every day, it is a sign that the destructive power of God has been at work and that we have been delivered from the thing that hindered us growing. The view people have of sin is always the test of their view of salvation, and today, views are creeping into God's Book that never came from Him. Sin must be destroyed, not corrected; it is the destruction of something in order to lead to emancipation. It is always God rescuing Israel from Babylon, always Jesus Christ rescuing His people from their sin.

The Element of Direction in Salvation

[Go] away, do not stand still.

To study the teaching of our Lord in connection with the verb *to go* would amaze us. How often do you hear in meetings the word *go*, and how often do you hear the word *get*? We emphasize *get*; the New Testament emphasizes go. If you have escaped the edge of the sword, go!

(a) The Paralysis of Sin

Slaves born in slavery and suddenly freed will often prefer to go back. When the slaves in America were freed, they did not know what to do with their freedom, they were amazed and dazed and stupid; they had never been master of themselves before, and many pleaded with their masters to be taken back. That moment of paralysis is the natural result of being suddenly delivered. Sinners when first delivered from sin have such moments, they wish God would take them safe to heaven where they would be secure from temptation. We may not say it, but it is common to us all to look at things in this way in the implicit region, if not in the explicit: "Yes, I believe God does deliver from sin and fill with the Holy Spirit, and if He would only take me straight to heaven it would be all right, but I have to live amongst people who are wrong, in the midst of a people of unclean lips and the memory of how continually I fell in the past makes me fear I shall do it again in the future." Satan takes advantage of these moments of paralysis; consequently there is need for direction. A snare in many evangelistic meetings is that people are taught to say, "Thank God, I am saved," or, "Thank God I am sanctified," but no line of direction is given. The counsel in God's Book is: Testify to the truth God has revealed to you, and go on. People begin to degenerate because they don't know what to do; the direction given in God's Book has never been put in its right place. The direction is summed up in this one word: *Go*.

(b) The Pain of the Saved

When a limb that has long been cramped is released, there is the experience of excessive pain, but the pain is the sign of life. The first moment of realizing God's truth is usually a moment of ecstasy, the life is brimming over with joy and happiness and brightness, there is no pain, nothing but unspeakable, unfathomable joy. Then the verb *to go* begins to be conjugated, and we experience the growing pains of salvation, and Satan comes as an angel of light and says, "Don't go on, stand still, and," in the language of the hymn, " 'sing yourself away to everlasting bliss!' "

We do not consider enough the necessity of learning how to walk spiritually. Remember, when we are saved, we have been cramped in sin. Paul puts it in this way: "You used to use your members as servants for sin, now you are emancipated from sin, use your members as servants to righteousness" (Romans 6:19, paraphrased); that is, use them in a different way. If one has used one's arm only for writing, and then becomes a blacksmith, one will groan for days with the tremendous pain in the deltoid muscle until by practice the time comes when there is no more pain because the muscle has become rightly adjusted to its new work. The same thing happens spiritually—God begins to teach us how to walk and over and over again we begin to howl and complain. May God save us from the continual whine of spiritual babes: "Teach us the same things over and over again, don't give us the revelations of God that are painful, give us the 'simple gospel'—that is, what we have always believed, don't tell us of things we have never thought about before, because that causes pain" (compare Hebrews 5:12). Of course it does. Thank God there is a pain attached to being saved, the pain of growing until we come to maturity where we can do the work of a son or a daughter of God.

(c) The Passion in the Saving

The application of our Lord's phrase, "Behold, we are going up to Jerusalem" (Luke 18:31), is this passion not to stand still but to go on. Look back over your life in grace, whether long or short, and ask yourself which are the days that have furthered you most in the knowledge of God—the days of sunshine and peace and prosperity? Never! The days of adversity, the days of strain, the days of sudden surprises, the days when the earthly house, this tent, was strained to its last limit—those are the days when you learned the meaning of this passion of "Go." Any great calamity in the natural world—death, disease, bereavement—will awaken a person when nothing else would, and the person is never the same again. We would never know the "treasures of darkness" if we were always in the place of placid security. Thank God, salvation does not mean that God turns us into milksops; God's salvation makes us for the first time into men and women. The passion of the Holy Spirit means that we go on with God exactly on the lines God wants; the Holy Spirit will give the direction, and if we do not know it we are to blame. "My people do not consider," says God (Isaiah 1:3); they won't heed this Book. We say, "I don't like studying these subjects, I have no affinity for them." We do not say it actually, but over and over again these thoughts keep us from going on with God. The Holy Spirit will make us face subjects for which we have no affinity naturally in order that we may become full-orbed as God's servants.

The Elements of Discipline in Salvation

Remember the LORD afar off, and let Jerusalem come to your mind.

In the midst of an alien land, afar off from the home of God, the remembrance of the Lord will make you strong with the strength of ten. Note carefully in this connection our Lord's use of the phrase "Do this in remembrance of Me" (Luke 22:19). The ordinance of the Lord's Supper is not a memorial of One who has gone but of One who is always here.

(a) The Dangerous Infatuation

Infatuation means a stupid sense of my own security. Sick people often have the dangerous infatuation that they are all right. This danger overtakes a saint on what Bunyan calls "the enchanted ground" (compare 2 Peter 1:12–13). Whenever we come to the state of feeling, "Well, it's all right now and I can rest here," we are in danger. There is only one point of rest, and that is in the Lord, not in our experiences. We are never told to rest in the experience of salvation or of sanctification or in anything except the Lord Himself. Whenever you rest in the dangerous infatuation, "Thank God, I know I am all right," you will go down as sure as Satan is Satan and you are you.

(b) The Divine Imperative

Remember the LORD afar off.

The command to remember does not simply mean to recall but to re-identify yourself in imagination with your Lord. The passive stage is a great danger:

When obstacles and trials
  seem like prison walls to be,
I lay me down and go to sleep
  and leave it all to Thee!

That is the stage of spiritual dry rot. There is nothing more difficult to get rid of than the encroachments of this spiritual sickness; it is not physical weariness—that will come over and over again—but spiritual weariness, and spiritual weariness coins such phrases as: Once in grace always in grace, no matter how disgraceful you are; The Lord is far too good to let me go; I have been so much used in days gone by I am all right. It is rather a certainty that you are spiritually sick. Jesus said, "I have come that they may have life" (John 10:10), not laziness. Whenever we are in danger of nestling in spiritual armchairs, the clarion voice of the Lord comes and bids us neither sit nor stand but go! Look back over your life and you will see whenever there was the danger of spiritual dry rot or of getting off onto enchanted ground, God in mercy to your soul allowed an earthquake to come, and the whole thing went to pieces and you with it; for a while you were dazed and amazed, and then all of a sudden He set you on your feet again. "For here we have no continuing city" (Hebrews 13:14). To remember the Lord afar off means to remember that we have to be like Him.

(c) The Devoted Intellect

"And let Jerusalem," the God-lit city, "come to your mind." Ask yourself: "What do I let come to my mind?" If one lets one's garden alone, it pretty soon ceases to be a garden, and if saints let their minds alone, those minds will soon become garbage patches for Satan's scarecrows. Read the terrible things that Paul says will grow in saints' minds unless they look after them (for example, Colossians 3:5). The command to let Jerusalem come to mind means we have to watch our intellect and devote it for one purpose; let only those things come in that are worthy of the God-lit city. "Let": it is a command. See to it by the careful watching of your mind that only those thoughts come in that are worthy of God. We do not sufficiently realize the need to pray when we lie down at night, "Deliver us from the evil one" (Matthew 6:13). It puts us in the attitude of asking the Lord to watch our minds and our dreams, and He will do it.

Reality

It seems to me that some-
    where in my soul
There lies a secret self as yet
    asleep;
No stranger hath disturbed its
    slumber deep,
No friend dispersed the
    clouds that round it roll.
But it is written on my For-
    tune's scroll
That should some hand the
    chords of being sweep
And speak a certain sound,
    this self would leap
To fullest life and be awake
    and whole.

Then He said to them all, "If anyone desires to come after Me,
let him deny himself, and take up his cross daily, and follow Me."
Luke 9:23

By *reality* we mean that all the hidden powers of our lives are
in perfect harmony with themselves and in perfect harmony
with God. None of us are real in the full sense of the word;
we become real bit by bit as we obey the Spirit of God. It is
not a question of sham and reality or of hypocrisy and reality,
but of sincerity being transformed into reality. It is possible
to be perfectly real to ourselves but not real to God; that is
not reality. It is possible to be perfectly real to ourselves and

real to other people, but not real in our relationship to God; that is not reality. The only reality is being in harmony with ourselves and other people and God. That is the one great reality toward which God is working and toward which we are working as we obey Him.

Self-Realization—Naturally

> If anyone desires to come after Me . . .

It is a painful process becoming conscious of one's self; we are not conscious of ourselves at the beginning of life. Children have no realization of themselves as distinct from those round about them, consequently they are in complete harmony. When children begin to realize themselves they become self-conscious and their distress begins; they begin to find they are different from others and think that no one understands them, and they become either conceited or depressed.

(a) Sense of Individualism

The critical moment in people's lives is when they realize they are individually separate from other people. When I realize I am separate from everyone else, the danger is that I think I am different from everyone else. As soon as I think that, I become a law to myself; that means I excuse everything I do—but nothing anyone else does. "My temptations are peculiar," I say, "my setting is very strange; no one knows but me the peculiar forces that are in me." When first that big sense awakens that I am different from everyone else, it is the seed of all lawlessness and all immoralities.

(b) Sense of Intuition

This sense that I know what other people do not know, that I have a special intuition that tells me things, is even more dangerous than the sense of individualism, because it leads to spiritual deception in a religious nature and to hard intellectual conceit in a natural nature.

(c) Sense of Isolation

When a person realizes he or she is alone the danger of inordinate affection arises. Have you ever noticed the remarkable phrase in the Song of Songs: "Do not stir up nor awaken love until it please" (2:7; 3:5)? The forces of the world, the flesh, and the devil are set to do that one thing, to awaken the soul's love before the true Lover of the soul, the Lord Jesus Christ, has been revealed. It would serve us well if we thought a great deal more from the ethical side of our Christian work than we do. We think of it always from the spiritual side because that is the natural way for us, but when we think of it from the ethical side we get at it from a different angle. More damage is done because souls have been left alone on the moral side than Christian workers ever dream, simply because their eyes are blinded by seeing only along the spiritual line. When once the powers of a nature, young or old, begin to awaken it realizes that it is an individual, that it has a power of knowing without reasoning, and it begins to be afraid because it is alone and looks for a companion, and the devil is there always to supply the need. Remember the old proverb: "If you knock long enough at a door the devil may open it." The Bible indicates that there is a wrong as well as a right perseverance.

Self-realization naturally means I must develop my nature along its natural line: I am an individual, therefore I shall take care that no one who is not like me teaches me; I have gifts of soul that make me feel a strong affinity for certain natures— those I shall foster; I feel very much alone, therefore I shall select another person or persons to comrade me. The Spirit of God counteracts these tendencies of the nature that He has created until they flow into the right channels.

There are many signs of religiosity in a young life that arise simply from natural physical development and are not spiritual at all. Boys and girls in their teens often show amazingly religious tendencies and these are mistaken for the real work of the Spirit of God; they may or may not be. The need for spiritual discernment on this point in those of us who are workers is intense. Whenever there is real spiritual life, Jesus Christ is in the first place; when it is not the work of the Spirit of God there are vague notions about God, aspirations after this and that, and great strivings that may end anywhere, toward God or not. The great need is for the Holy Spirit to introduce Jesus Christ. The supreme moment for our Lord in any life is when that individual life is beginning to awaken. The incalculable power of intercession comes in here. A Christian father or mother or teacher or friend can anticipate that moment in the life of his or her child or student or friend, so that when the awakening comes, the Spirit of God in answer to believing prayer holds off the world, the flesh, and the devil and introduces the Friend of friends, the Lord Jesus Christ. I wish I could convey to you the imperative importance of intercessory prayer. If the devil is anxious about one thing, he is anxious not to allow us to see this; if we will only say, "Well, prayer does not much matter; they are very young and inexperienced." Forestall the time; hold off the devil! We do not know when a nature begins to awaken along the line of self-realization; it may be very early in life or later on, but I do believe that by intercessory prayer, as Jesus Himself has told us, the great power of God works in ways we cannot conceive. I think sometimes we will be covered with shame when we meet the Lord Jesus and think how blind and ignorant we were when He brought people around us to pray for or gave us opportunities of warning, and instead of praying we tried to find out what was wrong. We have no business to try and find out what is wrong, our business is to pray, so that when the awakening comes Jesus Christ will be the first they meet. The one who meets a nature at its awakening has the opportunity of making or marring that life. As soon as Jesus Christ touches "the chords of being," the nature is fascinated by Him, as the early disciples were—no work of regeneration as yet, simply the holding of the nature entranced by Jesus Christ. The chances for the devil in that life are very poor indeed; but if the world, the flesh, and the devil get the first touch, a long line of havoc may follow before Jesus Christ has His chance.

Christ-Realization

let him deny himself . . .

Jesus is talking to people who have reached the point of self-realization naturally; now He is requiring from them an identification with Him.

It is not only that they identify themselves in a fidelity which is indistinguishable from that which is due to God alone, but that He, in the most solemn, explicit, and overpowering words, requires from them that identification, and makes their eternal destiny depend upon it.

—Denny

Self-realization naturally cares nothing about God, it does not care whether Jesus lived or died or did anything at all. For ourselves we live and for ourselves we die; that is self-realization that leads to death and despair; it is absolutely and radically opposed to Christ-realization. True self-realization is exhibited in the life of our Lord, perfect harmony with God and a perfect understanding of humanity, and He prays "that they may be one just as We are one" (John 17:22).

(a) Power of Asceticism

Asceticism is the passion of giving up things and is recognizable in a life not born again of the Spirit of God. It is all very well if it ends in giving up the one thing God wants us to give up, namely, our right to ourselves, but if it does not end there, it will do endless damage to the life. In a sanctified soul the power of asceticism shows itself in an understanding of the mighty place of martyrdom in our Lord's program for a disciple. "Let him deny himself." These words of Jesus reveal the line He continually worked on when He talked to the disciples; He introduced the closest ties and said that at times even these have to be severed if we are to be true to Him. That sounds harsh to anyone who has not come into the understanding of Jesus that we get after sanctification.

> Consider how great this Person is who declares that the final destiny of men depends on whether or not they are loyal to Him, and who demands absolute loyalty though it involve sacrifice of the tenderest affections, and the surrender of life in the most ignominious death.
>
> —Denny

(b) Passion of Absorption

When Jesus Christ is seen by a newly awakened nature His fascination is complete—no conviction of sin, no reception of the Holy Spirit, no believing, even, but an absorbing passion for Jesus Christ. There are a great number of Christians in this immature stage, they write books and conduct meetings along the line of being absorbed in Jesus, but we have the feeling as we listen: "There is something lacking—what is it?" What is lacking is the realization that we have to be brought by means of the death of Jesus into the relationship to God that our Lord Himself had. The hymns that are written by people in this stage emphasize the human aspect of Jesus, but there is no real, gripping power in them for the saint.

The passion of absorption is also recognizable in the initial stages of sanctification, perhaps more so than at any other stage; there is no consciousness of a separate life. To talk about suffering and cross-bearing and self-denial is not only outside the soul's vocabulary but outside the possibility of its thinking; the soul seems to be absolutely absorbed in Christ. This stage is excessively dangerous unless it leads to one thing, identification with the death of Jesus.

(c) Perseverance of Adoration

When Jesus touches a nature, a long series of devotional hours characterizes the life—always wanting times of being alone with God, always wanting to pray and read devotional books. In some natures it goes as far as ecstasy. After sanctification the characteristic of the life is clear—Jesus Christ first, Jesus Christ second, and Jesus Christ third, all that the Lord wants; the life goes on with a flood of intense energy, adoration unspeakable. Said Paul: "It is no longer I who live, but Christ lives in me" (Galatians 2:20). The identity is changed, the very faith, the very nature that was in Jesus is in us now, and we with all other saints may grow into the full realization of God's purpose in Redemption: "till we all come to the unity of the faith" (Ephesians 4:13). We cannot attain it alone.

Self-Realization—Spiritually

. . . and take up his cross daily, and follow Me.

In the first experience of sanctification we lose altogether the consciousness of personal identity—we are absorbed in God; but that is not the final place, it is merely the introduction to a totally new life. We lose the natural identity and consciously gain the identity that Jesus had, and it is when God begins to deal with sanctified souls on that line that darkness sometimes comes and the strange misunderstanding of God's ways. They are being taught what God taught Abraham:

My goal is God Himself, not
   joy, nor peace,
Nor even blessing, but Himself, my God.

Jesus said to His disciples, "I still have many things to say to you, but you cannot bear them now" (John 16:12). They could not bear them until the Holy Spirit brought them into the realization of who Jesus was.

(a) Patient Dedication

> and take up his cross . . .

The immature stage of the life of sanctification merges into a clear, patient dedication to Jesus Christ; free from all hurry spiritually and all panic, there is a slow and growing realization of what Jesus meant when He said, "As the Father has sent Me, I also send you" (John 20:21). Our cross is the steady exhibition of the fact that we are not our own but Christ's, and we know it and are determined to be unenticed from living lives of dedication to Him. This is the beginning of the emergence of the real life of faith.

(b) Plain Daylight

> daily . . .

The life of manifestations is a critical stage in the saint's experience. The real life of the saint on this earth, and the life that is most glorifying to Jesus, is the life that steadfastly goes on through common days and common ways, with no moun-taintop experiences. We read of John the Baptist "looking at Jesus as He walked"—not at Jesus in a prayer meeting or in a revival service, or Jesus performing miracles; he did not watch Him on the Mount of Transfiguration, he did not see Him in any great moment at all; he saw Him on an ordinary day when

Jesus was walking in an ordinary, common way, and he said, "Behold, the Lamb of God!" (John 1:36). That is the test of reality. Mounting up with wings like eagles, running and not being weary (see Isaiah 40:31) are indications that something more than usual is at work. Walking and not fainting is the life that glorifies God and satisfies the heart of Jesus to the full—the plain daylight life, unmarked, unknown; only occasionally, if ever, does the marvel of it break on other people.

(c) Persistent Devotion

... and follow Me.

This is the life of martyrdom with the glowing heat of perfect love at its heart. Only one figure ahead and that the Lord Jesus; other people, saints or sinners, shadows. The mark of this life of devotion is its persistence. Spasms are a sign of returning or departing life. The continual feeling, "I must wind myself up, I have been letting things go, I must screw my life up and get to work," may be a sign that we are coming nearer the source of the true life or it may be exactly the opposite—it may be a sign that we are declining into death. God and we ourselves are the only judges of that. The one thing to fix on is that the life Jesus lived is the pattern of what our lives will be when once we come to the place of self-realization spiritually.

> No one is worthy of Jesus who does not follow Him, as it were, with the rope round his neck—ready to die the most ignominious death rather than prove untrue.
>
> —Denny

The idea of martyrdom is the very essence of the saint's life. Jesus Christ always used the figure of martyrdom when He spoke of this stage of the Christian life (see John 21:18). The saint at this stage is leagues beyond the point of asking, "Am I doing God's will?" That saint *is* God's will; leagues beyond the point of saying, "I do want God to bless me here and use me there"; leagues beyond the point of saying, "I have got the victory" and praising God for it; that saint is in the place where God can make him or her broken bread and poured-out wine, just as He made His Son broken bread and poured-out wine for us.

May this message make clear to our hearts and minds the purpose of God in our salvation and sanctification. God's purpose is to make us real, that is, to make us perfectly at one with all our own powers and perfectly at one with God, no longer children but understanding in our heads as well as in our hearts the meaning of the Redemption and slowly maturing until we are a recommendation to the redeeming grace of our Lord Jesus Christ. As the angels look down on us, do they see something that makes them marvel at the wonderful workmanship of Jesus Christ: "When He comes . . . to be glorified in His saints and to be admired among all those who believe" (2 Thessalonians 1:10).

Judgment

Oh, we're sunk enough here, God knows!
　　But not quite so sunk that moments,
Sure tho' seldom, are denied us,
　　When the spirit's true endowments
Stand out plainly from its false ones,
　　And apprise it if pursuing
Or the right way or the wrong way,
　　To its triumph or undoing.

—Robert Browning

And this is the condemnation, that the light has come into the world, and men loved the darkness rather than light, because their deeds were evil. John 3:19

The healthiest exercise for the mind of a Christian is to learn to apprehend the truth granted to it in vision. Every Christian with any experience at all has had a vision of some fundamental truth, either about the Atonement or the Holy Spirit or sin, and it is at the peril of the soul that he or she loses the vision. By prayer and determination, we have to form the habit of keeping ourselves soaked in the vision God has given. The difficulty with the majority of us is that we will not seek to apprehend the vision; we get glimpses of it and then leave it alone. "I was not disobedient to the heavenly vision," said Paul (Acts 26:19). It is one of the saddest things to see men and women who have had visions of truth but have failed to apprehend them, and it is on this line that judgment comes. It is not a question of intellectual discernment or of knowing how to present the vision to others but of seeking to apprehend the vision so that it may apprehend us. Soak and soak and soak continually in the one great truth of which you have had a vision; take it to bed with you, sleep with it, rise up in the morning with it, continually bring your imagination into captivity to it, and slowly and surely as the months and years go by God will make you one of His specialists in that particular truth. God is no respecter of persons.

The Master Meaning of Crisis

> And this is the condemnation . . .

That is, this is the critical moment. People are not judged by their ordinary days and nights because in these they are more or less creatures of drift, but a crisis is immediately the test. A crisis is a turning point that separates, and it will always reveal character. If, after a crisis is passed, you will take the trouble to go back, you will find there was a moment away back when a clear idea was given you of what God wanted you to do, and you did not do it; the days have gone on and suddenly the crisis comes, and instantly judgment is passed. The thing that tells is the crisis. The generality of people drift along without bothering their heads about anything until a crisis comes, and it is always critical.

(a) The Critical Issue

> But when Herod heard, he said, "This is John, whom I beheaded; he has been raised from the dead!" Mark 6:16

The crisis in the case of Herod was brought about by the disciples' preaching of Jesus; when "His name had become well known" (v. 14), Herod was mastered and made known to himself; the crisis revealed a terror-stricken conscience. Herod was a Sadducee, and the Sadducees say "there is no resurrection" (12:18), but when the name of Jesus was noised abroad, he was superstitiously terrified and said, "This is John, whom I beheaded; he has been raised from the dead."

(b) The Convicting Idea

John had said to Herod, "It is not lawful for you to have your brother's wife." 6:18

The convicting idea was produced by what Herod heard; the truth had been spoken to him, he had been convicted by it: "he did many things, and heard him gladly" (v. 20), but not the one thing. Herod refused to obey the light when it was given, and it was that moment that determined how he would show himself in the crisis.

(c) The Confirming Intention

Then an opportune day came . . . verse 21

The opportune day will always come, the opportune day for the satisfaction of sin. This is a general principle that the generality of Christian workers do not seem to realize. Sin has got to be satisfied or else strangled to death by a supernatural power. Hell is the satisfaction of all sin. Sentimentalism arises in the nature that is unused to facing realities. A person will pile on Christian work, will do anything, will slave endlessly, rather than let you touch the thing that is wrong. Great oceans of penitence and confession are shown, but when all that is through you find there is one fact more, one blind spot that the person you are dealing with refuses to look at or to let you look at. If you are a servant of God, you must ruthlessly rip up the sentimental humbug and go direct to the one thing.

These three things play their parts in every crisis. Be careful to note, however, that a crisis does not make character; a crisis reveals character. No sane person is allowed by God to live continually in the light of the conscience. The characteristic of the life of a saint is essential, elemental simplicity.

Apart from moments of crisis, character is not consciously known. You can see this every day you live; we all say: "If I had been in your place, I would have done so and so." You have no means of knowing what you would have done; the nature of a crisis is that it takes you unawares, it happens suddenly, and the line you take reveals your character; it may also reveal something that amazes you. For instance, you may think a certain person selfish, self-interested, and self-satisfied, but a crisis comes, bereavement or a business disaster or sickness, and to your amazement you find he or she is not the self-interested person you thought at all, there are whole tracts of generosity in that individual's nature of which you knew nothing. Or you may think someone very generous and kind and loving, and when a crisis occurs, to your amazement and everyone else's, the person is shown to be mean and selfish and cruel. The crisis is always the judgment.

The Moral Majesty of the Criterion

that the light is come into the world . . .

What does Jesus Christ say the standard of God's judgment is for us all? The light that has come into the world. Who is the Light of the world? The Lord Jesus Christ, Son of God and Son of Man.

To judge is to see clearly, to care for what is just, and therefore to be impartial and impersonal.

—Amiel

A few moments' consideration will reveal what a difficult task the Holy Spirit has in bringing even the best of saints to this impersonal standard of judgment. This idea, which shows our personal ways of looking at things, is always lurking about us:

"Oh, well, God knows I really meant to devote myself to Him and to obey Him, but so many things have upset me; I have not had the opportunities I should have had."

310   *The Philosophy of Sin*

"I don't really mean to speak and act as I do, but I shall not count it this time."

All this shows how difficult it is for the Holy Spirit to bring us to apply the standard of Jesus Christ to ourselves; we will apply His standard to other people, but Jesus Christ brings it home to us. Am I willing to obey the light? We have to beware of personal interests that blur our minds from accepting our Lord's standard. To walk in the light, as God is in the light, is the one condition of being kept cleansed from all sin (see 1 John 1:7).

(a) The Standard for the Heathen

> That was the true Light which gives light to every man coming into the world. John 1:9; see also Matthew 25:31–46; Romans 2:11–16

The first thing to ask in regard to this standard is—what about the people who have never heard of Jesus Christ and may never hear of Him, how are they judged? The passages given all refer to God's standard of judgment for the heathen, namely, the light they have, not the light they have never had and could not get. Conscience is the standard by which men and women are to be judged until they have been brought into contact with the Lord Jesus Christ. The call to preach the gospel to the heathen is not the frenzied doctrine that the heathen who have never known Jesus Christ and never had the chance of knowing Him are going to be eternally lost, but the command of Jesus Christ: "Go into all the world and preach the gospel to every creature" (Mark 16:15).

(b) The Standard for Christendom

> He who believes in Him is not condemned; but he who does not believe is condemned already, because he has not believed in the name of the only begotten Son of God. John 3:18

The standard for the judgment of Christendom is not the light it has received but the light it ought to have received. Every country in Christendom has had plenty of opportunity of knowing about Christ, and the doom of a soul begins the moment it consciously neglects to know Jesus Christ or consciously rejects Him when He is known. Beware of applying our Lord's words in Matthew 25 to Christians; Matthew 25 is not the standard for the judgment of Christians, but the standard for the judgment of the nations that do not know Christ. The standard for the judgment of Christians is our Lord.

(c) The Standard for the Church

> And He Himself gave some to be apostles, some prophets, some evangelists, and some pastors and teachers, for the equipping of the saints, . . . for the edifying of the body of Christ, till we all come to the unity of the faith. Ephesians 4:11–13

These verses do not refer to individual Christian lives but to the collective life of the saints. The individual saint cannot be perfected apart from others. "He Himself gave some to be apostles," for what purpose? To show how clever they were, what gifts they had? No, "for the equipping of the saints." In looking back over the history of the church we find that every one of these "gifts" has been tackled. Paul says that apostles, prophets, evangelists, pastors and teachers, are all meant for one thing by God, namely, "for the equipping of the saints, . . . for the edifying of the body of Christ." No saint can ever be perfected in isolation or in any other way than God has laid down. There are very few who are willing to lay hold of that for which they were laid hold of (see Philippians 3:12–13), they thank God for salvation and sanctification and then stagnate, consequently the perfecting of the saints is hindered.

The Making Moment of Choice

> And men loved darkness rather than light, because their deeds were evil.

The choice is indelibly marked for time and eternity. What we decide makes our destiny—not what we have felt nor what we have been moved to do or inspired to see, but what we decide to do in a given crisis—it is that which makes or mars us. Sooner or later there comes to every life the question, Will I choose to side with God's verdict on sin in the cross of Christ? I may say "I won't accept," or "I will put it off," but both are decisions, remember.

(a) The Prejudice for Darkness

> If therefore the light that is in you is darkness, how great is that darkness! Matthew 6:23

Your disposition determines the way you will decide when the crisis comes, but the only One who knows your disposition other than you yourself is God. The unaltered, natural disposition of a person is called by our Lord "darkness," that means prejudice against the light.

(b) The Persistence of Direction

> And the king was exceedingly sorry; yet, because of the oaths and because of those who sat with him, he did not want to refuse her. Immediately the king sent an executioner and commanded his head to be brought. Mark 6:26–27

John the Baptist represented the voice of God to Herod; Herod decided to silence the voice of God. He had one subsequent twinge (see vv. 16–18), then his conscience never bothered him again, and Jesus Christ and all He represented became a farce to him. We read in Luke 23:8–9 that "when Herod saw Jesus, he was exceedingly glad; for he had desired for a long time to see Him, . . . and he hoped to see some miracle done by Him. Then he questioned Him with many words, but He answered him nothing." Herod had ordered the voice of God to be silent, and it was, and now all sails are set for perdition. His was "a ghastly smooth life, dead at heart." That is the awful condition to which a person may get where she or he no longer believes in goodness or purity or justice; but the Bible never allows that someone can get there without being culpable in God's sight. Whenever you see a soul in danger of closing over one sin, go at it, no matter how it hurts or how annoyed that soul is with you, go at it until the sin is blasted right out, never palliate it or sympathize. Very few voices rise up against the sins that make for the seal of silence on men and women and churches.

This is what is lacking today.

(c) The Pronouncement of Destiny

> Then he questioned Him with many words, but He answered him nothing. Luke 23:9

The reason "He answered him nothing" is found in Mark 6:26–27. Herod decided to silence the voice of God in his life, and when the Son of God stood before him, he saw nothing in Him; there was no more compunction of con-science. Whenever one makes the decision that Herod made: "I don't want to hear any more about the matter," it is the beginning of the silence of God in one's soul. To silence the voice of God is damnation in time; eternal damnation is that forever. "God . . . does not answer me anymore" (1 Samuel 28:15) is an expression of damnation in time. Divine silence is the ultimate destiny of anyone who refuses to come to the light and obey it.

It is a terrible thing in the spiritual career not to be appre-hended by the light that has been given; it may have been at some midday or midnight, in childhood or in the early days of your Christian life, or as recently as last week—you know exactly when it was, it is between you and God—are you going to decide along that line: "My God, I don't know all that it means, but I decide for it"? Whenever any light is given you on any fundamental issue and you refuse to settle your soul on it and apprehend it, your doom is sealed along that particular line. If a clear, emphatic vision of some truth is given you by God, not to your intellect but to your heart, and in spite of it all you decide to take another course, the vision will fade and may never come back.

There are men and women who ought to be princes and princesses with God, but they are away on God's left; they may even be sanctified, but they are left at a particular stage because they chose to be left; instead of obeying the heavenly vision, the natural, judicious decisions of an average Christian life have been preferred. It has nothing to do with salvation but with lost opportunities in service for God. "Many are called, but few chosen" (Matthew 22:14), that is, few prove themselves the chosen ones. Whenever the vision comes, let me plead with you, as though God were entreating by me, do not be disobedient to it, because there is only one purpose in our lives, and that is the satisfaction of the Lord Jesus Christ.

Backsliding

John 6

The tendencies that make temptation possible are inherent in humanity as God created us, Adam and our Lord Jesus Christ being witnesses; and we have to bear in mind that regeneration does not remove those tendencies but rather increases them. The possibility of temptation reaches its height in Jesus Christ.

Tendency to Repose

> It takes so much effort to maintain one's self in an exceptional point of view that one falls back into prejudice by pure exhaustion.

The tendency to repose physically is a right law of human physical nature; morally and spiritually it is a tendency toward immorality and unspirituality.

(a) The Desire for Rest—The Arrest of Desire John 6:10–15

The desire at the heart of true spiritual life is for union with God; the tendency to rest in anything less than the realization of this desire becomes the arrest of desire. Whenever we seek repose in any blessing spiritually, sleeping sickness begins. The tendency to rest in any of the blessings that are the natural outcome of union with God is the beginning of backsliding. Is my desire for union with God, or am I like the people who sought to make Jesus king—for what purpose? If

Jesus could feed their bodies without their having to work, that was the very thing they wanted. The incident is symbolic of the tendency to repose that is inherent in human nature, but if this desire were satisfied it would be the destruction of all character.

(b) The Decay of Reality—The Dawn of Death verses 30–31

Reality means that which is in perfect accord with God. If I accept any blessing of God, for example, sanctification, as the final end and aim of my life, from that moment decay begins in my spiritual life. Sanctification is the gateway to real union with God, which is life unutterable. Peter points out this very thing in his epistles; he says, you know these things and are established in the truth, but you are going to sleep, you are in danger of mistaking this for the final place; it is not, it is only the introduction (see 2 Peter 1:12–13). Are we sufficiently well taught of the Holy Spirit to stir up souls who have gotten right with God, until they come to the reality of realities, absolute oneness with God?

The tendency to backslide begins right in the very secret places. No wonder Jesus urged His disciples to watch and pray, "lest you enter into temptation" (Matthew 26:41; Mark 14:38). The possibility of backsliding is so full of peril that the only safety is to look to Jesus, relying on the Holy Spirit, and never to allow the repose, which is a necessity physically, to come into the life of the spirit. The arrest of desire begins when I want to rest in spiritual blessings, and the dawn of death in spiritual life begins when I become smugly satisfied with my attainments: "This is all God wants of me." What God wants of me is all that He has revealed in Jesus Christ. "till we all come . . . to the measure of the stature of the fullness of Christ" (Ephesians 4:13). The rest that is the outcome of entire sanctification is not the rest of stagnation but the rest of the reality of union with God.

(c) The Dreams of Repose—The Night of Disaster

> Then they said to Him, "Lord, give us this bread always."
> And Jesus said to them, "I am the bread of life. He who comes to
> Me shall never hunger, and he who believes in Me shall never
> thirst." John 6:34–35

These words of our Lord are a puzzle to an unspiritual
mind, and an unspiritual mind is produced by allowing
visions and dreams of spiritual repose that Jesus Christ continually discourages. What do I dream about and allow my
mind to fancy when in communion with God? One of the
greatest snares in spiritual life is to foster dreams and fancies
of our own that do not tally with the statements of Jesus,
instead of bringing every thought into captivity to the obedience of Christ. People who go off at a tangent and are led
astray by Satan as an angel of light are deceived just here.
Disaster spiritually follows whenever the tendency to repose
is yielded to. "Forgetting those things which are behind and
reaching forward to those things which are ahead" (Philippians 3:13) is the only attitude for a saint.

The Tendency to Revert

> Is not life the test of our moral force, and all these untold waver-
> ings—are they not temptations of the soul?

In all organic life there is a tendency to revert to the original type. Flowers and plants may be highly developed and
cultivated, but if afterwards they are left alone year after year
they will revert to the original type from which they sprang.
The spiritual application of this is that there is the possibility
in every child of God of reverting to the original type of self-
interest; but thank God there is also the possibility of being
transformed into the image of God's Son (see Romans 8:29).

(a) The Possibility of Offense

> The Jews therefore quarreled among themselves, saying, "How
> can this Man give us His flesh to eat?" John 6:52

The possibility of offense can only come when two persons have somewhat the same natures. People who have no affinity with Jesus run no risk of being offended with Him; but no Christian is ever free from that possibility (compare Matthew 11:6). Satan comes to us with suggestions: "Surely God would never ask you to do such and such a thing? God would never guide you in such a way?" But God does. The possibility of offense is there as soon as I become a child of God.

(b) The Perversity of the Offended verses 60–61

Perversity means to turn away from one to whom I have been devoted because he or she says things that do not suit my ideas. There is a stage in spiritual experience, it may be before or after sanctification, when this perversity is possible. Someone comes with an exposition of a truth of God I have never realized before, and at once the possibility of perversity is awakened, and I say, "No, I am sure God would never have revealed this truth to you if He has not revealed it to me." The possibility of offense is always there, and perversity is the next step. As soon as I am offended I become perverse, my eyes are blinded, and I see only along the line of my prejudices. There are saints, for instance, who resolutely shut their minds against the truth that they can draw upon the Lord's life for their bodies or against the need for being continually renewed in their minds. This will lead not only to stagnation spiritually, but to perversity. The only safety is to keep in the light as God is in the light.

(c) The Perfidy of the Offended

From that time many of His disciples went back and walked with Him no more. verse 66

Reversion to self-will and insisting on my own way of serving God is not only utter faithlessness to Jesus Christ, but active working against the particular truth that has offended me. The people who are most perverse against the truth are those who know it. This is stated in its most extreme form in Hebrews 6:4–6.

If God were to remove from us as saints the possibility of disobedience there would be no value in our obedience, it would be a mechanical business. To say after sanctification, "Now I can do what I like," is a perilously dangerous statement. If it were true, it would never have been recorded that "even Christ did not please Himself" (Romans 15:3). The possibility of disobedience in a child of God makes her or his obedience of amazing value. The one who is not a child of God is the slave of the wrong disposition and has not the power to obey; as soon as God delivers someone from the wrong disposition, that individual is free to obey and consequently free to disobey, and it is this that makes temptation possible. Temptation is not sin; temptation must always be possible for our parent-child relationship to be of worth to God. It would be no credit for God to bring mechanical slaves to glory: "for it was fitting for Him . . . in bringing many sons to glory"—not slaves, not useless channels, but vigorous, alert, wide-awake men and women, with all their powers and faculties devoted absolutely to God.

Tendency to Revolt

The independence which is the condition of individuality is at the same time the eternal temptation of the individual.

Spiritual revolt means the deliberate forsaking of God and signing on under another ruler. We must distinguish between degeneration and revolt. We have been dealing with the tendencies that lead to degeneration, no positive side has been taken yet, but there is a distinct disinclination to go on further; "I am thankful I am here, and here I am going to stay"— without realizing that we cannot stay where we are, we must either go on or go back—and that leads ultimately to revolt, not mere declension but a deliberate signing on under another ruler. "For My people have committed two evils: they have forsaken Me the fountain of living waters"—that is not backsliding, that is degeneration; "and hewn themselves cisterns— broken cisterns that can hold no water" (Jeremiah 2:13)— these two things together constitute backsliding. The words God uses in connection with backsliding are terrible. He uses words that shock us, as moral individuals, in order to portray what backsliding is in His sight.

(a) The Reaction of the Unattained John 6:41, 52

When souls realize the truth of God and fail to attain it, there lies within them a power of reaction that not only means they will try no more, but they will dissuade others. If once we have had a vision from God of His purpose for us and we leave it unattained, the tendency is to say, "Oh, well, it may be meant for other people, but it isn't for me." This tendency is in every one of us, we scarcely discern it, but it is there. For anyone to leave unattained anything our Lord has revealed as possible for him or for her is the beginning of Satan's chance over that soul. Our Lord makes no allowance for not attaining because by means of His cross we have all the marvelous grace of God to draw upon, all the mighty life of the Lord Jesus Christ to enable us to attain. A great many of us try and attain without having received the life of Jesus and we are bound to fail; that is not a matter of reaction, it is inevitable. But if we have received the life of Jesus, it is unconscious blasphemy in God's sight to stop short of attaining anything He reveals as possible for us. Our Lord's illustration of salt that has lost its flavor is applicable. "You are the salt of the earth; but if the salt loses its flavor, how shall it be seasoned? It is then good for nothing but to be thrown out and trampled underfoot by men" (Matthew 5:13). Flavorless salt is a most cursed influence in the physical world, and a saint who has lost saintliness is a pestilential influence in the spiritual world. We lose saintliness whenever we take our eyes for one second off the Source of life, the Lord Jesus Christ. Whenever we do, all these errors begin to be possible. But if we keep in the light with God, the life is that of a child, simple and joyful all through. It is sufficient for children to know that their parents wish them to do certain things and they learn to draw on a strength greater than their own and attain and attain; if they do not, they run the risk of becoming prodigals.

(b) The Reviling of the Unreached John 6:61

If people have really tasted the life of God and know God's purpose for them—or did know it months or years ago—but have never fulfilled that purpose through obedience, the tendency to revile the standard is irresistible. We must revile a standard we have not reached when we know we ought to have reached it. It is not something that can be prevented, it is inevitable. If once we deliberately stop short and refuse to let God's life have its way with us, we shall revile the truth because it has not been reached.

There are two things that keep us from going on with God—first, the "show business"; by the show business we mean the desire to appeal to the largest number; if you do that, you will have to lower the standards of Jesus Christ—and second, sympathy. Sympathy with one another that does not spring from sympathy with God's interests in one another will always end in reviling some standard of God's truth. It will not mean you use reviling language, you may use very pious and sighing language—"Oh, no, I could never attain to that." You may preach entire sanctification and your message may be couched in beautiful language, then you say—"This is God's standard, but of course I am not there." There can be only one result in the souls of those who listen, and that is the reviling of the standard, for which you and I will be called to account. The glibness and ease with which people proclaim the great standards of Jesus Christ and then sweep them away by saying, "God forbid I should say I am there," makes one tremble, because such a statement implies Jesus Christ cannot bring me there, it is an ideal to which I cannot attain. When we come to the New Testament there is the quiet and grandly easy certainty that we can attain. All God's commands are enablings. Never sympathize with a soul who cannot get through to God on Jesus Christ's lines. The Lord is never hard nor cruel, He is the essence of tender compassion and gentleness. The reason any soul cannot get through is that there is something in the soul that won't budge; as soon as it does, Jesus Christ's marvelous life will have its way.

(c) The Renunciation by Unbelief John 6:70–71

Not only is it possible for a soul to revile the standards set up by Jesus, but it is possible to do what Judas did, renounce Him by unbelief. It is easy to make Judas the arch-sinner, but he is the type of what is possible in every one of us. Thank God that the apostle Paul is also a possible type for every one of us, but do not forget that Judas is a possible type too.

These are terrible truths, but it is the terrors of the dark night that drive us closer to the haven of unutterable security, the Lord Jesus Christ. No wonder God's Book says, "the way of the unfaithful is hard" (Proverbs 13:15). Could God have made it more terrible than He has for people to go astray? Could He have put the danger signals more clearly than He has? The way is absolutely strewn with alarm signals; it is impossible to go wrong easily.

Thus in new ways we learn the profound beauty of our Lord's words: "Come to Me" (Matthew 11:28); "I am the way, the truth and the life" (John 14:6).

Temptation

1 Corinthians 10:12–13

Let him who thinks he stands take heed lest he fall. No temptation has overtaken you except such as is common to man; but
God is faithful, who will not allow you to be tempted beyond
what you are able, but with the temptation will also make the
way of escape, that you may be able to bear it.

The word *temptation* has come down in the world, we use it
wrongly nowadays. Temptation is not sin, it is the thing we
are bound to meet if we are human; not to be tempted would
be to be beneath contempt. Temptation is something that
exactly fits the nature of the one tempted and is therefore a
great revealer of the possibilities of the nature. Every person
has the setting of his or her own temptation. A good illustration of temptation is the way steel is tested. Steel can be
"tired" in the process of testing, and in this way its strength is
measured. Temptation means the test by an alien power of
the possessions held by a personality. This makes the temptation of our Lord explainable: He held in His person the fact
that He was to be the King of humanity and the Savior of the
world, and the alien power that came to test Him on these
lines is called in the Bible, Satan.

Temptation is also a severe test to fulfill the possessions
of personality by a shortcut. Temptation trains innocence
into character or else into corruption. There are some temptations, however, by which we have no business to be
tempted any longer; we should be on a higher plane dealing
with other temptations. We may have our morality well

324

within our own grasp and be comparatively free from temptation, but as soon as we are regenerated by the Spirit of God
we begin to understand the force of spiritual temptations of
which we were unconscious before.

Temptation versus Sin

James 1:12–15

Temptation and sin are profoundly different. Temptation
is a pathway to the end desired, but it leads to a perplexing
situation, inasmuch as it makes a person decide which factor
to obey in the dilemma. The possibility of sin and the inclination to sin are different things. Everyone has the possibility
of committing murder, but the inclination is not there. The
inclination is as the deed, whether it is carried out or not
(Romans 2:1; 1 John 3:15). Satan had the possibility of disobedience, and when the temptation producing the dilemma
came, he inclined to rebellion against God. Adam had the
possibility of disobedience, and when temptation came to
him producing the dilemma, he deliberately inclined to disobedience, and the disposition to disobey God became the
inheritance of the whole of the human race: "Through one
man sin entered the world, and death through sin, and thus
death spread to all men, because all sinned" (Romans 5:12).
The disposition of sin is fundamental anarchy against God's
rule over me, and as long as that disposition remains, temptation finds an inclination to sin in me; but when our Lord
delivers me from the disposition of sin, the hour of temptation discovers no inclination to sin, it tests the door of possibility only. "But now having been set free from sin, and
having become slaves of God, you have your fruit to holiness, and the end, everlasting life" (Romans 6:22). Our Lord
Jesus Christ had the possibility of disobedience, but when
the temptation producing the dilemma came to Him, it found
no inclination to disobedience, and everyone that is saved by

Him is put in the position He was in when He was tempted (see Hebrews 2:11; 4:15–16). Until one is regenerated and sanctified, the general character of our Lord's temptation is unguessed.

The sinless perfection heresy arises out of this confusion—it says that because the disposition of sin is removed, it is impossible to sin. The inclination to sin, thank God, is removed, but never the possibility. If the power to disobey were removed, our obedience would be of no value, for we would cease to be morally responsible. It is gloriously possible not to sin, but never impossible to sin, because we are moral agents. Morality must be militant in this order of things, but we can be "more than conquerors" (Romans 8:37) every time.

The temptation James speaks of is the temptation we know naturally: "Each one is tempted when he is drawn away by his own desires and enticed" (1:14). Until we are born again we only understand this kind of temptation, but by regeneration we are lifted into another realm and have other temptations to face, namely, the kind of temptations our Lord faced. The temptations of Jesus have no home at all in the natural human nature; they do not appeal to us. One's disposition on the inside, that is, what one possesses in one's personality, determines by what one is tempted on the outside, and the temptation will always come along the line of the ruling disposition. Sin is a disposition of self love that obeys every temptation to its own lordship. Sin is literally self-centered rule, a disposition that rules the life apart from God.

Naturally we are taught by this disposition to lust for what we desire, and lust will warp character from rectitude to ruin: "drawn away by his own desires and enticed." The destiny of lust is peculiarly fascinating. It presents a wild reach of possibility, and lust stampedes when it is not constrained by the consideration that it will lead the character to infamy, not fame. Lust means "I must have it at once, I will have my desire satisfied and will brook no restraint." Temptation yielded to is the birth of sin in the personal life and ends in death. The verses in James 1 are the natural history of temptation. Lustful desire is used in other ways in the Bible than merely of immorality—it is the spirit of "I must have it at once," no matter what it is. Temptation yielded to is lust deified.

The period of temptation in our Lord's life came immediately after a time of spiritual exaltation (see Matthew 3:16–17; 4:1); it was a period of estimating forces, and the historic temptations of Jesus Christ are pictorial records of wrong ways to the kingdom of God. At His baptism Jesus Christ accepted the vocation of bearing away the sin of the world, and immediately He was put by God's Spirit into the testing machine of the devil. But He did not "tire"; He went through the temptations "without sin" and retained the possessions of His personality intact.

"Then the devil left Him, and behold, angels came and ministered to Him" (Matthew 4:11). The sign that you have gone through temptation rightly is that you retain your affinity with the highest.

Temptation and Jesus Christ

Matthew 4:1, 11; Hebrews 2:18; 4:15–16

External circumstances are made to form an exact counterpart of the internal desire, which is different in different people. For example, the temptation of our Lord was quite different from the temptation of Judas Iscariot, because the inner disposition was different. We have to beware of saying that because Jesus was Divine, temptation to Him was not real. If that is so, then the record in the Bible of our Lord's temptations is a mere farce and is misleading, and the writer to the Hebrews is untrue when he says of Jesus, "tempted . . . yet without sin" (4:15).

Could Jesus Christ be tempted? Undoubtedly He could, because temptation and sin are not the same thing. The temptation James speaks of and the temptation of Jesus are very different in character. The temptations that beset us as ordinary people gather round the disposition of sin.

In Luke 3:23 we read: "Now Jesus Himself began His ministry at about thirty years of age." That is the time in human life when people reach maturity and all their powers are perfected, the time when they are spared no requirement of their adulthood. Up to that time, life is full of promise; after that it is a matter of testing and attainment. After the baptism of Jesus and the descent of the Holy Spirit upon Him, God, as it were, took His sheltering hand off Him and let the devil do his worst.

Our Lord's temptation and ours move in different spheres until we are born again and become His brothers and sisters (see Hebrews 2:11). The records of the temptation of Jesus are the records of how God as human being is tempted, not of how we are tempted as human beings. The temptations of Jesus are not those of a human as human but the temptation of God as human. Jesus Christ was not born with a heredity of sin: "Therefore, in all things He had to be made like His brethren" (v. 17). His "brethren" are those in whom He is born. It is nowhere said that Jesus Christ was tempted as we are as ordinary human beings. By regeneration the Son of God is formed in us, and He has the same setting in our physical lives as He had when He was on earth. Are we remaining loyal to Him in the things that beset His life in us? The devil does not need to bother about the majority of us—we have enough lust on the inside to keep us in sin—but when one is born from above, the temptations alter instantly, and one realizes where the temptation is aimed, namely, at the disposition.

Our Lord was tested for the fulfillment of what He held in His own personal life, namely, the Saviorhood of the world and the Kingship of humanity, and the temptation by Satan was that He should fulfill these by a shortcut. Our Lord's temptations were set by His disposition; He could not be tempted by lust, but He was tempted to the fulfillment of His incarnation along a line other than that marked out by His Father. Satan came to Him as an angel of light, and the central citadel of the temptations was: "You are the Son of God, then do God's work in Your own way." And at the heart of every one of our Lord's answers is this: I came to do My Father's work in His way, not in My own way (see Matthew 4:3–11). Satan was right every time in his promise of what would happen if our Lord took his suggested shortcuts (see John 6:15); but our Lord would not be King of humanity on that line. He deliberately chose the long, long trail, evading none of the suffering involved (see Hebrews 2:9–10).

Temptation, the Sinner, and the Saint

Matthew 26:41; Luke 22:28; James 1:14–15

We all of us suffer from temptations we have no business to be suffering from, simply because we refuse to let God lift us to a higher plan—where we would have other temptations to face of another type. The temptations of Jesus are removed from any affinity with the natural, but when we are born again we realize the meaning of our Lord's words to Peter, "Satan has asked for you, that he may sift you as wheat" (Luke 22:31).

In our natural lives we possess the possibility of self-realization: "I am going to get the best out of myself and train myself for my own ends." Until we are born from above, the highest standpoint we have is that of self-realization, and the particular possessions of our personalities will be tested by the alien power to see whether that power can "tire" them. Temptation is not toward what we understand as evil, but toward what we understand as good (compare Luke 16:15).

Temptation is something that for a while completely baffles us, we do not know whether it is toward a right thing or not.

Spiritual life is attained not by a necromantic magic pill but by moral choices, whereby we test the thing that pre-sents itself to us as being good. The basis of natural life and moral and spiritual life is the same. The way we maintain health in each of these domains is by fight. Health is the bal-ance between my physical life and external nature. If the fighting force on the inside begins to dwindle or is impaired, I get diseased, things outside begin to disintegrate my vital force. The same is true of my moral life: everything that does not partake of the nature of virtue is the enemy of virtue in me, and it depends on how much moral caliber I have whether I overcome and produce virtue. The same is true spiritually; if I have enough spiritual fighting capacity, I will produce a character like Jesus Christ's. Character must be attained, it is never given to us.

The devil does not tempt to wrong things, he tries to make us lose what God has put into us by regeneration, namely, the possibility of being of value to God. The central citadel of the devil's attack on Jesus Christ is the same in us when we are born from above, namely, my right to myself. Satan's aim is to dethrone God, and his whole purpose through the disposition of sin is to get us to the same place. Satan is never represented in the Bible as being guilty of sins, of doing wrong things; he is a wrong being.

There is a limit to temptation. "God is faithful, who will not allow you to be tempted beyond what you are able." God does not save us from temptations, but He succors us in the middle of them. In Hebrews 4:15, the writer is not referring to the temptations common to people as fallen beings but to the temptations common to the sanctified soul. And when our Lord taught His disciples to pray, "Do not lead us into temptation" (Matthew 6:13; Luke 11:4), He was not referring to the temptation James refers to but to the temptation He Himself was led into by the Spirit of God. After the baptism of Jesus and the descent of the Holy Spirit upon Him, God, as it were, took His sheltering hand off Him. So also after the work of sanctification, when the life of the saint really begins, God lifts His hand off and lets the world do its worst, for He is assured that "He who is in you is greater than he who is in the world" (1 John 4:4; see Romans 8:31).

Conscience

Conscience is that innate faculty in one's spirit that attaches itself to the highest one knows, whether one is an atheist or a Christian. The highest the Christian knows is God; the highest the atheist knows is his or her principles. That conscience is the voice of God is easily proved to be absurd. If conscience were the voice of God, it would be the same in everyone. "Indeed, I myself thought," said Paul, "that I must do many things contrary to the name of Jesus of Nazareth" (Acts 26:9). Paul acted according to his conscience, and our Lord said, "Whoever kills you will think that he offers God service" (John 16:2)—people will obey their consciences in putting you to death.

The eye in the body records exactly what it looks at. The eye simply records, and the record is according to the light thrown on what it looks at. Conscience is the eye of the soul, which looks out on what it is taught is God, and how conscience records depends entirely upon what light is thrown upon God. Our Lord Jesus Christ is the only true light on God. When one sees Jesus Christ one does not get a new conscience, but a totally new light is thrown upon God, and conscience records accordingly, with the result that one is absolutely upset by conviction of sin.

The Articles of Conscience

By the "articles" of conscience we mean the regulations of conscience in people fresh from the hand of their Creator, and those articles are: God is Love, God is Holy, God is Near. The Bible records that "God is love" (1 John 4:16), but it must be borne in mind that it is the love of God, and that love, which is inexpressible bliss to a Being like Jesus Christ or to a being like Adam as God created him, is a veritable hell of pain to those of us who are not like either. To know that God is love, God is holy, God is near, is pure delight to people in their innocent relationship to God, but a terror extreme since the Fall. God can never leave people until He has burned them as pure as He is Himself. It is God's love that forbids He should let us go.

These regulations of conscience are ingrained in the spirits of the fallen as they are in the spirits of those who are born from above.

The Attitudes of Conscience

When God is revealed as love, as holy, and as near, it is the conscience that alarms a person from the sleep of death; it makes hell for someone instead of a life of peace. "Do not think that I came to bring peace on earth. I did not come to bring peace but a sword" (Matthew 10:34). Wherever Jesus comes He reveals that people are away from God by reason of sin, and they are terrified at His presence. That is why people will put anything in the place of Jesus Christ, anything rather than let God come near in His startling purity, because as soon as God comes near, conscience records that God is holy and nothing unholy can live with Him, consequently His presence hurts sinners. "If I had not come and spoken to them, they would have no sin, but now they have no excuse for their sin" (John 15:22).

(a) Self-Consciousness

The first thing conscience does is to rouse up self-consciousness, and that produces embarrassment. Little children are full of winsome beauty because they are utterly free from self-consciousness; when they begin to be conscious of themselves they become awkward and shy and do all kinds of affected things; and when once the human conscience is roused by the presence of God, it produces a consciousness of self that makes us scuttle out of His presence like bats out of the light. Most of us know much too little about what conscience succeeds in doing when we stand in the presence of God. We talk much too lightly about sin. Stand one second in the presence of God, in the light of conscience with the Spirit of God illuminating it, without Jesus Christ, and instantly you are conscious of what is stated in Genesis 3:7, namely, your kinship with the brute creation, with no God-quality in you.

(b) World-Consciousness

One effect of the disturbance caused by the light of conscience is to drive us into the outside hubbub of things. In the early days of Christianity people brooded on their sins; nowadays psychologists tell us the more wholesome way is to forget all about sin—fling yourself into the work of the world. Rushing into work in order to deaden conscience is characteristic of the life we live today. "Live the simple life, keep a healthy body, never let your conscience be disturbed—for any sake keep away from religious meetings; don't bring before us the morbid tendency of things." We shall find that the morbid tendency of things is the conviction of the Holy Spirit.

(c) God-Consciousness

The consciousness of God will break out in spite of all our sense of uncleanness, in spite of all our rush and interest in the work of the world, and in spite of all our logic; the implicit sense of God will come and disturb our peace.

We are laying down the fundaments of the way God has constituted human beings. God is holy, therefore nothing that does not partake of His holiness can abide in His presence, and that means pain. When conscience begins to be awakened by God, we either become subtle hypocrites, or saints; that is, either we let God's law working through conscience bring us to the place where we can be put right, or we begin to hoodwink ourselves, to affect a religious pose, not before other people, but before ourselves, in order to appease conscience—anything to be kept out of the real presence of God because wherever He comes, He disturbs.

The Awakening of Conscience

(a) Armored in Sin

The majority of people are dead in trespasses and sins. Our Lord illustrates this: "When a strong man, fully armed guards his own palace, his goods are in peace. But when a stronger than he comes upon him and overcomes him, he takes from him all his armor in which he trusted, and divides his spoils" (Luke 11:21–22). When the prince of this world rules, people are armored in sin, not necessarily in wrongdoing but in the wrong attitude, consequently they have no disturbance, no trouble, no perplexity. As the psalmist says, "There are no pangs in their death. . . . They are not in trouble as other men, . . . they have more than heart could wish" (Psalm 73:4–7).

(b) Awakened in Sin

How is conscience in people like that to be awakened? No one can awaken someone else; the Spirit of God alone can awaken anyone. Our Lord did not say that the strong battles with the stronger; He said, "When a stronger than he comes upon him and overcomes him." When once the Spirit of God shows Jesus Christ to people in that condition, their armor is gone, and they experience distress and pain and upset, exactly as Jesus said they would. Before, they had been armored with the peace of the prince of this world and their consciences recorded that everything was all right. As soon as Jesus Christ is presented, conscience records what people are in the light of God, and the garrison within is disturbed, their peace and joy are gone, and they are under what is called conviction of sin.

(c) Awakening to Holiness

"And when He has come He will convict the world of sin" (John 16:8). We are apt to put conviction of sin in the wrong place in someone's life. The one man of all people who experienced conviction of sin was the saintly apostle Paul. "I was alive once without the law, but when the commandment came, sin revived and I died" (Romans 7:9). There is no mention of conviction of sin in Paul's account of his conversion, only conviction of darkness and distress and of being out of order. But after Paul had been three years in Arabia with the Holy Spirit blazing through him, he began to write the diagnoses of sin that we have in his epistles. The sense of sin is in proportion to the sense of holiness. The hymn has it rightly:

> And they who fain would
>   serve Thee best
> Are conscious most of wrong
>   within.

It does not mean that indwelling sin and indwelling holiness abide together—indwelling sin can never abide with indwelling holiness; it means exactly what Paul said: "I know that in me (that is, in my flesh) nothing good dwells" (Romans 7:18); "Yes we had the sentence of death in ourselves, that we should not trust in ourselves" (2 Corinthians 1:9). The majority of us have caught on the jargon of holiness without the tremendous panging pain that follows the awakening to holiness. The Spirit of God brings us to face ourselves steadily in the light of God until sin is seen in its true nature. If you want to know what sin is, don't ask the convicted sinner, ask the saint, the one who has been awakened to the holiness of God through the Atonement; the saint is the one who can begin to tell you what sin is. The people writhing at the penitent form are affected because their sins have upset them, but they have very little knowledge of sin. It is only as we walk in the light as God is in the light that we begin to understand the unfathomable depths of cleansing to which the blood of Jesus Christ goes (see 1 John 1:7). Every now and again the Spirit of God allows the saint to look back as the apostle Paul did when he said, "I was formerly a blasphemer, a persecutor, and an insolent man" (1 Timothy 1:13). Paul was a mature saint at this time, but he was looking back into what he was before Jesus Christ apprehended him.

Conscience is the internal perception of God's moral law. Have you ever been convicted of sin by conscience through the Spirit of God? If you have, you know this—that God dare not forgive you and be God. There is a lot of sentimental talk about God forgiving because He is love; God is so holy that He cannot forgive. God can only destroy forever the thing that is unlike Himself. The Atonement does not mean that God forgives sinners and allows them to go on sinning and receiving forgiveness; it means that God saves sinners and turns them into saints, that is, destroys the sinner out of them, and through the conscience they realize that by the Atonement God has done what He never could have done apart from it. When people testify you can always tell whether they have been convicted by the Spirit of God or whether their equilibrium has been disturbed by doing wrong things. When people are convicted of sin by the Spirit of God through the conscience, their relationships to

other people are absolute child's play. If, when you were convicted of sin, you had been told to go and lick the dust off the
boots of your greatest enemy, you would have done it willingly. Your relationship to people is the last thing that bothers you. It is your relationship to God that bothers you. I am
completely out of the love of God, out of the holiness of God,
and I tremble with terror when I think of God drawing near.
That is the real element of conviction of sin, and it is one of
the rarest things nowadays because people are not uplifting
the white light of Jesus Christ upon God, they are uplifting
arbitrary standards of right. They are uplifting, for instance,
the conduct of one person to another; they are telling us we
should love other people. The consequence is the majority of
us get off scot-free, we begin to feel very self-righteous: "But
they, measuring themselves by themselves, and comparing
themselves among themselves, are not wise" (2 Corinthians
10:12). But when conscience is illuminated by the Holy
Spirit, these three amazing articles—God is Love, God is
Holy, God is Near—are brought straight down to our inner
lives, and we can neither look up nor down for terror. When
people begin the life with God there are great tracts of their
lives that they never bother their heads about, but slowly
and surely the Spirit of God educates them down to the tiny
little detail. Every crook and cranny of the physical life,
every imagination and emotion is perfectly known to God,
and He demands that all these be blameless. That brings us to
absolute despair unless Jesus Christ can do what He claims
He can. The marvel of the Atonement is just this very thing,
that the perfect Savior imparts His perfections to me, and as I
walk in the light as God is in the light, every part of bodily
life, of affectionate life, and of spirit life is kept unblameable
in holiness; my duty is to keep in the light, God does all the
rest. That is why the life of God within the saint produces
agony every now and again, because God won't leave us

alone—He won't say, "Now that will do." He will keep at us, blazing and burning us, He is a "consuming fire" (Hebrews 12:29). That phrase becomes the greatest consolation we ever had. God will consume and shake, and shake and consume, till there is nothing more to be consumed, but only Him—incandescent with the presence of God.

Humanity

Psalm 2

> God does His business, do yours.
>
> —Amiel

The tendency nowadays is to take the management of the universe out of God's hands, while at the same time neglecting our business, namely, the government of the universe within.

Enthusiasm for Humanity

Psalm 2:2

The main line indicated in the Bible with regard to the human race and God's purpose for it is that God allows the human race full liberty, and He allows the spirit of evil, namely, Satan, nearly full liberty also. Peter says that God is "longsuffering" (2 Peter 3:9); He is giving us ample opportunity to try whatever line we like, both in individual and in national life, but the Bible reveals that in the final end of all things, humanity will confess that God's purpose and His judgment are right. We must disabuse our minds of the idea that God sits like a Judge on a throne and batters humanity into shape. He is sometimes presented in that way, not intentionally, but simply because the majority of people have forgotten the principle laid down by Jesus that "there is nothing covered that will not be revealed, and hidden that will not be known" (Matthew 10:26; Luke 12:2), and that in the end, God's judgments will be made utterly plain and clear, and people will agree that they are right. Meantime, God is giving humanity and the devil ample opportunity to try and prove that His purposes and His judgments are wrong.

Enthusiasm means intensity of interest. Enthusiasm for humanity is one thing; enthusiasm for saints is another— God's purpose is the latter. In order that we may see exactly the forces and the problems that are at work morally, we will look at these heads:

(a) The Master Man

> Through one man sin entered the world, and death through sin, and thus death spread to all men, because all sinned. Romans 5:12

Adam stands as the federal head of the race, he is the master key to the virtues that still remain in sinful humanity. These virtues must be understood as remnants left of God's original design and not promises of what humanity is going to be. The moral problem comes in this way: we inherit by nature certain strong cardinal virtues, but these are not the slightest atom of use to us, and when a man or a woman is born again of the Spirit of God, these virtues are nearly always a hindrance instead of a benefit. Think of the virtues that Jesus Christ demands in His teaching and compare them with the cardinal virtues left in us as the remnants of a ruined humanity, not as promises of the new humanity, and you will see why it is that we cannot patch up our natural virtues to come anywhere near Jesus Christ's demands. We must be remade on the inside and develop new virtues entirely, a new man in Christ Jesus. This is one part of the problem that no teacher outside the Bible deals with. Books on ethics and morals take the natural virtues as promises of what humanity is going to be; the Bible indicates that they are remnants of what humanity once was, and the key to these virtues is Adam, not Jesus Christ. This accounts for our Lord's attitude, a strange, perplexing attitude until we understand this point. Jesus loves the natural virtues, and yet He refers to them in a way that makes them seem utterly futile. Take the natural virtues in the rich young ruler; we read that Jesus, looking on him, "loved him" (Mark 10:21). Natural virtues are beautiful in the sight of Jesus, but He knows as none other could know that they are not promises of what humanity is going to be, but remnants, "trailing clouds of glory," left in human beings, and are not of the slightest atom of practical use to them. Jesus Christ told the rich young ruler that he must strip himself of all he possessed, give his humanity to Him, and then come and follow Him; in other words, he must be remade entirely.

(b) The Muddle of Men

> Death spread to all men, because all sinned. Romans 5:12

The human muddle refers to the whole of the human race since Adam; we are all a muddle, "because all sinned." Since Adam, humanity, individually and collectively, presents a muddle morally that has puzzled everyone; the Bible is the only Book that tells us how the moral muddle has been produced, namely, by sin. In those in whom the cardinal virtues are strong and clear, there is another element that the Bible calls sin (no one else calls it sin), and it is this element that makes men and women a complete muddle; you do not know how to sort them out. In some particulars they are good, and in others they are bad, and the problem arises when you fix on one point of their personalities as if it were the only point. For example, when Oscar Wilde wrote De Profundis in prison, he allowed one point of his personality to have way, namely, his sentimental, intellectual interest in Jesus Christ, and the book was written from that point of view. He wrote sincerely, but he overlooked all the other points of his personality that contradicted that particular one, and when he came out of prison it was those other points that dominated. That is what we mean by the human muddle, and everyone who touches it, outside the Bible, instead of clearing it up makes it worse. The muddle is explained by one word: *sin*.

(c) The Mystery Man

That Day will not come unless . . . the man of sin is revealed, the son of perdition, who opposes and exalts himself above all that is called God. 2 Thessalonians 2:3-4

The Bible reveals that the sin that muddles people and society is ultimately going to appear in an incarnation called the "man of sin," or the Antichrist. The enthusiasm of humanity for itself in its present state simply means irrevocable disaster ultimately. Nowadays people talk about the whole human race being in the making, that our natural virtues are promises of what we are going to be; they take no account at all of sin. We have to remember that an enthusiasm for humanity that ignores the Bible is sure to end in disaster; enthusiasm for the community of saints means that God can take hold of the muddle and can remake people, not simply in accordance with the master man before the Fall, but "conformed to the image of His Son" (Romans 8:29).

The Embarrassment of Humanity

He who sits in the heavens shall laugh; The Lord shall hold them in derision. Psalm 2:4; see also verses 5-6

(a) Bastard Solidarity

The LORD saw that the wickedness of man was great . . . and that every intent of the thoughts of his heart was only evil continually. Genesis 6:5

If you are without chastening, . . . then you are illegitimate and not sons. Hebrews 12:8

Solidarity means consolidation and oneness of interest; the solidarity of the human race means that every member of the race has one point of interest with every other member. Notice how the whole of Scripture is knit together over this false solidarity of sin. It is quite possible for the human mind to blot God out of its thinking entirely and to work along the line of the elements that are the same in everyone and to band the whole of the human race into a solid atheistic community. The only reason this has not been done up to the present is that the human race has been too much divided, but we shall find that these divisions are gradually resolving themselves. There are elements in human nature that are the same in everybody, and if once the human mind succeeded in obliterating God, the whole of the human race would become one vast phalanx of atheism.

(b) Babel of Souls

> And they said, "Come, let us build ourselves a city, and a tower whose top is in the heavens; let us make a name for ourselves, lest we be scattered abroad over the face of the whole earth."
> Genesis 11:4; see verses 1–9

This is the first time solidarity was attempted, away in hoary antiquity. What encumbers and embarrasses humanity is an uncomfortable feeling that God is laughing at it all the time, and in the history of humanity up to the present time the hindrance to perfectly organized atheism has been the saints who represent the derision of God: if they were removed, we should find perfectly organized atheism.

(c) Body of sin

> Our old man was crucified with Him, that the body of sin might be done away with, that we should no longer be slaves of sin.
> Romans 6:6

The body of sin is this tremendous possibility of solid atheism underlying humanity; the share of individual men and women in that body is called "the old man." Every time a man or a woman by identification with Jesus enters into the experimental knowledge that the old man is crucified with Christ, the ultimate defeat and destruction of the body of sin becomes clearer. The body of sin is not in people; what is in people is the old man, the carnal mind that connects them with the body of sin. The solidarity of sin forms the basis of the power of Satan, and it runs all through humanity, making it possible for the whole human race to be atheistic. Sin in its beginning is simply being without God. Paul's argument is that the purpose of the old man being crucified with Christ is that the body of sin might be destroyed, that is, that the connection with the body of sin might be severed. Everyone who becomes identified with the death of Jesus Christ aims another blow at Satan and at the great solidarity of sin. There are two mystical bodies—there is the mystical body of Christ and the mystical body of sin, which is anticipated in the "man of sin." When a person begins to go wrong, he or she says, "I can't help it"; perfectly true. God's Book reveals the great oracle of evil, the tremendous power behind wrongdoing; it is a supernatural power antagonistic to God. We do not battle against flesh and blood but "against principalities, against powers, against the rulers of the darkness of this age, against spiritual hosts of wickedness in the heavenly places" (Ephesians 6:12). A person who is saved and sanctified is severed from the body of sin, and consequently all the powers of darkness backed by Satan make a dead set for that soul. The only thing that can keep a sanctified soul is the almighty power of God through Jesus Christ, but kept by that power that soul is perfectly safe. When once the saints are removed, the world will be faced with the menace of the solidarity of sin and atheism.

> The question of the moment is: A God that serves Humanity, or a Humanity that serves God?
>
> —Forsyth

When people depart from the Bible, they call humanity "god" in differing terms; the use of the term *God* means nothing to them, God is simply the name given to the general tendencies that further people's interests. This spirit is honeycombing everything, we find it coming into the way we talk of Christian experience; there is creeping in the idea that God and Jesus Christ and the Holy Spirit are simply meant to bless us, to further our interests. When we come to the New Testament we find exactly the opposite idea, that by regeneration we are brought into such harmony and union with God that we realize—with great joy—that we are meant to serve His interests.

The Embroilment of Humanity

Psalm 2:7–9

Embroilment means to involve in perplexity. It is the presence of the saints that upsets the calculations of Satan, and it is the presence of Jesus that involves not only Satan but humanity in all kinds of distractions. If humanity and Satan could only get rid of Jesus Christ, they would never be involved in perplexity, never be upset. Jesus put it very clearly: "If I had not come and spoken to them, they would have no sin, but now they have no excuse for their sin" (John 15:22). The greatest annoyance to Satan and to humanity is Jesus Christ. Twenty centuries ago the apostle John wrote, "Every spirit that does not confess [that dissolves Jesus by analysis] that Jesus Christ has come in the flesh is not of God. And this is the spirit of the Antichrist, which you have heard was coming" (1 John 4:3). Watch the tendency abroad today; people want to get rid of Jesus Christ, they cannot prove that He did not live or that He was not a remarkable person, but they set to work to dissolve Him by analysis, to say He was not really God Incarnate. Jesus Christ always upsets the calculations of humanity; that is what made Voltaire say, "Crucify the wretch, stamp Him and His crazy tale out," because He was the stumbling-block to all the human reasonings. You cannot work Jesus Christ into any system of thinking. If you could keep Him out, everything could be explained. The world could be explained by evolution, but you cannot fit Jesus Christ into the theory of evolution. Jesus Christ is an annoyance to Satan, a thorn in the side of the world at large, an absolute distress to sin in the individual. If we could crucify Him and stamp Him out, the annoyance would cease. In dealing with the carnal mind, Paul says it "is enmity against God" (Romans 8:7).

(a) The Past Watchword—A religion that utilizes humanity

The error in the past on the part of religious teachers has been to present God as a great sovereign power who utilizes humanity without rhyme or reason.

(b) The Present Watchword—A humanity that utilizes God

The present error is the opposite, namely, that God is a great, aimless, loving tendency that humanity utilizes to forgive itself, to cleanse itself, and to justify itself.

(c) The Persistent Word—A Christ who unites God and humanity in love

Through both the errors is this, the Lord Jesus Christ, who can unite a holy God and an unholy humanity by means of His wonderful redemption. In this connection, Jesus Christ stands as the type of person, and the only type of person, who can come near to God. "Christ is the central figure for a glorified humanity to develop by Christ's aid the innate spiritual resources of a splendid race." Jesus Christ is the One who has the power to impart His own innate spiritual life, namely, Holy Spirit, to unholy people and develop them until they are like Himself. That is why the devil hates Jesus Christ and why he tries to make people calculate without Him.

The Emancipation of Humanity

Psalm 2:10–12

When any sinful soul accepts morally the verdict of God on sin in the cross of Christ, that soul becomes emancipated. A moral decision is different from a mental decision, which may be largely sentiment. A moral decision means, "My God, I accept Your verdict against sin on the cross of Jesus Christ, and I want the disposition of sin in me identified with His death"—as soon as someone gets there, all that we understand by the Holy Spirit working in His tremendous power through the Redemption takes place, and the emancipation of humanity is furthered. "Christ is the central figure for a glorious God, and humanity's chief end is to develop from reconciliation, redemption, and subjection to God's will."

(a) The Second Man

For as by one man's disobedience many were made sinners, so also by one Man's obedience many will be made righteous. Romans 5:19; see verses 17–19

God emancipates the human race through this second Man, the Lord Jesus Christ. That is why Paul called Jesus Christ "the Last Adam." If the First Adam is the key to the human muddle, Jesus Christ, the Last Adam, is the key to human emancipation. Jesus Christ stands for all that a person should be, and to the saints He stands for all that God is.

(b) The Sanctified People

God . . . made us sit together in the heavenly places in Christ Jesus. Ephesians 2:4, 6; see verses 1–10

A sanctified person has not only had the disposition of sin crucified, but is emancipated from connection with the body of sin and is lifted to the heavenly places where Jesus lived when He was here. This marvelous revelation is summed up in

1 John 1:7, "if we walk in the light as He is in the light, we have fellowship with one another, and the blood of Jesus Christ His Son cleanses us from all sin." This is the enthusiasm for the communion of saints in contrast to the enthusiasm for humanity. It is by thinking along these lines that we are enabled to prove experimentally what we know in our minds, and we would live with far greater power if only we would let our pure minds be stirred up by way of reminder (see 2 Peter 3:1). While we are on this earth, living in alien territory, it is a marvelous emancipation to know that we are raised above it all through Jesus Christ and that we have power over all the power of the Enemy in and through Him.

(c) The Supreme Mystery

> This is a great mystery, . . . Christ and the church. Ephesians 5:32

Around the saints is the great power of God that keeps watch and ward over them so that the Wicked One does not touch them (see 1 John 5:18). What is true of saints individually is true of all saints collectively, namely, that the elements that, under Satan, make for the solidarity of atheism, make for the solidarity of holiness under God. "Do not fear, little flock; for it is your Father's good pleasure to give you the kingdom" (Luke 12:32), a tiny insignificant crowd in every age. Christianity has always been a forlorn hope because the saints are in alien territory, but it is all right; God is working out His tremendous purpose for the overthrow of everything Satan and sin can do. "He who sits in the heavens shall laugh" (Psalm 2:4). Everything that sin and Satan have ruined is going to be reconstructed and readjusted through the marvelous redemption of our Lord Jesus Christ.

Harmony

Health—Physical Harmony *Peace of Fact*

Genesis 2:1–9, 15–17

Harmony means a fitting together of parts so as to form a connected whole, agreement in relation. Health, or physical harmony, was God's plan from the very beginning. The first mention of any subject in the book of Genesis colors every allusion to that subject throughout the Bible. Health (physical harmony), happiness (moral harmony), and holiness (spiritual harmony) are all divergent views as to what is the main aim of a person's life. Health, or physical harmony, is a perfect balance between the human organism and the outer world.

(a) The Cult of the Splendid Animal

> He does not delight in the strength of the horse; He takes no pleasure in the legs of a man. Psalm 147:10

There always have been and always will be people who worship splendid, well-groomed health. This verse reveals that God places health, or physical harmony, in a totally different relationship from that which it is put in by people. The modern name for the worship of physical health is Christian Science. The great error of the healthy-minded cult is that it ignores a person's moral and spiritual life.

(b) The Cult of the Sick Attitude

> Surely every man walks about like a shadow. . . . I am consumed by the blow of Your hand. . . . Surely every man is vapor. Psalm 39:6–11

A great many people indulge in the luxury of misery; their one worship is of anguish, agony, weakness, and sensitivity to pain. The cult of the sick attitude is well established in human history by the fact that most of the great men and women whose personalities have marked the life of their times have been to some degree deranged physically. Amiel, a highly sensitive and cultured person, almost too morbid to exist, was a lifelong invalid, and he wrote thus in his journal: "The first summonses of illness have a divine value, so that evils though they seem, they are really an appeal to us from on high, a touch of God's Fatherly scourge." The healthy-minded do not agree with that attitude, and the sick are inclined to worship it. The attitude to sickness in the Bible is totally different from that of those who believe in faith healing. The Bible attitude is not that God sends sickness or that sickness is of the devil but that sickness is a fact usable by both God and the devil. Never base a principle on your own experience. My personal experience is this: I have never once in my life been sick without being to blame for it. As soon as I turned my mind to asking why the sickness was allowed, I learned a lesson that I have never forgotten, namely, that my physical health depends absolutely on my relationship to God. Never pin your faith to a doctrine or to anyone else's statement; get hold of God's Book, and you will find that your spiritual character determines exactly how God deals with you personally. People continually get into fogs because they will not take God's line, they will take someone else's line. God's Book deals with facts. Health and sickness are facts, not fancies. There are cases recorded in the Bible, and in our own day, of people who have been marvelously healed—for what purpose? For us to imitate them? Never, but in order that we might discern what lies behind, namely, the individual relationship to a personal God. The peace arising from fact is unintelligent and dangerous; for example, people who base on the fact of health are at peace, but it is often a peace that makes them callous. On the other hand, people who accept the fact of being sick are inclined to have a jaundiced eye for everything healthy. For a person to make health a god is to put himself or herself merely at the head of the brute creation.

I am purposely leaving the subject vague and without an answer; there can be no answer. The great difficulty is that people find answers that they say came from God. You cannot prove facts; you have to swallow them. The fact of health and the fact of sickness are there; we have nothing to do with choosing them, they come and go. We have to get onto another platform, the moral platform, and then the spiritual platform, before we can begin to get an explanation of these facts.

Happiness—Moral Harmony *Peace of Principle*

Happiness, or moral harmony, is a perfect balance between the inclination and the environment. The peace of principle keeps a person's moral nature in a state of harmony.

(a) *The Pride of Integrity*

> The Pharisee stood and prayed thus with himself, "God, I thank You that I am not like other men—extortioners, unjust, adulterers, or even as this tax collector." Luke 18:11

Integrity means the unimpaired state of anything, and pride in the integrity of one's morality will produce happiness. Such people have no need of prayer, or if they do pray it is a soliloquy of peace before high heaven. The Pharisee in our Lord's parable was happy; he was not praying to God or that others might hear; he was praying "with himself, 'God, I thank You that I am not like other men—extortioners, unjust, adulterers, or even as this tax collector.' " Look at him, then put your own name behind him and you have got his portrait exactly; you know where he lives and everything about him.

Beware of calling this type of happiness self-righteousness; the phrase that gives the true meaning would be happy satisfaction with my intellectual and moral conduct. That happiness is impregnable to God and to the devil; its true emblem is ice. If you want to find an analysis of every kind of moral and immoral character, the Bible is the place to look for it. This picture in Luke 18 is not the picture of a person of the world but of a religious person. As Christians we have to beware of Pharisaic holiness along the line of sanctification.

(b) The Pain of Iniquity

> The tax collector, standing afar off, would not so much as raise his eyes to heaven, but beat his breast, saying, "God, be merciful to me a sinner!" verse 13

This is the stage when the peace of principle has broken down. "When with rebukes You correct man for iniquity, You make his beauty melt away like a moth" (Psalm 39:11). According to the steadily reiterated teachings of Jesus Christ, one who is in moral harmony with oneself without being rightly related to Jesus Christ is much nearer the devil than a bad-living person.

Harmony, both physical and moral, is God-ordained, that is, it is God's will that human bodies, with all their component parts, should be in perfect harmony with themselves and with the outer world, and it is God's will that people should be in moral harmony with themselves and happy in that sense, and yet, as we have pointed out, the Bible reveals that people can have physical health at the cost of their moral welfare and happiness at the cost of their spiritual welfare.

Holiness—Spiritual Harmony *Peace of God*

Holiness, or spiritual harmony, is a perfect balance between the human disposition and all the law of God. Never trust your temperament, that is, your sensibility to things. When God makes saints He plants a new disposition in them, but He does not alter their temperaments; the saints have to mold their temperaments according to the new disposition. Take your own experience, think of the time before you knew God, before God gave you the Holy Spirit, before you entered into the life of sanctification—your temperament and your sensibilities produced in you a horror for certain things that now you look at from a totally different attitude, and you begin to say, "Why, I must be getting callous!" Nothing of the sort, you have a new disposition with which your temperament is being brought into harmony, and that disposition, being God-given, is bringing you into sympathy with God's way of looking at things so that you are no longer the creature of your sensibilities. If you have begun to get discouraged over the difficulty of disciplining your sensibilities, don't be discouraged, get at it again. At the beginning we are apt to be tripped up by our sensibilities because they have not yet been brought into complete subjection to the Lord Jesus Christ. Remember, although Jesus Christ is on the throne, you are "prime minister" under Him.

(a) Untouched by Panic

> He will not be afraid of evil tidings; his heart is steadfast, trusting in the LORD. Psalm 112:7

Our Lord never suffered from physical or moral or intellectual panics, because He was fixed in God. "But Jesus did not commit Himself to them, because He knew all men, . . . for He knew what was in man" (John 2:24–25). Look at your own experience and see how your sensibilities will run you into panics and try and make you believe a lie. It is through their sensibilities that Satan tries to get hold of the saints. God said to Satan about Job, "Behold, all that he has is in your power; only do not lay a hand on his person" (Job 1:12). For our present argument, may this not mean that Satan cannot touch the ruling disposition but that if we are not on the watch at all the loopholes, he will get hold of the sensibilities and try to bring us into bondage? Whenever you feel bond-age spiritually, smell brimstone—you are on a wrong tack. Panics are always wrong, there is nothing in them. What a blessing it is to know someone who never gets into a panic, someone you can always depend on. You go to him or to her in a flurry, with fired and jangled nerves, brain like cotton wool, heart panting like a butterfly nearly dead, and in two or three minutes everything is quieted. What has happened? The difference in you has come about because that man or that woman is paying no attention to personal sensibilities but only to the one bedrock reality of the life, namely, God. Holiness is untouched by panic. "In tumults," says Paul (2 Corinthians 6:5; see 11:23–29). What is a tumult? Watch a porridge pot boiling, that is a tumult; to be inside that, undis-turbed, means something, and that type of character is the only one that can stand as a worker for God in this world. A man or a woman with that disposition within can stand where Jesus Christ stood, because it is His own disposition that is within, and that disposition cannot be upset, it cannot be made to take account of the evil. In the eyes of the world the way a saint trusts God is always absurd, until there is trouble on, then the world is inclined to kneel down and worship the saint.

(b) Undeterred by Persecution

> The wicked will see it and be grieved; he will gnash his teeth and melt away. Psalm 112:10

God's Book reveals all through that holiness will bring persecution from those who are not holy. Our Lord taught His disciples to be conspicuous. "You are the light of the world. A city that is set on a hill cannot be hidden" (Mat-thew 5:14), and He taught them never to hide the truth for fear of wolfish people (see 10:16). Personal experience bears out the truth that a testimony to holiness produces either rage or ridicule on the part of those who are not holy. We are all cowards naturally; we are only not cowards when God has altered our dispositions, because the disposition God puts in keeps us fixed in a right relationship to Him. The one dominant note of the life of a saint is first of all sympathy with God and God's ideas, not with human beings. A two-fold line runs all through God's Book, and especially in the epistles of Saint Paul, with regard to public preaching and teaching and dealing with people in private: Be as stern and unflinching as God almighty in your preaching, but as tender and gentle as a sinner saved by grace should be when you deal with a human soul. Today the order is being reversed and modern teaching is amazingly "easy-osy." Look at the standard of the preaching of today—sympathy with human beings is put first, not sympathy with God, and the truth of God is withheld. It must be withheld, it dare not be preached, because as soon as the fullness of a personal salvation is preached—which means I must be right with God, must have a disposition that is in perfect harmony with God's laws and that will enable me to work them out—it produces conviction and resentment and upset. Jesus Christ taught His disciples never to keep back the truth of God for fear of persecution. When we come to dealing with other people, what is the attitude to be? Remember yourself, remember who you are and that if you have attained to anything in the way of holiness, remember who made you what you are. "By the grace of God I am what I am," says the apostle Paul (1 Corinthians 15:10). Deal with infinite pity and sympathy with other souls, keeping your eye on what you once were and what, by the grace of God, you are now.

In dealing with yourself be as patient as God is with you. Beware of the spiritual sulks that spring from thinking that because I, a two-year-old in sanctifying grace, am not as big and mature and strong as the twenty-year-old in grace, I can't be sanctified rightly! There is more danger there than most saints think (see Hebrews 12:5–11). The devil tries to make us think that when we have entered into the sanctified life, all is done; it is only begun. We have entered into Jesus Christ's finished work, but remember, says Paul, you have attained to nothing yet; everything is perfectly adjusted, now begin to attain and to "grow up in all things into Him" (Ephesians 4:15).

These three things develop slowly together: first, the basis of spiritual holiness; second, the building of moral happiness; and third, the decoration of physical health. A full-grown person in Christ Jesus is one who has become exactly like Christ Jesus. "Till we all come. . . to the measure of the stature of the fullness of Christ" (v. 13).

Note to the Reader

The publisher invites you to share your response to the message of this book by writing Discovery House Publishers, Box 3566, Grand Rapids, MI 49501, USA. For information about other Discovery House books, music, or videos, contact us at the same address or call 1-800-653-8333. Find us on the Internet at http://www.dhp.org/ or send e-mail to books@dhp.org.